MEXICO

CHAPTER I

A FIRST RECONNAISSANCE

Romance of history—Two entrance ways—Vera Cruz—Orizaba—The Great Plateau—Fortress of Ulua—Sierra Madre—Topographical structure—The Gulf coast—Tropical region—Birds, animals, and vegetation of coast zone—*Tierra caliente*—Malaria—Foothills—Romantic scenery—General configuration of Mexico—Climatic zones—Temperate zone—Cold zone—The Cordillera—Snow-capped peaks—Romance of mining—Devout miners—Subterranean shrines—The great deserts—Sunset on the Great Plateau—*Coyotes* and *zopilotes*—Irrigated plantations—Railways—Plateau of Anahuac—The cities of the *mesa central*—Spanish-American civilisation—Romance of Mexican life—Mexican girls, music, and moonlight—The *peones* and civilisation—American comparisons—Pleasing traits of the Mexicans—The foreigner in Mexico—Picturesque mining-towns—Wealth of silver—Conditions of travel—Railways—Invasions—Lerdo's axiom—Roads and horsemen—Strong religious sentiment—Popocatepetl and Ixtaccihuatl—Sun-god of Teotihuacan—City of Mexico—Valley of Mexico—The Sierra Madre—*Divortia aquarum* of the continent—Volcano of Colima—Forests and ravines—Cuernavaca—The trail of

Cortes—Acapulco—Romantic old *haciendas*—Tropic sunset—Unexplored Guerrero—Perils and pleasures of the trail—Sunset in the Pacific Ocean.

Mexico, that southern land lying stretched between the Atlantic and Pacific Oceans, upon the tapering base of North America, is a country whose name is fraught with colour and meaning. The romance of its history envelops it in an atmosphere of adventure whose charm even the prosaic years of the twentieth century have not entirely dispelled, and the magnetism of the hidden wealth of its soil still invests it with some of the attraction it held for the old Conquistadores. It was in the memorable age of ocean chivalry when this land was first won for Western civilisation: that age when men put forth into a sunset-land of Conquest, whose every shore and mountain-pass concealed some El Dorado of their dreams. The Mexico of to-day is not less interesting, for its vast territory holds a wealth of historic lore and a profusion of natural riches. Beneath the Mexican sky, blue and serene, stretch great tablelands, tropic forests, scorching deserts, and fruitful valleys, crowned by the mineral-girt mountain ranges of the Sierra Madres; and among them lie the strange pyramids of the bygone Aztecs, and the rich silver mines where men of all races have enriched themselves. Mexico is part of that great Land of Opportunity which the Spanish-American world has retained for this century.

There are two main travelled ways into Mexico. The first lies across the stormy waters of the Mexican Gulf to the yellow strand of Vera Cruz, beyond which the great "star-mountain" of the Aztecs, Citlaltepetl,[1] rears its gleaming snow-cap in mid-heavens, above the clouds. It was here that Cortes landed, four centuries ago, and it is the route followed by the tide of European travellers to-day. Otherwise, the way lies across the Great Plateau, among the arid plains of the north, where, between the sparsely-scattered cities and plantations of civilised man, the fringe of Indian life is spread upon the desert, and the shadowy forms of the *coyote* and the cactus blend into the characteristic landscape. Both ways are replete with interest, but that of Vera Cruz is the more varied and characteristic. Here stands Ulua, the promontory-fortress, where more than one of Mexico's short-lived rulers languished and died of yellow fever, and which was the last stronghold of Spain. Beyond it arise the white buildings and towers of Vera Cruz, a dream-city, as beheld from the Gulf, of interest and beauty; and to the west, are the broad coastal deserts, bounded by the foothills and tropic valleys of the *tierra caliente* of the littoral. Piled up to the horizon are the wooded slopes and canyons of the great Sierra Madre, topped by the gleaming Orizaba, towering upwards in solitary majesty. We stand upon a torrid strand, yet gaze upon an icy mountain.

1 Orizaba, 18,250 feet altitude.

A country of singular topographic structure is before us. The Mexican Cordillera conceals, beyond and above it, the famous Great Plateau; the *mesa central*, running to the northwards eight hundred miles or more, and reaching westwardly to the steep escarpments of the Pacific slope. These plutonic and volcanic ranges encircle and bisect the great tableland, and enclose the famous Valley of Mexico and its beautiful capital, lying far beyond the horizon, above the clouds which rest upon the canyons and terraces of that steep-rising country to the west. Our journey lies upwards to this Great Plateau of Anahuac over the intervening plains and mountain range.

It is a tropical region of foliage, flowers, and fruits, of rugged countryside and rushing streams, this eastern slope of Mexico; and the blue sky and flashing sun form the ambient of a perpetual summer-land. We traverse the sandy Tertiary deserts of the coast, and thence enter among groves of profuse natural vegetation, interspersed with cultivated plantations. In these the gleam of yellow oranges comes from among the foliage, and the graceful leaves of the plátanos and rubber-trees fan their protecting shade over young coffee-trees. But away from the haunts of man along the littoral is a region of startling beauty—of rivers and lagoons and hills, their shores and slopes garmented with perennial verdure, the forest-seas bathing the bases of towering peaks. Beautiful birds of variegated and rainbow colours, such as Mexico is famous for, people these tropic southern lands of Vera Cruz. Along the shores and in the woods and groves, all teeming with prolific life, which the hot sun and frequent rains induce, the giant cranes and brilliant-plumaged herons disport themselves, and gorgeous butterflies almost outshine the feathered denizens. From the tangled boughs the pendant boa-constrictor coils himself, and hissing serpents, basking crocodiles, and prowling jaguars people the untrodden wilds of jungle and lagoon. In these great virgin forests tribes of monkeys find their home, and the tapir and the cougar have their being. Mangroves, palms, rubber-trees, mahogany, strange *flora*, and ungathered fruits run riot amid this tropical profusion, and flourish and fall almost unseen of man. And here the malarias of the lowlands lurk—those bilious disorders which man is ever fighting and slowly conquering. This is Mexico's *tierra caliente*.

But our way lies onwards towards the mountains. A wildness of landscape, unpictured before, opens to the view. Here rise weird rock-forms, Nature's cathedral towers and grim façades magnificent in solitude and awe-inspiring, as by steep bridle-paths we take our way along the valleys, and draw rein to gaze upon them. Ponderous and sterile, these outworks and buttresses of the great Sierra Madre rise upwards, fortifications reared against the march of tropic verdure beneath, cloud-swathed above and bathed below by forest-seas. Born in that high environment of rains and snows, rippling streams descend, falling in cascades and babbling rapids adown romantic glens, and their life-giving waters, with boisterous ripple or murmuring softly, take their way over silver sand-bar and polished ledge of gleaming quartz or marble, winding thence amid corridors of stately trees and banks of verdant vegetation, to where they fill the irrigation-channels of white-clad peasants, far away on the plains below.

Still onwards and upwards lies the way. One of the most remarkable railways in the world ascends this steep zone, and serpentines among sheer descents to gain the summits of abrupt escarpments, from which—a remarkable feature of the topography of the eastern slope of Mexico—the traveller looks down as into another country and climate, upon those tropical valleys which he has left below. This is the Mexican Vera Cruz railway.

THE ATLANTIC SLOPE: TUNNEL AND BRIDGE OF THE INFIERNILLO CAÑON, ON THE MEXICAN RAILWAY, IN THE STATE OF VERA CRUZ.

Let us pause a moment and gain a comprehensive idea of the character of Mexico's configuration and climate. It is to be recollected that Mexico, like other lands of Western America, is a country of relatively recent geological birth. The form of the country is remarkable. It shares the topographical features of others of the Andine countries of America—of tropical lowlands and temperate uplands, in which latter nearness to the heat of the Equator is offset by the coolness of the rarefied air of high elevations above sea-level. This structure is the dominant note of the scheme of Nature in Mexico—as it is in Peru and other similar countries—and the anthropo-geographical conditions are correspondingly marked. The region first passed is known as the *tierra caliente*, or hot lands. Its climatic limit extends up the slopes of the Sierras to an elevation of some 3,000 feet or more, embracing the lowlands, hot and humid generally, of the whole of the Gulf coast and of the peninsula of Yucatan, all of which regions are subject to true tropical conditions—the dense forests, the great profusion of animal life, the wonderful abundance and colour of Nature, and in places the swamps and their accompanying malarias, shunned by the traveller. But yellow fever and malaria are much less dreaded now than heretofore. In the city of Vera Cruz and in Tampico the new era of sanitation, brought about by British and American example and seconded by the Mexican authorities, has almost banished these natural scourges.

Rising from the *tierra caliente*, the road enters upon the more temperate zone, the *tierra templada*, extending upwards towards the Great Plateau. The limit of this climatic zone is at the elevation of 6,000 feet above sea-level, and here are evergreen oaks, pine, and the extraordinary forms of the organ cactus, as well as orchids. It is, indeed, a transition zone from the hot to the cold climates, and the zone embraces the greater part of the area of Mexico. Rising rapidly thence up to and over the escarpments of the Sierra Madre and the high plains, we shall enter upon the *tierra fria* or cold lands, ranging from 6,000 feet to 8,000 feet above sea level. Above this rise the high summits of the Mexican Cordilleras, with their culminating peaks, some few of which penetrate the atmosphere above the limit of perpetual snow. Thus, three diverse climatic zones are encountered in Mexico, which, ever since the advent of the Spaniards, have been designated as the *tierra fria*, *tierra templada*, and *tierra caliente* respectively. These conditions, as will be seen later, are also encountered upon the Pacific slope.

We now ascend the steep upper zone of the Sierra Madre, and cross it, descending thence to the Great Plateau or *mesa central*, the dominating topographical feature of the country. Here lies the real Mexico of history, and here is the main theatre of the new land of industrial awakening. Within the mountain ranges—that which we have crossed, and those which intersect this vast tableland and bound it on three sides—lies the great wealth of minerals —gold, silver, and others—which have attracted men of all races and all times since Cortes came. Here the true fairy tales of long ago, of millions won by stroke of pick, had their setting, and indeed, have it still. Upon these hills the thankful miner reared temples to his saints, and blessed, in altar and crucifix, the mother of God who graciously permitted his enrichment! And as if such devotion were to be unstinted, he also places his shrines within the bowels of the mines, and pauses as he struggles through the dark galleries, with heavy pack of silver rock upon his back, to bend his knee a moment before the candle-lighted subterranean altar.

And now great desert plains unfold to view. Upon their confines arise the blue mountain ranges which intersect them, their canyons and slopes, though faint in distance and blurred by shimmering heat arising from the desert floor, yet cast into distinct tracery by the rays of the sun. Towards the azure vault overhead, as we behold the arid landscape, eddying dust-pillars whirl skywards upon the horizon, or perhaps a cloud of dust, far away upon the trail which winds over the flat expanse, denotes some evidence of man—horseman or ox-cart pursuing its leisurely and monotonous way. Upon the edges of the dry stream-beds, or *arroyos*, which descend from the hills and lose themselves in wide alluvial fans upon the sandy waste, a fringe of scant vegetation appears, nourished by the water which flows down them in time of rain.

Beneath our horses' hoofs the white alkali crust which thinly covers the desert floor, crumbles and breaks. Gaunt cacti stretch their skinny branches across the trail, which winds among foothills and ravines, and the horned toads and the lizards, the only visible beings of the animal world here, play in and out of their labyrinths as we pass. We are upon the Great Plateau. All is vast, reposeful, boundless. The sun rises and sets as it does upon some calm ocean, describing its glowing arc across the cloudless vault above, from Orient to Occident. Sun-scorched by day, the temperature drops rapidly as night falls upon these elevated steppes, 7,000 feet or more above the level of the sea, and the bitter cold of the rarefied air before the dawn takes possession of the atmosphere. The shivering *peones* of the villages rise betimes to catch the sun's first rays, and stand or squat against the eastern side of their adobe huts, what time the orb of day shows his red disc above the far horizon. *La capa de los pobres*—"the poor man's cloak"—they term the sun, as with grateful benediction they watch his coming, and stamp their sandalled feet.

THE GREAT PLATEAU: NIGHTFALL IN THE DESERT.

Impressive and melancholy is the nightfall upon the Great Plateau. The opalescent tints of the dying day, and the scarlet curtains flung across the Occident at the sun's exit give place to that indescribable depth of purple of the high upland's sky. The faint ranges of hills which bound the distant horizon take on those diminishing shades which their respective distances assign them, and stand delicately, ethereally, against the waning colours of the sunset, whilst the foreground rocks are silhouetted violet-black against the desert floor. The long shadows which were projected across the wilderness, and the roseate flush which the setting sun had cast upon the westward-facing escarpments behind us, have both disappeared together. Impenetrable gloom lurks beneath the faces of the cliffs, the mournful howl of the *coyotes* comes across the plain, and their slinking forms emerge from the shadow of the rocks. There is a shapeless heap, the carcass of some dead mule or ox, some jetsam of the desert, lying near at hand, at which my horse was uneasy as I drew rein in contemplation, and which explains the nearness of the beasts of prey, and the long line of *zopilotes*, or buzzards, which I had observed to cross the fading gleam of the firmament. All is solitary, deserted, peaceful. The day is done, the night has come, "in which no man can work."

At daylight the uncultivated desert gives place to human habitations; and we approach the *hacienda* of a large landowner, with its irrigated plantations, and adobe buildings which form the abodes of the workers. All around are vast fields of *maguey*, or plantations of cotton, stretching as far as can be seen. Great herds of cattle, rounded up by picturesque *vaqueros* with silver-garnished saddles and strange hats and whirling lassoes, paw the dusty ground, shortly to writhe beneath the hot imprint of the branding-iron. Long irrigation ditches, brimming with water from some distant river, and fringed with trees, wind away among the plantations; and white-clad *peones*, hoe in hand, tend the long furrows whose parallel lines are lost in perspective. Centre of the whole panorama is the dwelling-house of the *hacendado*, the owner of the lands; and almost of the bodies and souls of the inhabitants! Quaint and old-world, the place and its atmosphere transport the imagination to past centuries, for the aspect of the whole still bears the stamp of its mediæval beginning, save where the new Mexican millionaire-landowner has planted some luxurious abode, replete with modern convenience.

But these are not isolated from the world upon this Great Plateau so much as might appear at first glance. There is a puff of smoke upon the horizon, and the whistle of a locomotive strikes upon the ear. The railway which links this great oasis of cultivated fields with others similar, and with the world beyond, runs near at hand, and will bear us, do we wish it, away to the confines of the Republic in the north, to the United States, and in five days to New York. Southwards it winds away to the great capital City of Mexico, to Vera Cruz, and thence on towards the borders of Guatemala. But let us avoid the railway yet. Not thus, in the comfort of the Pullman cushions, do we know the spirit and atmosphere of Mexico; but the saddle and the dusty road shall be our self-chosen portion. Indeed, it will be so from sheer necessity, for our way will lie onwards to the Pacific Ocean, and no railway of the plateau quite reaches this yet.

Throughout the Great Plateau of Anahuac, separated by long stretches of dusty wilderness, unclothed except by scanty thorny shrubs, and scarcely inhabited except by the *coyote* and the *tecolote*,[2] are handsome cities with their surrounding cultivation and characteristic life. As we top the summit of a range and behold these centres of population from afar, a bird's-eye view and philosophical comprehension of their *ensemble* is obtained. Seen from the outside, they present a picturesque view of cathedral spires and gleaming domes and white walls; the towers rising from the lesser buildings amid groves of verdant trees, forming a striking group, all backed by the blue range of some distant sierra. The main group shades off into a fringe of *jacales*—the squalid habitations of the *peones*, and of the city's poor and outcast, with rambling, dusty roads bordered by hedges of prickly pear, or *nopales*; picturesque, quaint, the roads ankle-deep in white adobe dust, which rises from beneath our horse's hoofs and covers us with an impalpable flour upon traversing the environs of the place. Clattering over the cobble-paved streets, we rapidly approach the central pulse of the town, the *plaza*. Singular shops, where fruits and meats and clothing are displayed in windowless array, line the streets, and quaint dwelling-houses, with iron grilles covering their windows, giving them the mediæval Hispanic aspect familiar to the Spanish-American traveller. Into these we gaze down from the height of the saddle in passing, and perchance some dark-haired Mexican damsel, who has been snatching a moment from her household duties to gaze at the outside world, retires suddenly from the balcony with well-simulated haste and modesty before the rude gaze of the approaching stranger. Indians or *peones* in loose white garments of cotton *manta*, with huge Mexican straw hats, and scarlet blankets depending from their shoulders, stalk through the street, or issue from ill-smelling *pulque* shops, whose singularly-painted exteriors arrest the attention. Gaunt dogs prowl about and lap the water of the open *acequias*, or ditch-gutters, between the road and the footpath, fighting for some stray morsel thrown into the street from the open doors of the shops aforesaid. Of stone or of adobe—generally the latter—according to the geology of the particular neighbourhood, the houses are whitened or tinted outside, with flat roofs, or *azoteas*. Through the wide entrance-door a glimpse is obtained of an interior paved *patio*, adorned, in the better-class homes, with tubs of palms and flowers; and before one of such a character we draw rein—the *meson* or *fonda*, the hotel under whose roof temporary shelter shall be sought. This abode faces the *plaza*, and opposite rises the quaint church—or cathedral if it be a State capital city—which is the dominating note of the community.

2 Mexican night owl.

ON THE GREAT PLATEAU: VIEW OF THE CITY OF DURANGO.

Exceedingly picturesque are the fine cities which form Mexico's chief centres of civilisation along the Great Plateau—Chihuahua, Durango, Guadalajara, Puebla, and many others. They have that quaint, old-world air ever characteristic of Spanish-America, unspoilt by the elements of manufacturing communities. Their shady *plazas* are centres of recreation and social life, always in evidence, distinctive of Spanish-American civilisation, where music is a part of the government of the people; a feature far more prominent than in Britain or the United States. The cathedrals, the quaint architecture of the streets, the barred windows, and the picturesque dress of the working class, form an atmosphere of distinctive life and colour. Let us halt a moment in the *plaza*. The band is discoursing soft music, varied by some stirring martial air; the Mexican moon has risen, and now that the sunset colours pale, vies with the lamps of the well-lit promenade to illumine a happy but simple scene. Its rays shine through the feathery boughs of the palms, and glisten on the broad, elegant leaves of the *plátanos*—which grow even in the upland valleys—whilst the scent of orange-blossoms falls softly through the balmy air, as in ceaseless promenade fair maidens and chatting youths, with coquetry and stolen glance, pass round the square untiringly. White dresses and black eyes and raven tresses—the olive-complexioned beauties of the Mexican uplands take their fill of passing joy. The moment is sweet, peaceful, even romantic; let us dally a moment, nor chafe our cold northern blood for more energetic scenes. Do we ask bright glances? Here are such. Shall we refuse to be their recipient? And moonlight, palms, and music, and evening breeze, and convent tolling bell, and happy crowd—no, it is not a scene from some dream of opera, but a phase of every-day life in Mexico.

In many respects it is an atmosphere of charm and interest which the traveller encounters in Mexican life, especially if he has recently arrived from among the prosaic surroundings of Mexico's great northern neighbour, the United States. Indeed, the transition from the busy Anglo-Saxon world which hurries and bustles in strenuous life northward from the Rio Grande, to that pastoral and primitive land of Spanish-America is as marked as that between Britain and the Orient. Yet it is only divided by a shallow stream—the Rio Grande. As the traveller crosses this boundary he leaves behind him the twentieth century, and goes back in time some hundreds of years—a change, it maybe said *en passant*, which is not without benefit, and attractive in some respect. The brusque and selfish American atmosphere is left behind, the patience and courtesy of Mexico is felt. The aggressive struggle for life gives place to the recollection that to acquire wealth is not necessarily the only business of all men and all nations; for the patient *peon* lives in happiness without it. You may scorn him, but he is one of Nature's object-lessons.

Singularly un-American—that is if United States and Canadian manners and customs shall be considered typical of America—are the customs of the Mexican. The influence and romance of the long years of Spanish domination and character have been crystallised upon the Mexican soil. The mien and character of the race created here in New Spain is marked for all time as a distinctive type, which may possess more for the future than the votary of Anglo-Saxon civilisation and strenuous commercialism may yet suspect. Whatever critical comparison may be applied to these people, the foreigner will acknowledge the pleasing trait of courtesy they invariably show. The elegance and grace of Spanish manners, wafted across the Atlantic in the days of ocean chivalry, were budded to the gentle courtesy of the native; and the brusque Anglo-Saxon is almost ashamed of his seeming or intended brusqueness before the graceful salutation of the poorest *peon*. Hat in hand, and with courteous or devout wish for your welfare on his lips, the poor

Mexican seems almost a reproach to the harbinger of an outside world which seemingly grows more hard and commercial as time goes on.

The picturesque and the simple are, of course, bought at the expense, too often, of hygiene and comfort, and Mexico does not escape this present law. Yet it is remarkable how soon the Briton or the American in Mexico adapts himself to his surroundings, and grows to regard them with affection. It is true that the government of the country is practically a military despotism, yet the foreigner is respected, and none interfere with him. On the contrary, he is often looked up to as a representative of a superior State, and if he be worthy he acquires some of the demeanour of race-*noblesse oblige*.

There are cities set on steep hill-sides, which we shall enter. Terrace after terrace climb the rocky ribs of arid hills. Houses, interspersed with gardens; communities backed by the soft outlines of distant ranges, seen adown the widening valley; and walls, houses, streets, people, landscape; all are of that distinctive colour and character of the Mexican upland, over-arched by the cloudless azure of its sky. Clustered upon these same steep mineral-bearing hills—and, indeed, they are the *raison d'être* of the town at all in that spot—are the great mining places, ancient and modern, which form so important a feature of the life of the country on the Great Plateau.

Fabulous wealth of silver has been dug from these everlasting hills. Grim and abandoned mine-mouths, far away like black dots upon the slopes, and strange honeycombed galleries and caverns far beneath the outcropping of the lodes, have vomited rich silver ore for centuries: and the clang of miners' steel and the dropping candle are now, as ever, the accompaniment of labour of these hardy *peones*. The very church, perhaps, is redolent of mining, and was raised by some pious delver in the bowels of the hill whereon it stands—a thank-offering for some great luck of *open sesame* which his saints afforded him.

But we will not linger here; Guanajuato and Zacatecas and Pachuca shall be our theme in another chapter, and the tale of toil and silver which they tell. For the moment the way lies down the Great Plateau, among its intersecting ranges of hills, through the fertile valleys, which alternate with the appalling sun-beat deserts.

The conditions of travel in this great land of Mexico—it is nearly two thousand miles in length—are, perhaps, less arduous than in Spanish-American countries generally. Mexico has lent itself well to the building of railways in a longitudinal direction, upon the line of least resistance from north-west to south-east, paralleling its general Andine structure. Several great trunk lines thus connect the capital City of Mexico and the southern part of the republic with the civilisation of the United States, over this relatively easy route. Yet the earliest railway of Mexico, that from Vera Cruz to the City of Mexico, traverses the country in the most difficult direction, transversely, rising from tide-water and the Atlantic littoral, and ascending the steep escarpments of the Eastern Sierra Madre to fall down into the lake-valley of Mexico, bringing outside civilisation to that isolated interior world. But Mexico's singular topographical position did not secure her from invasion. Three times the city on the lakes has fallen to foreign invaders—the Spaniards of the Conquest, the French of Napoleon, and the Americans of the United States. Indeed, the flat and arid tableland stretching away for such interminable distances to the north was formerly a more potent natural defence than the Cordilleran heights which front on the Atlantic seas; and the axiom of Lerdo is well brought to mind in considering the geographical environment: "Between weakness and strength—the desert!"

ORIZABA, CAPPED WITH PERPETUAL SNOW: VIEW ON THE MEXICAN RAILWAY AT CORDOVA.

But away from the railways, and the roads where *diligencias* ply their lumbering and dusty course, the saddle is the only, and indeed the most characteristic, mode of travel; and the *arriero* and his string of pack-mules is the common carrier, and the mountain road or dusty desert trail the means of communication from place to place. Along these the horseman follows, day after day, his hard but interesting road, for to the lover of Nature and incident the saddle ever brings matter of interest unattainable by other means of locomotion. The glorious morning air, the unfolding panorama of landscape —even the desert and the far-off mountain spur which he must round ere evening falls, are sources, of exhilaration and interest. The simple people and their quaint dwellings, where in acute struggle for life with Nature they wrest a living from rocks and thorns—are these not subjects, even, worthy of some passing philosophical thought? Not a hilltop in the vicinity of any human habitations—be they but the wretched *jacales* or wattle-huts of the poorest peasants—but is surmounted by a cross: not a spring or well but is adorned with flowers in honour of that patron saint whose name it bears; and not a field or hamlet or mine but has some religious nomenclature or attribute. For the Mexicans are a race into which the religion of the Conquistadores penetrated indelibly, whose hold upon them time scarcely unlooses. The creeds of the priests, moreover, are interwoven with the remains of Aztec theistic influence, and the superstitions of both systems hold the ignorant peasantry of Mexico in enduring thrall. Much of beauty and pathetic quaintness there is in this strong religious sentiment, which no thinking observer will deride; much of retrograde ignorance, which he will lament to see.

The Great Plateau tapers away towards the south, terminating in the Valley of Mexico, bounded by the snowy Cordillera of Anahuac. Within this range are two great volcanic uplifts, two beautiful mountain peaks, crowned with perpetual snow—the culminating orographical features of the Sierras, and the highest points in Mexico. The loftiest of these is Popocatepetl, "the smoking mountain," and its companion is Ixtaccihuatl, the "sleeping woman," both of poetical Indian nomenclature. These beautiful solitary uplifts rise far above the canyons and forests at their bases: penetrate the clouds which sometimes wreath them, terminating in a porcelain-gleaming summit of perpetual snow. The mid-day sun flashes upon them, rendering them visible from afar, and its declining rays paint them with that carmine glow known to the Andine and Alpine traveller, which arrests his vision as evening falls. So fell, indeed, the morning rays of the orb of day upon the burnished golden breastplates of the image set on the sacred pyramid of Teotihuacan: the sun-god, Tonatiuah, as in the shadowy Toltec days he faced the flashing east.

Prehistoric fact and fable press hard upon us as we approach the famous Valley of Mexico and its fine capital. This is the region where that singular "stone age" flourished, of pyramid-building and stone-shaping peoples. Here both geology and history have written their pages, as if Nature and Fate had conspired together to mark epochs of time and space in ancient temple, dead revolution, and slumbering volcano. And now below us lies the City of Mexico. From the wooded uplands and hill-summits—redolent of pine and exhilarating with the tonic air—which form the rim of the valley, the panorama of the capital and its environs lies open to the view. Plains crossed by white streaks of far-off roads, intersecting the chequered fields of green *alfalfa* and yellow maize; *haciendas* and villages embowered in luxuriant foliage; the gleam of domes and towers, softened in the glamour of distance and bathed by a reposeful atmosphere and mediæval tints—such is Mexico, this fair city of the West.

PINE-CLAD HILLS FORMING THE RIM OF THE VALLEY OF MEXICO, 8,000 FEET ELEVATION ABOVE SEA-LEVEL.

The City of Mexico, like most centres of human habitation in whatever part of the world, is most beautiful when seen from afar, and in conjunction with Nature's environment. But the old Aztec city, the dark, romantic seat of the viceroys, the theatre of revolutionary struggle, and the modern centre of this important Mexican civilisation, is a really handsome and attractive city. Indeed, the capitals of many Spanish-American republics, and their civilisation and social *régime*, are often in the nature of a revelation to the traveller from Europe or the United States, who has generally pictured a far more primitive State. With its handsome institutions and public buildings, and extensive boulevards and parks, and characteristic social, literary, and commercial life, the City of Mexico may be described as Americo-Parisian, and it is rapidly becoming a centre of attraction for United States tourists, who, avid of historical and foreign colour, descend thither in Pullman-car loads from the north. The city lies some three miles from the shore of Lake

Texcoco, which, with that of Chalco and others, forms a group of salt- and fresh-water lagoons in the strange Valley of Mexico. At the time of the Conquest the city stood upon an island, connected with the mainland by the remarkable stone causeways upon which the struggles between the Spaniards and the Aztecs took place, during the siege of the city at the time of the Conquest. But these lakes, after the manner of other bodies of water, generally, in the high elevations of the American Cordilleras—Titicaca, in Peru, to wit—are gradually perishing by evaporation, their waters diminishing century by century. The Valley of Mexico, however, of recent years has received an artificial hydrographic outlet in the famous drainage canal and tunnel, which conducts the overflow into a tributary of the Panuco river, and so to the Gulf of Mexico.

The Valley of Mexico is surrounded by volcanic hills, forming a more recent formation of the Andine folds, of which the Sierra Madres compose the Mexican Cordilleras. We have now to cross this, for our faces are set towards the Pacific Ocean. We ascend and pass the Western Sierra Madre, the *divortia aquarum* of the Pacific watershed, leaving the intra-montane plateau of Anahuac and the *mesa central* behind us. Again the climate changes as the downward journey is begun, and again the *tierra caliente* is approached. The culminating peaks—the beautiful Popocatepetl and Ixtaccihuatl—sink now below the eastern horizon, but as we journey to the west Colima's smoking cone will rise before the view. The descent from the highlands to the west coast is even more rapid than to the east, and the temperate climate of the valleys, and the bitter cold of the early morning on the uplands, soon give place to tropical conditions. Extensive forests of oak and pine, clothing the sides of the canyons and *barrancas* of the high Sierra Madre, are succeeded by the profuse vegetation of the torrid zone. Down in the soft regions of the west, where tropical agriculture yields its plentiful and easily-won harvests, are romantic old *haciendas* and villages hidden away in the folds of the landscape, such as are a delight to the traveller and the lover of the picturesque. The "happy valley" of Cuernavaca is reached by railway from the capital, but beyond this the road to the seaboard is still that ancient trail which Cortes used, which descends to Acapulco, for the railway builders have not yet completed their works to the Pacific waters.

Away from the main route of travel lie sequestered old sugar estates, and villages of romantic and picturesque charm, yet untouched by speculator or capitalist. Antique piles of stone buildings are there, redolent of that peculiar poetry of the pastoral life of Mexico in the tropics. The old Spaniards built well; their solid masonry defies the centuries; and their most prosaic structures were invested with an architectural charm which the rapid money-seeker of to-day cares little for, in his corrugated iron and temporary materialism. Near to the arches, columns, and turrets of the old *haciendas* the garden lies, replete with strange fruits and flowers. The gleam of oranges and limes comes from the tangled groves; grapes and pomegranates vie with each other in unattended profusion. The iguana sports among the old stone walls of the great garden, and humming-birds and butterflies hover in the subtle atmosphere. The tropic sunset throws a peaceful glamour and serenity over all. The cocoanut palms, with feathery grace above and slender column upward rearing, stir not against their ethereal setting as we watch, and the passing water in the old aqueduct scarce breaks the tropic silence, or if, perchance, it whisper, murmurs of centuries past, a low refrain.

But we shall journey away from the haunts of man again, and penetrate the deep dark *barrancas* and little-known mountain-fastnesses of the western slope of the State of Guerrero. Here are great uninhabited and unexplored stretches of country, rugged and wild, replete with matters of interest, whether for hunter, sportsman, or archæologist. Indeed, it would be difficult to find a region offering so varied a nature of resource and interest in any part of the world, except possibly in the still less accessible wilds of the Amazonian slopes of the Peruvian Andes. The botanist will find on this Pacific side of Mexico an unstudied *flora*, and the ethnologist and the antiquarian a number of native races, speaking strange separate languages; and the ruins of thousands of the habitations of prehistoric man. The climate in these rugged regions ranges from the heat of the fierce tropical sun to the bitter cold of the mountain summits. Abundant *bosques* or forests of oak cover the higher regions, and the wild and broken nature of the country renders it difficult to traverse, and calls for the adventurous spirit of the pioneer and explorer, without which the traveller will but meet with discomfort and danger.

Yet the true traveller finds pleasure in these matters. The impressive grandeur of the mountain landscape, the endless forests, the profound ravines do but serve to divert his mind from the peril and discomfort of the trail. Here he may revel in Nature's untamed handiwork of mountain, forest, and flood, as day after day he journeys onward in the saddle towards the Pacific Ocean. Here are the imposing *barrancas* of Jalisco which he traverses, and marks how they are buried in the profuse vegetation which presses up to the very border of the lava of smoking Ceboruco. Thence the myrtle forests of Tepic are penetrated. On the tropic lakes thousands of log-like alligators lie, gloomily awaiting their prey. From the verge, which rich forests fringe, and where brilliant water-weeds encircle the shoals, dainty pink and white herons rise, and below the blue surface gleams the sheen of myriad fish. Far to the southwards the fitful volcanic flames of Colima light up the landscape at night. A day's journey more across the coastal plains, and our reconnaissance is finished. The long-drawn surf beats upon the shore of the vast western ocean, for we have crossed the continent; and the sun's glowing disc dips to the blood-red waves—sunset in the Pacific.

TYPICAL VILLAGE OF THE PACIFIC COAST ZONE: STATE OF COLIMA.

CHAPTER II

THE DAWN OF MEXICO: TOLTECS AND AZTECS

Lake Texcoco—Valley of Anahuac—Seat of the Aztec civilisation—Snow-capped peaks—Pyramids of Teotihuacan—Toltecs—The first Aztecs—The eagle, cactus, and serpent—Aztec oracle and wanderings—Tenochtitlan—Prehistoric American civilisations—Maya, Incas—Quito and Peru—The dawn of history—The Toltec empire—Rise, *régime*, fall—Quetzalcoatl—Otomies—Chichemecas—Nezahualcoyotl—Astlan—The seven tribes and their wanderings—Mexican war-god—The Teocallis—Human sacrifices—Prehistoric City of Mexico—The Causeways—Aztec arts, kings, and civilisation—Montezuma—Guatemoc—Impressions of the Spaniards—The golden age of Texcoco—Vandalism of Spanish archbishop—The poet-king and his religion—Temple to the Unknown God—Aztecs and Incas compared—The Tlascalans—The Otomies—Cholula—Mexican tribes—Aztec buildings—Prehistoric art—Origin of American prehistoric civilisation—Biblical analogies—Supposed Asiatic and Egyptian origins—Aboriginal theory.

Like the misty cloud-streaks of the early dawn, the beginning of the story of the strange empire of prehistoric Mexico unfolds from fable and fact as we look back upon it. We are to imagine ourselves upon the shores of Lake Texcoco, in the high valley-plateau of Anahuac, "the land amid the waters." It is the year 1300, or a little later, of the Christian era. The borders of the lake are marshy and sedgy, the surrounding plain is bare and open, and there is no vestige of man and his habitation. Far away, east, west, and north, faint mountain ranges rise, shimmering to the view in the sun's rays through the clear upland air, whilst to the south two beautiful gleaming snow-capped peaks are seen,[3] and over all is the deep blue vault of the tropic highland sky.

3 Ixtaccihuatl and Popocatepetl.

We have said that there are no vestiges of man or his structures to be seen, yet upon gazing penetratingly towards the north-east there might be observed the tops of two high ruined pyramids,[4] the vestiges of the civilisation of the shadowy Toltecs. But we are not for the moment concerned with these ruined structures, for, as we watch, a band of dusky warriors, strangely clad, comes over the plain. They come like men on some set purpose, glancing about them, at the shores of the lake, at the horizon, expectantly, yet with a certain vague wistfulness as of deferred hope. Suddenly their leader halts and utters an ejaculation; and with one hand shading the sun's rays from his eyes he points with outstretched arm towards the water's edge. His companions gaze intently in the direction indicated, and then run forward with joyous shouts and gesticulations. What is it that has aroused their emotions? Near the lake-shore a rock arises, overgrown with a thorny *nopal*, or prickly-pear cactus, and perched upon this is an eagle with a serpent in its beak.

4 Teotihuacan: pyramids of the sun and moon.

Who are these men and whence have they come? They are the first Aztecs, and they have come "from the north"; and for centuries they have been wandering from place to place, seeking a promised land which their deity had offered them, a land where they should found a city and an empire. The hoped-for oracle is before them, the promised symbol which they had been bidden to seek, by which they should know the destined spot—an eagle perched upon a *nopal* with a serpent in its beak: and their wanderings are at an end. Here they pitched their camp, and here as time went on the wonderful city of Tenochtitlan arose, the centre of the strange Aztec civilisation. Thus, fable records, was first established the site of Mexico City; prehistoric, despotic, barbaric, first; mediæval, dark, romantic, later; handsome and interesting to-day.

THE FINDING OF THE SITE FOR THE PREHISTORIC CITY OF MEXICO BY THE FIRST AZTECS.
(From the painting in Mexico.)

But whence came these men? That, indeed, who shall say? Whence came the strange civilisation of the American races—Maya, Toltec, Aztec, Inca? To Mexico and Yucatan and Guatemala, to Quito and Peru, whence came the peoples who built stone temples, pyramids, halls, tombs, inscribed hieroglyphics, and wrought cunning arts, such as by their ruins, relics, and traditions arouse our admiration even to-day. History does not say, yet what glimmerings of history and legend there are serve to take us farther back in time, although scarcely to a fixed starting-point, for the thread of the tale of wanderings and developments of these people of Mexico—a thread which seems traceable among the ruined structures of Anahuac.

The first glimmerings of this history-legend refer to an unknown country "in the north." About the middle of the third century of the Christian era there proceeded thence the people known as the Mayas, who traversed Mexico and arrived in Yucatan; and they are the reputed originators of the singular and beautiful temples encountered there, and the teachers of the stone-shaping art whose results arouse the admiration of the archæologist and traveller of to-day, in that part of Mexico. The descendants of the Mayas are among the most intelligent of the native tribes inhabiting the Republic, doubtless due to the influence of the polity and work of their ancestors. Time went on. About the middle of the sixth century A.D. another people came "out of the north"—the famous Toltecs, and in their southward migration they founded successive cities, ultimately remaining at Tollan, or Tula, and to them are attributed the remarkable pyramids of Teotihuacan, Cholula, and other structures. Tula is some fifty miles to the north of the modern city of Mexico, and it formed the centre of the powerful empire and civilisation of this cultured people. Eleven monarchs reigned, but the Toltec Empire was overthrown; the people dispersed, and they mysteriously disappeared at the beginning of the twelfth century A.D., after some 450 years of existence. None of these dates, however, can be looked upon as really belonging to the realm of exact history.

PREHISTORIC MEXICO: TOLTEC PYRAMID OR TEOCALLI OF THE SUN AT SAN JUAN, TEOTIHUACAN.
(Exploration and restoration work being carried on.)

Tradition also has it that the Toltecs were dispersed by reason of a great famine due to drought, followed by pestilence, only a few people surviving. Banished from the scene of their civilisation by these disasters, the few remaining inhabitants made their way to Yucatan and Central America; and their names and traditions seem to be stamped there. Beyond this little is known of the Toltecs. Possibly some of them found their way still further south to Ecuador and Peru, and influenced the Inca civilisations of the South American continent. To the Toltecs is ascribed the most refined civilisation of prehistoric America, a culture which was indeed the source of the far inferior one of the Aztecs, which we shall presently observe. The Toltecs wrought cleverly in gold and silver, and in cotton fabrics; whilst the remarkable character of their buildings and structures is shown by the ruins of these to-day, as at Cholula and Teotihuacan. The art of picture-writing is attributed to them; and the famous Calendar stone of Mexico has also been ascribed to these people. From amid the shadowy history of the Toltecs the traditions of the deity which so largely influenced prehistoric Mexican religion arose: the mystic Quetzalcoatl, the "god of the air," "the feathered serpent." This strange personage was impressed upon the people's mind as a white man of a foreign race, with noble features, long beard, and flowing garments; and he taught them a sane religion, in which virtue and austerity were dominant, and the sacrifice of human beings and animals forbidden. This singular personage, runs the fable, disappeared after twenty years' sojourn among them, in the direction of the rising sun, having promised to return. When the Spaniards came out of the East their coming was hailed as the return of Quetzalcoatl, and the reverence and superstition surrounding these supposed "children of the sun" protected the Spaniards and permitted their advance into the country, and indeed, was at length conducive to the downfall of Montezuma and the Aztec Empire.

So pass the cultured, shadowy Toltecs from our vision. They had been preceded in their southward migration by the Otomies, in the seventh century A.D., an exceedingly numerous and primitive people who almost annihilated the Spaniards during the Conquest, and whose descendants to-day occupy a vast region, and still largely speak their own language, rather than Spanish. The Toltecs were succeeded by yet another tribe "from the north," the Chichemecas, who came down and occupied their civilisation of Tula. These people, warlike and inferior in culture to the Toltecs, allied themselves with the neighbouring Nahua tribes, and an empire came into being, with its capital at Texcoco, on the shore of the great lake. The famous Nezahualcoyotl, the poet-king of this empire, who ascended the throne of Texcoco in 1431, was one of the most remarkable figures of prehistoric Anahuac, and his genius and fortunes recall the history of Alfred of England, to the student's mind. He built a splendid palace at Texcotzinco, and ruins of its walls and aqueducts remain to this day. His life is sketched in these pages subsequently, and something of the beauty of his philosophy set forth.

And thus history has brought us again to the Aztecs, the founders of Tenochtitlan by the lake-shore, on the spot indicated by their oracle. They had come "from the north," one of seven tribes or families, all of which spoke the Nahuatl or Mexican tongue. This unknown country, called Astlan, or "the land of the herons," was the home of these seven tribes—the Mexicas, or Aztecs, the Tlascalans, Xochimilcas, Tepanecas, Colhuas, Chalcas and Tlahincas—and has been varyingly assigned a locality in California, and in Sinaloa. Why the Aztecs left their northern home is not known, even in legend, but they were instigated to their wanderings, tradition says, by their fabled war-god, Huitzilopochtli, or Mexitl, from whom came the name "Mexica" or "Azteca," by which these people called themselves. From the beginning of the tenth to the beginning of the thirteenth century A.D. this tribe journeyed and sojourned on its southward way, from valley to valley, from lake to lake, from Chapala to Patzcuaro, and thence to Tula, the old Toltec capital. Once more dispersed, they wandered on, and, guided by their oracle, reached their final resting-place at Tenochtitlan. This name, by which they designated their capital, was derived either from that of Tenoch, their venerated high priest, or from the Aztec words meaning "stone-serpent," in reference to the emblem they had followed.

The first work of the people was to raise a great temple to their god—the bloodthirsty Huitzilopochtli—who had led them on. It was begun at once, and around it grew the habitations of the people, the huts made of reeds and mud called *xacali*, such as indeed to-day form the habitations of a large part of Mexican people under the name of *jacales*.[5] This great Teocalli, or "house of god," at the time of the arrival of the Spaniards, was a structure pyramidal in form, built of earth and pebbles and faced with cut stone, square at base, its sides—300 to 400 feet long—facing the cardinal points of the heavens. Flights of steps on the outside, winding round the truncated pyramid, gave access to the summit. Here in the sanctuary was the colossal image of the Aztec war-god—the abominable conception of a barbaric people—and the stone of sacrifice upon which the sacrificial captives were laid. Upon its convex surface the unhappy wretches were successively bound, their breasts cut open with obsidian knives, and the still beating hearts, torn forth by the hand of the priest, were flung smoking before the deity!

5 *X* and *j* are often interchangeable in Spanish.

Upon the marshy borders of this lake, set in the beautiful and fertile valley of Anahuac, the city rose to elegance and splendour. The *jacales* gave place to buildings of brick and stone, founded in many cases upon piles, and between them were streets and canals, giving access to the city from the lake. Centre of all was the great Teocalli.

The position of the city was peculiar. It was founded upon an island, and was subject to inundations from the salt waters of the lake; for the Valley of Mexico had at that time no outlet for its streams. It formed a hydrographic entity; and in this connection it reminds the traveller of the birthplace of that other strange, prehistoric American civilisation, three thousand miles away to the south-east—Lake Titicaca and the cradle of the Incas. To protect the city from these inundations embankments were made, and other works which attest the engineering capabilities of the people. Four great causeways gave access to the marshy island upon which the capital was situated—structures of stones and mortar, the longest being some four or five miles in length. To-day one of these forms part of a modern street, and the waters of the lake have retired more than two miles from the city.

THE VALLEY OF MEXICO: VIEW ON LAKE TEXCOCO; THE MODERN CITY OF MEXICO IN THE DISTANCE.

The habitations of the principal people were built of stone, and the interior of polished marbles and rare woods. Painting and sculpture embellished these interiors and exteriors, although these were generally crude and barbaric in their execution and representation. Around the city and upon the shores of the lakes, numerous villages arose, surrounded by luxurious gardens and orchards, and the singular *chinampas*, or floating gardens, were made, with their wealth of flowers, such as the early Mexicans both loved and demanded for sacrificial ceremonies.

Naturally, all this development took time. Yet the rise of this civilisation must be considered rapid—probably it was largely inherited in principle. The first Aztec government was the theocratic and military *régime* established in the fourteenth century under Tenoch, a military priest and leader who died in 1343. Less than two hundred years afterwards the city of Tenochtitlan was in the zenith of power and culture at the moment when it fell before the Spaniards. Ten kings followed Tenoch, the first being Itzcoatl, who may be considered the real founder of the empire. He was followed by the first

Montezuma, who greatly extended its sway, dying in 1469. Then came Axayacatl, who is considered to be the constructor of the famous Mexican Calendar stone. Tizoc, his successor, hoped to win the favour of the war-god by the reconstruction of the great Teocalli, whose service was inaugurated by the infamous Ahuizotl in 1487 and at whose dedication an appalling number of human sacrifices were made. Then at the beginning of 1500 the throne was ascended by Montezuma the Second, who further extended the beauty and power of the Aztec capital, but who, vacillating and weighed down by the fear of destiny, lived but to witness the beginning of the fall of Mexico before the Spaniards in 1519. The brave Guatemoc, the last of his line, strove vainly to uphold the dynasty against the invaders.

There is no doubt that the Aztecs created a remarkable centre of semi-barbaric civilisation, and the descriptions given by the Spanish historians—whether those who accompanied Cortes, as Bernal Diaz, or those who drew their colouring from these accounts—are such as to arouse the interest and enthusiasm even of the reader of to-day. In this connection, of course, it is to be recollected that Cortes and his followers were not all men of education or trained knowledge of the great cities of the civilised world, and there is no doubt that they lacked somewhat the faculty of comparison, and over-estimated what they beheld. Let us translate from Clavijero, a Spanish historian and Jesuit who wrote later, and who describes the scene which the Spaniards beheld from the summit of the great Teocalli as "many beautiful buildings, gleaming, whitened, and burnished; the tall minarets of the temples scattered over the various quarters of the city; the canals; verdant plantations and gardens—all forming a beautiful whole which the Spaniards never ceased to admire, especially observing it from the summits of the great temples which dominated not only the city immediately below, but its environs and the large towns beyond. No less marvellous were the royal palaces and the infinite variety of plants and animals kept there; but nothing caused them greater admiration than the great market plaza." "Not a Spaniard of them," according to Bernal Diaz, the soldier-historian of the Conquest, who was there and saw it all, although he wrote about it long afterwards, "but held it in high praise, and some of them who had journeyed among European cities swore they had never seen so vast a concourse of merchants and merchandise."

Returning to our history, it is not to be supposed that this powerful Aztec nation, with their fine capital of Tenochtitlan, were the only people inhabiting the land of Anahuac at that time. Several other peoples held sway there. On the eastern side of Lake Texcoco, a few leagues away, lived the Texcocans, already mentioned; one of the tribes who also had come "from the north" in early days and who had settled there. They also had developed or inherited a civilisation akin to that of the Toltecs, far more refined and important than that of their neighbours and kindred, the Aztecs. It was about the end of the twelfth century when the Texcocans established themselves, building a splendid capital and developing an extensive empire. But misfortune fell upon them as the centuries went on. Soon after the beginning of the fifteenth century they were attacked and overwhelmed by the Tepanecas, another of the seven kindred tribes: their city reduced and their monarch assassinated. But there arose a picturesque figure, the saviour of his country—Prince Nezahualcoyotl, son of the dead king. The prince passed years in disguise, as a fugitive, but at length was permitted to return to the capital, where he led a life of study. But his talents aroused the jealousy of the Tepanec usurper, who saw a danger of the people acclaiming him as their rightful lord and throwing off the yoke of the strangers. Nezahualcoyotl again became a fugitive, having escaped with his life by a stratagem, disappearing through a cloud of incense into a secret passage. But as the years went on the Texcocans, goaded to revolt by grievous taxation, arose: and seizing the moment, the outlawed prince put himself at the head of his people and regained his rightful position, largely with the assistance of the neighbouring Mexicans of Tenochtitlan.

Then followed what has been termed the golden age of Texcoco. Its art, poets, and historians became renowned throughout Anahuac, and its collected literature was the centre of historical lore. Indeed, this it was that was so perversely destroyed by the first Archbishop of Mexico, Zumarraga, after the Conquest—an irremediable loss. The prince or emperor was a philosopher and a poet, and he has left some remarkable examples of his philosophical prayers to the "Unknown God," in whom he believed, abhorring the human sacrifices of his neighbours the Aztecs. He has been termed the "Solomon of Anahuac," although the severe code of laws he instituted have earned him a harsher name in addition.

Under this *régime* agriculture prospered exceedingly, and a large population cultivated all the available ground, just as under the Incas of Peru the Andine slopes were terraced and cultivated. Splendid buildings were erected, and a style of luxurious living inaugurated somewhat after the fashion of Oriental history, and the descriptions of the magnificence of the royal appurtenances fill pages of the historians' accounts. Most of this history was written by the famous Ixtlilxochitl, son of this great emperor, who occupied the throne at the time of the Conquest and became an ally of the Spaniards against the Aztec. It is upon the writings of this prince-historian that much of the material of the later writers of the history of Mexico and the Conquest is founded.

In the construction of his palaces and buildings Nezahualcoyotl employed vast bodies of natives, after the manner of an Egyptian potentate of old. Baths, hanging-gardens, groves of cedar, harems, villas, temples formed the beautiful and luxurious Texcotzinco, the prince's residence, as described by its historian. To-day the mounds and *débris* of sculptured stone which formed the place scarcely arrest the traveller's attention. In the midst of his luxury the emperor fell a prey to a passion for the betrothed of one of his subjects, a beautiful maiden. The unhappy individual who had thus become his monarch's rival—he was a veteran chief in the army—was needlessly sent on a military expedition, where he fell, and the hand of his promised bride was free for the monarch's taking. So was enacted upon these high regions of Anahuac a tragic episode, as of David and Uriah, to the blemish of an otherwise noble name and of a mind above the superstitions of his time.

"Truly, the gods which I adore; idols of stone and wood: speak not, nor feel, neither could they fashion the beauty of the heavens—the sun, the moon, and the stars ... nor yet the earth and the streams, the trees and the plants which beautify it. Some powerful, hidden, and unknown God must be the Creator of the universe, and he alone can console me in my affliction or still the bitter anguish of this heart."[6] So spake Nezahualcoyotl.

6 I have translated this from the Spanish of Ixtlilxochitl as quoted by Prescott.—C. R. E.

Urged probably by the feelings of the philosopher (whose ponderings on the infinite may occasion him more anguish perhaps than the ordinary vicissitudes of life), the monarch raised up a temple to the "Unknown God," in which neither images nor sacrifices were permitted.

After somewhat more than half a century of his reign, and at a time calculated as the beginning of the last quarter of the fifteenth century, this remarkable philosopher-king died, and was succeeded by his son Nezahualpilli, who in a measure followed in his father's footsteps. But he also passed away, his life having been overshadowed to some extent by the singular belief or prediction of the fall of his people in the coming of the white man from the East—a belief which influenced both the Texcocans and the Aztecs. His son Ixtlilxochitl, the historian above named, was in power at the time of the conquest by the Spaniards, but he hated the Aztecs with a bitter hatred in consequence of their influence upon his people, and the installing by the machinations of Montezuma of an elder brother upon the throne, which had plunged the kingdom into civil war. This was in the second decade of the sixteenth century.

The Texcocans, in conjunction with yet another and smaller people living on the west side of the lake at Tlacopan, formed with the Aztecs a confederation or triple alliance of three republics, by which they agreed to stand together against all comers, and to divide all territory and results of conquest in agreed proportion. They carried on war and annexation around them for a considerable period, extending their sway far beyond the Valley of Mexico, or Anahuac, which formed their home, passing the Sierra Madre mountains to the east, until about the middle of the fifteenth century—under Montezuma —the land and tribes acknowledging their sway reached to the shores of the Gulf of Mexico. To the south their arms and influence penetrated into what are now Guatemala and Nicaragua, whilst to the west they exercised sovereignty to the shores of the Pacific.

THE LAND OF THE AZTEC CONQUEST: MAIZE FIELDS NEAR ESPERANZA, STATE OF PUEBLA.

These conquered territories were not necessarily of easy subjugation. On the contrary, they were plentifully inhabited by races of warrior-peoples, many of them with strong and semi-civilised social and military organisations. The analogy between this confederation of the Aztecs and the extending area of their dominion and civilisation, and the Incas of the Titicaca plateau of Peru, surrounded on all sides by savage warlike tribes, presents itself to the observer in this as in other respects. Like the Incas, the Aztec emperors[7] returned from campaign after campaign loaded with trophies and embarrassed with strings of captives from the vanquished peoples who had dared oppose this powerful confederation. The rich tropical regions of both the eastern and western slopes of the tableland of Anahuac thus paid tribute to the Aztecs, as well as the boundless resources of the south.

7 Both these nations have been likened to the Romans in this respect.

But not all the nations of Anahuac fell under the dominion of the Aztecs. Far from it. The spirits of the people of Tlascala would rise from their graves and protest against such an assertion! Tlascala was a brave and warlike little republic of mountaineers—a kind of Switzerland—who inhabited the western slopes of the Eastern Sierra Madre and the eastern part of the plateau of Anahuac, under the shadow of the mighty Malinche, whose snow-crowned head arises on the eastern confines of the tableland. Tlascala, indeed, was a thorn in the side of Montezuma and the Aztecs. The latter had demanded that the little republic pay homage and tribute, and acknowledge the hegemony of the dominant nation, to which the Tlascalans made reply, "Neither our ancestors nor ourselves ever have or will pay tribute to any one. Invade us if you can. We beat you once and may do it again!" or words to that effect, as recorded by the historians. For in the past history of the Tlascalans—who were of the same original migratory family as the Aztecs—a great conflict had been recorded, in which they had vanquished their arrogant kindred.

Deadly strife and hatred followed this, but Tlascala withstood all attacks from without, and, moreover, was strengthened by an alliance with the Otomies, a warlike race inhabiting part of the great *mesa* or central tableland north of Anahuac. These were the people who so grievously harassed the Spaniards after the *Noche Triste* and against whom the heroic battle of Otumba was fought. Except to the east, whence approach was easy from the coast, the territory of Tlascala was surrounded by mountains, and this natural defence was continued by the building of an extraordinary wall or fortification at the pregnable point. Through this the Spaniards passed on their journey of invasion, and, indeed, its ruins remained until the seventeenth century. The name of the Tlascalans well deserves to be written on the pages of the history of primitive Mexico, for it was largely due to their alliance with the Spaniards that the conquest of Mexico by Cortes and his band was rendered possible.

In addition to these various and petty powers and independent republics upon the tableland of Anahuac and its slopes, must be mentioned that of Cholula, a state to the south of Tenochtitlan, in what now is the State of Puebla. This region, which contains the remarkable mound or pyramid bearing its name—Cholula—the construction of which is ascribed to the Toltecs, was, with its people, dominated by and under tribute to the Aztecs. So was the nation of the Cempoallas, upon the Vera Cruz coast, who rendered assistance to the landing *Conquistadores*; and, indeed, almost all the natives of that vast region acknowledged the sway and lived in awe of the empire of Montezuma.

It is seen that Mexico, in prehispanic times, was fairly well populated—comparatively speaking, of course. Indeed, at the present time there are ten times as many Indians in that part of North America which forms modern Mexico, as ever existed in the whole of the much vaster area which forms the United States. The inhabitants of Mexico were divided into two main classes—those living under a civilised or semi-civilised organisation, such as the Aztecs and others already enumerated, and those which may be looked upon as savages. These latter were exceedingly numerous, and at the present day something like 220 different tribal names have been enumerated. This serves to show the wide range of peoples who inhabited the land before the Conquest, principally as clans, or *gentiles*, as in South America also.

Having seen, thus, what were the anthropo-geographical conditions of primitive Mexico, we may cast a brief glance at the arts and institutions of these semi-civilised peoples. Their buildings—most indelible records of these civilisations—cover a considerable range of territory, as has been observed: yet the antiquities of less important nature cover one very much greater. The true stone edifices, the real mural remains, are, however confined to certain limits—between the 16th and 22nd parallel of north latitude—that is to say, the southern half of Mexico. Roughly, these buildings may be divided into three classes—*adobe*, or sun-dried earthen brick, unshaped stone and mortar, and cut and carved stone. In some cases a combination of these was used in the same structure. The best elements of construction do not seem to have been used. Domes and arches were not known to these builders, although they had a system of corbelling-out over openings, which, in the case of the Maya "arch," approximates thereto. They also used lintels of stone and wood, and these last were the weak points, and their decaying has sometimes brought down part of the façade. The work of the sculptor is crude, like that of the Incas of Peru, of which it reminds the traveller in some cases, but shows signs of evolving power and a sense of the beautiful, as has been averred by the most learned antiquarians who have studied it. It is held that there were several schools of architecture represented.

The various kinds of structures and relics found throughout the country include pyramids, temples, tombs, causeways, statues, fortifications, terraced hills, rock-sculpture, idols, painted caves, calendar stones, sacrificial stones, habitations, canals, pottery, mummies, *cenotes*, or wells, &c. The northernmost point where any monument in stone is encountered is at Quemada, in the State of Zacatecas, which seems to mark the limit of the stronger civilisation of Southern Mexico, in contrast to the less virile civilisation which seems to be indicated by the clay and *adobe* structures of the northern part of Mexico and of the adjoining territory embodied at the present day in Arizona, California, and New Mexico, beyond the Rio Grande.

PREHISTORIC MEXICO: RUINS OF EL FOLOC AT CHICHEN-YTZA, YUCATAN.

But once more we ask, "Where did these people come from originally?" It has been said that the origin of the people of a continent belongs not to the realm of history but of philosophy. Well may it be so, but we are not content. What was the origin of the first peoples of the Americas, and where did the principle of their barbaric civilisation come from? There were the fables of the lost continent of Atlantis—of which, geologically, part of North America is a portion—to be considered: and perchance, so thought the earlier thinkers, these peoples, remnants of its population. But the generally accepted theory assigns Eastern Asia as the source, and analogies are adduced in architecture, customs, religions, physiognomy, and a multitude of conditions. As to language, careful study has shown, on the other hand, that none of the numerous indigenous tongues of the present-day Mexican aborigines bear any resemblance whatever to Asiatic tongues, except that some likeness between Otomie and Chinese is traced: whilst some points of similarity are

Further similarities are adduced in matters relating to the system of chronology—that used by the Aztecs having analogy to that of the Mongol family, and to some extent of the Persians and Egyptians. Indeed, in the architecture of these prehistoric American ruins resemblance is traced to Egypt, as well as similarity in other matters; and this more strongly perhaps in Peru than in Mexico. In general terms it may be said that many points of prehistoric Mexican civilisation suggest analogy with Egypt and with Hindustan, and it has been said that, from his head-dress to his sandalled feet, the native Mexican is Hispano-Egyptian. But be it as it may, their civilisation seems to have come from the West, not from the East. These aboriginal people and their attributes have nothing in common with Europeans or negroes, whilst they are not unlike Asiatics. I have often been surprised by the strong "Japanese" or Mongol character in the Mexican face. How and when such prehistoric immigrants came, whether by the approaching shores of Behring Straits, whether in that geological time when land connection between North America and Asia was intact, is buried in oblivion. Beyond these theories there still remains that of an autochthonous origin; and who shall yet affirm that both the people and their civilisation may not have sprung and evolved upon the soil of the world which we call new? Time and advancing knowledge may yet reveal these secrets.

CHAPTER III

THE STRANGE CITIES OF EARLY MEXICO

Principal prehistoric monuments—Aztec capital of Tenochtitlan—Pyramids of Teotihuacan—Toltec sun-god—Pyramid of Cholula—Pyramids of Monte Alban—Ruins of Mitla—Remarkable monoliths and sculpture—Beautiful prehistoric stone-masonry—Ruins of Palenque—Temple of the Sun, and others—Stone vault construction—Tropical vegetation—Ruins of Yucatan—Maya temples—Architectural skill—Temples of Chichen-Ytza—Barbaric sculpture—Effect of geology on building—The Aztec civilisation—Land and social laws—Slavery—Taxes, products, roads, couriers—Analogy with Peru—Aztec homes and industries—War, human sacrifice, cannibalism—History, hieroglyphics, picture-writing—Irrigation, agriculture, products—Mining, sculpture, pottery—Currency and commerce—Social system—Advent of the white man.

The most remarkable of the remaining monuments in stone of the peoples who successively or contemporaneously inhabited Mexico, are those well-defined and fairly well-known groups of ruins scattered at wide distances apart in the southern and south-eastern part of Mexican territory. The principal of these are: Teotihuacan, at Texcoco, in the Valley of Mexico; Cholula, in the State of Puebla; Monte Alban and Mitla, in the State of Oaxaca; Palenque, in the State of Chiapas; Uxmal and Chichen-Ytza, in the peninsula of Yucatan.

Of the Aztec city of Tenochtitlan, or Mexico, but little of antiquity remains, as, according to the historian of the Conquest, the place was almost entirely razed to the ground by Cortes. It is probable, however, that enduring stone edifices formed a much less considerable part of this city than has been supposed. Nevertheless, modern excavations continually lay bare portions of Aztec masonry, as well as sculptured monoliths. A short time ago a sculptured tiger, weighing eight tons, was unearthed and deposited in the museum in the capital. The principal building of the Aztec city was the great Teocalli, upon whose site the existing cathedral was built. This huge truncated pyramid has been described already. It was surrounded by a great wall, upon the cornice of which huge carved stone serpents and tigers were the emblematic ornaments. From this wall four gates opened on to the four main streets, which radiated away towards the cardinal points of the compass. Its dimensions are given as 365 feet long by 300 feet wide at the base, whilst the summit-platform was raised more than 150 feet above the level of the streets and square. Here was set the great image of the Aztec war-god, the idol of the abominable Huitzilopochtli which Cortes and his men, after their frightful hand-to-hand struggle with the Aztecs on this giddy platform, tumbled down the face of the pyramid into the streets below, among the astonished Indians. The grandeur, architecturally, of the ancient City of

Mexico has probably been somewhat exaggerated by the *Conquistadores* and subsequent chroniclers, whose enthusiasm sometimes ran riot.

The ruins of Teotihuacan are situated in the north-eastern part of the valley of Mexico, some miles from the shores of Lake Texcoco and twenty-five miles from the modern City of Mexico. They are generally ascribed to the Toltecs, or, at any rate, to a civilised nation greatly previous to the Aztecs; for the ruins were abandoned and their origin unknown when these people arrived. Cortes and his Spaniards, defeated and fleeing after the terrible struggle of the *Noche Triste*, passed near to the great earth pyramids of the Sun and the Moon, which are the main structures of Teotihuacan; but even at that time they were—as they are to-day—mere mounds of earth, in which the pyramidal form has been partly obliterated by the action of time.

PREHISTORIC MEXICO: THE PYRAMID OF THE SUN AT TEOTIHUACAN, IN THE VALLEY OF MEXICO, SEEN FROM THE PYRAMID OF THE MOON.

The very extensive mounds and remains which constitute Teotihuacan are of numerous pyramids, and some ruined walls which have been excavated of recent years. All of these are formed of *adobe* and irregular pieces of the lava of which the adjoining hills are composed. Rude carved monoliths of deities have, however, been recovered from the *débris*. The main features of the ruins are, first, the "Pyramid of the Sun," a huge mound which forms the most colossal structure of prehistoric man in America. It measures, approximately, at its base—for its outlines are so indefined that no exact form can be adduced—some 700 feet on each side, rising upwards in the form of a truncated pyramid rather less than 200 feet above the level of the plain. Next, the "Pyramid of the Moon," a similar but smaller structure—about 500 feet at base—distant from the first some thousands of yards along a strange road or path across the plain, known as *Micoatl*, or the "Path of the Dead," some two miles in length. From the summit of the "Pyramid of the Moon" the beholder looks down into the great courtyard of an adjoining group of ruins; thence his eye travels along this pathway to where the huge "Pyramid of the Sun" arises, far off, on its left-hand side. Between these and indeed beyond them, and bordering on the "Path of the Dead"—probably so called in relation to human sacrifice—are numerous other mounds, which were formerly pyramids of similar character, but of much less magnitude. Probably, in ages past, they were all crowned by temples, and ascended by staircases and terraces—evidences of which, indeed, still remain—whilst the slopes were probably covered with stone and stucco. It is stated that upon the high summit of the great pyramid—that dedicated to Tonatiuh, the sun—a huge stone statue of this deity was placed, and that a plate of polished gold upon its front reflected back the first rays of the rising sun. The name Teotihuacan signifies the "house of the gods." Doubtless it was, in unknown centuries past, the centre of a thriving civilisation and busy and extensive agricultural population. To-day the great pyramid casts its shadow toward a small village of *jacales*, upon a semi-arid plain.

The pyramid of Cholula is of truncated form, like most of these numerous structures. Its height is 200 feet and its base measures 1,440 feet, which is greater than that of the pyramid of Cheops, and it forms the oldest and largest teocalli in Mexico. The presiding deity of this "house of God" was the mysterious Quetzalcoatl. In company with Teotihuacan at Texcoco, and Papantla, in the State of Vera Cruz, Cholula is ascribed to the Toltecs. The elevation above sea-level of the site of this structure is 7,500 feet, and at the time of Cortes the surrounding town is said to have contained a population of 150,000 inhabitants. Its summit is more than an acre in extension, and although partly obliterated and overgrown, the pyramid is crowned to-day with a Roman Catholic church of Spanish-American type. As has been described, these Teocallis were for purposes of religious rite and sacrifice, and upon their upper platforms were the sanctuaries, idols, and never-extinguished sacred fire, all reached by exterior staircases up the slope of the structure.

The State of Oaxaca—and part of the adjoining State of Guerrero—is remarkable for the numerous ruins of prehistoric inhabitants scattered upon its ridges and mountain crests. Terraces, pyramids, and walls crown the summits and extend down the slopes, actually clashing in some cases with the natural profiles of the hills, and causing the natural and artificial to mingle in a strange, and at first glance, scarcely distinguishable blend. These numerous ruins, and the small cultivated terraced patches on the almost inaccessible hill slopes, bring to mind the similar constructions of the old ruins and the singular "andenes" of the Andes of Peru.[8] They point to a busy and numerous population in former times, and in some cases the topography of whole mountain slopes has been remodelled by the hand of prehistoric man. No place was too inaccessible, and terrace and temple crown the Andine summits in Peru at more than 16,000 feet elevation above sea-level, and in Mexico in similar or greater profusion, but at less altitude.

   8 See my book, "The Andes and the Amazon."

Among the remarkable ruins of this nature, in Oaxaca, are those of Monte Alban, near the capital city of Oaxaca. Here are entire crests of mountains, cut away into terraces, quadrangles, and courts, and their great extent and strange environment create a sense of awe and amazement in the beholder. The utter abandonment and sense of solitude; the high ridges, thousands of feet above the valley, which, dim and distant through the atmospheric haze, glimmers below; the vast expanse of sky and landscape, without a sound or touch of life, invests the remains of those seemingly unreal or fairy cities of prehistoric man with a sense of mystery and unfathomed time. Pyramid after pyramid, terrace after terrace, the latter from 500 to 1,000 feet in length, extend along the ridge of the Alban hill—the numerous truncated pyramids rising, like the playthings of some prehistoric giant, from the levelled places. The beholder may imagine the chain of Teocallis which crowned them, lighted up at night by the glare of the never-extinguished sacred fires, as the thronging multitude of the great population of those barbaric peoples of pre-Columbian Mexico pressed along the streets below. He may fill in, in his mind's eye, the picture, fanciful and unreal, as if borrowed from the pages of some Eastern romance, were it not that the actual vestiges of that time are before him. Vast labour—probably directed by autocratic mandate without heed of native life, and working throughout generations—must have been employed to collect and raise up in place the stone, and earth, and *adobe* material of these pyramids, and to make the great levellings and excavations upon these inaccessible summits. They were cities, as well as mere places of religious ceremony, and a large number of people must have dwelt in these "mansions in the skies."

PREHISTORIC MEXICO: RUINS OF MITLA; FAÇADE OF THE HALL OF THE COLUMNS.
(The steps have been "restored" by the photographer.)

In the same State of Oaxaca are the famous ruins of Mitla, pride of the archæology of Mexico, situated some thirty miles from the state capital of Oaxaca. These famous ruins of Mitla are of a different character to the pyramidal structures of Monte Alban, although they have a low pyramidal base and were built mainly for religious purposes, it is probable, like most of these prehistoric monuments. They are situated in an inhabited valley, and the ruins consist of five main groups, some of which are exceedingly well preserved. Indeed, whilst the ruins of Mitla are by no means so extensive as others described, they are in the best state of preservation of any in the country. And this is due both to their method of construction and to their environment; for, unlike the low, tropical regions of Chiapas and Yucatan, this district is at a considerable altitude above sea-level. The great "palaces" or halls which these groups form, occupy an area of about 1,800 feet from north to south, by 1,200 feet from east to west. The principal groups are known as the "Hall of the Monoliths or Columns," the "Catholic group," and the "Arroyo group." Like some of the pyramids throughout Mexico, these are oriented, in this case the variation being but a few degrees from the cardinal points of the compass. The remarkable Hall of the Monoliths is a building some 125 feet long by 25 feet wide, with a row of great stone columns running down the centre. These columns are cut from a single piece of trachyte, 15 feet in height, and 3 feet in diameter at the base, tapering somewhat upwards, but of almost cylindrical form, without pedestal or capital. Whilst these columns are intact, the roof, which was doubtless supported on beams resting on the column, is gone. The weight of these monoliths is calculated at five or six tons, and they were cut from quarries in the trachyte rock of the mountains some five miles away, and more than 1,000 feet above the site of Mitla. In this quarry half-cut blocks for columns and lintels are still in place. Food for thought, even for the modern engineer, is this work.

PREHISTORIC MEXICO: RUINS OF MITLA; HALL OF THE MONOLITHS OR COLUMNS.

But the monolithic columns here are by no means the only remarkable features of the masonry of Mitla. The interior and exterior of these great halls are carved with a beautifully executed geometrical design—the Greek pattern enclosed in a quadrilateral, the blocks upon which they are cut being exactly fitted and adjusted in their places with scarcely visible joints. Indeed, at Mitla, as in other places in the Americas—Huanuco[9] and Cuzco, in Peru, for example—it seems to have been deemed an essential and peculiar art to adjust great blocks of stone with so great a nicety that no mortar was necessary and the joints almost invisible. This, of course, necessitated infinite time and patience—both of which were at the disposal of these prehistoric builders. It is to be recollected, in this connection, that each stone was generally an individual and not a counterpart, and so often had to be fitted to its fellows in the wall, by the laborious method of continually placing and removing. The remarkable and intricate nature of the mosaics and carved blocks at Mitla call forth the admiration of the observer. A vast number of separate stones have been employed, each requiring its respective forming, shaping, and placing, and one of the halls alone shows more than 13,000 such stones in its walls. The stone doorways to these halls are chaste, massive, and effective. The stone lintels in some cases are more than 12 feet long, and nearly 4 feet thick. Indeed, there exist at Mitla nearly a hundred examples of great monoliths, whether columns, lintels, or roof stones, some weighing as much as 15 tons, and up to 20 feet in length.

9 See the "Andes and the Amazon."

The earliest account of the ruins of Mitla, by Francisco de Burgoa, a priest of Oaxaca, who visited them in 1674, states that these beautiful halls were the scene, in prehistoric times, of the most diabolical rites. To-day the ruins are surrounded by a rude native population, most of whom dwell in wretched *jacales*, in a waterless and sun-beat valley—an environment in striking contrast to the antique splendour of these halls of the earlier occupiers of the land.

The ruins of Palenque, in the State of Chiapas, are situated at the base of the picturesque foothills of Tumbala, which border upon Guatemala, in a true tropical environment of luxuriant forest and brimming streams. From this setting the ruined temples and pyramids stand forth like a vision of a charmed or fabled story. Dense tropical undergrowth covers them, and grows again as soon as explorers, who have removed portions of Nature's persistent covering, leave the place. The main structures take the form of great truncated pyramids built up of earth, stones, and masonry, with temples and palaces of masonry upon their summits. Twelve of these pyramids have been discovered so far, and eight are crowned by buildings, the principal of which are known respectively as, the "Temple of the Sun," the "Temple of the Cross," "Temple of the Inscriptions," and the extensive group of ruins termed "The Palace." These temples and palaces consist of massive masonry walls, partly of roughly-shaped blocks, and partly of cut-and-carved stone, and stucco sculpture, with numerous doorways or openings on to the platform of the pyramid-summit. The interior of the buildings is a singular vault-like construction, covered with roofs of masonry carried by the vaulting. These vaults, however, do not embody the principle of the arch, but rather of the off-set, or lean-to, and are very high in proportion to their width. From the palace group arises a square tower of four storeys, about 40 feet in height, forming the centre of the group of extensive courts, buildings, and façades which surround it, all built upon the summit of a pyramid some 200 feet square. As in the Yucatan structures, the lintels over the doorway-openings in the walls were of wood, and their decay has largely been the cause of the façades having fallen into ruins, in many places. There are various interior staircases to these buildings, and the huge and unique reliefs of human figures are a remarkable feature of the interior. The beautiful figure known as the Beau Relief is compared to the relief sculptures of Babylon and Egypt. The material of construction was limestone, generally in unshaped blocks, not laid in regular courses, but with large quantities of mortar and stucco. The walls were lavishly painted and coloured. Indeed, the nature of the building has doubtless obeyed the character of the stone, which does not lend itself to careful cutting and carving like the easily-worked trachyte of Mitla. A very noteworthy structure of this prehistoric city, is the subterranean passage-way for the stream, which passes down the valley upon whose slopes the ruins of Palenque are situated. This, of stone-vaulted construction, after the manner before described, is somewhat less than 1,000 feet long, and the stream still flows through a portion of it. On every hand the extraordinary vigour of the tropical forest is evident, and the dense growth of trees, vines, and herbs which cover valley, pyramid, walls, and roofs, attest the power of the vegetable world.

The prehistoric structures of Yucatan—among the principal of which are those of Uxmal and Chichen-Ytza—are exceedingly numerous. Indeed, the traveller in this territory of the Mayas is rarely out of sight of crumbling pyramid or temple, as he traverses the dense forests of these curious flat and streamless limestone regions. Whilst most of these edifices were for purposes of religious ceremonial, the object of many of them can scarcely be conjectured. Their builders appear to have been people of a peaceful nature, and their dwellings do not generally bear evidence of defensive design. The architectural skill of the Mayas must have been of a very high order. Among the buildings which exist some are nearly perfect units of design, and seem almost to argue the use of "working drawings," as the plan and detail must have been perfected as a whole before the building was begun. This architectural skill of conception, however, has been common in many countries. Some of the buildings were in use when Cortes landed and fought on the shores of Yucatan, nearly four hundred years ago; nevertheless, they are in a remarkable state of preservation, notwithstanding the ravages both of Nature and of man, tending towards their destruction; for on the one hand, the roots of trees and profuse vegetation of a tropical region are efficient levers in the throwing down of the masonry, and on the other, the vandal ignorance of the surrounding inhabitants of the modern towns of the region permits them to make use of the stones in their own walls.

The ruins of Chichen-Ytza, the prehistoric city in the northern part of Yucatan, are among the most important and best preserved of any of the stone structures of the Americas. The ruins are grouped around two great natural wells, the *cenotes*, famous in this remarkable peninsula. Indeed, the derivation of the name of the old city is from Maya words meaning the "Mouth of the Well," and it serves to show the value in which these singular water-supplies were held in this riverless region of Yucatan. Among the most interesting of the structures of Chichen and Uxmal is that of the buildings known as El Foloc, or "the Church." Another is that known as the "House of the Nuns," and yet another the "Temple of the Tigers," which latter shows a sculptured procession of tigers or lynxes. Again, "the Castle" is remarkable, set upon a pyramid rising more than 100 feet above the plain. The "Governor's Palace," the "House of the Pigeons," and "House of the Turtles," are others of these remarkable structures.

The profuse and extraordinary, yet barbaric-appearing sculpture of the façades and interiors of these buildings arrests the observer's attention, and, indeed, fills him with amazement, as does their construction in general. What instruments of precision did a rude people possess who could raise such walls, angles, monoliths, true and plumb as the work of the mason of to-day?

It would be beyond the scope of this work to enter more fully into the details of these ruins. They have been minutely examined and described by famous archæologists, who have devoted much time thereto, and the student may be referred to their works. The foregoing is but a sketch, barely touching upon the extensive and beautiful handwork in stone of the ancient dwellers of this land. Indeed, the traveller may behold them for himself, without great risk or difficulty. He will observe them with admiration. Pyramids rising from the plains or forest-seas which surround them; strange halls where unknown people dwelt; great cities where busy races lived. The character of the various groups of ruins throughout the land shows the effect that the geology of the respective regions has had upon the stone-masonry of these prehistoric builders. As has been shown, the beautiful trachyte of Mitla, which, whilst it is tough and enduring, is soft, and lends itself readily to the chisel. The result has been handed down in the beautiful and exact sculpture of the blocks and *grecques* of the façades of these palaces: work which could not have been performed in a more refractory stone. Not a great distance away are the Monte Alban ruins, as described, which, although extensive and remarkable, show nothing of exact and intricate work in stone-shaping. The hard or silicious rocks which form the immediate region, and the quartzite and crystalline limestone, did not lend themselves, either in the quarry or under the chisel, to such work. In Chiapas, the unshaped and uncoursed masonry of Palenque is formed of a hard, brittle limestone, scarcely capable of being worked to faces. No invisible joints, such as are the beauty of some of the ancient stone structures of the Americas—North and South—were possible, and mortar and stucco were freely employed. Very different, however, was the limestone used in Yucatan. It was easily quarried from its bed, and was of such a texture as lent itself to the profuse and beautiful sculpture of those Maya cities of long ago. Again, the great pyramidal structures of Teotihuacan and surrounding ruins of the Toltec civilisation, had little for their composition but lavas of basaltic nature, which did not possess a character adaptable for exact stone-shaping. Thus it is seen how largely the existence, or non-existence, of freestone influenced the character of these prehistoric structures.

PREHISTORIC MEXICO: RUINS OF MITLA; THE HALL OF THE GRECQUES.

Of exceeding interest are these old buildings of the early Mexicans, whether upon the open plains of the uplands, or buried in the glades of the tropical forests. There they arise, great palace walls where sculptured tigers and serpents, and strange designs, run in barbaric riot around their ruined façades, above grim vaults, subterranean passages, and chambers of inexplicable purpose. There they stand, chapters in stone of the history of a people whose destiny it seems to have been to have formed no link in the purpose and evolution of man; a people who seem to have been upon the threshold of a true civilisation.

The form of government of the principal peoples of Anahuac, the Aztecs and Texcocans, was an uncommon one—that of an elected monarchy. The king or emperor was chosen, however, from among members of the royal family, whether brothers or nephews of the preceding sovereign, by the four appointed electors. He was installed with barbaric splendour, a main feature of the event being the great sacrifice of human beings in the Teocalli—that diabolical custom which ever robs the Aztec *régime* of the dignity of any appellation beyond that of semi-civilisation. Otherwise the Aztec *régime* may be considered as a military democracy. The land was held, to some extent, by great chiefs under a species of feudal system which carried with it certain obligations as to military service, but it was also assigned to the use of the people. The monarchy became of a despotic character, and legislative power lay with the sovereign, although a system of judicial tribunals administered justice throughout the cities of the Empire, and the Aztec civilisation had at least advanced far enough to acknowledge and uphold, by legal machinery, the rights and security of individuals and of property. Like the customs of the Incas of Peru, heavy penalties—generally of death—were meted out for bribery or corruption of the officers of justice.

Indeed, the great crimes were in most cases capital offences, as murder, adultery, thieving, as well as the misappropriation of funds, and the removal of land boundaries with intent to defraud. Marriage was a solemn and binding ceremonial, and divorce could be obtained only after a careful judicial inquiry and sanction. Slavery existed in several forms—captives of battles, reserved for the sacrifice; criminals, paupers, and debtors became slaves voluntarily; and children of poor parents who were sold into a species of mild servitude or dependency. No child, however, could be born into the condition of slavery—a somewhat unique proviso among systems of servitude.

The land system was, in some respects, similar to that which obtained amongst the Incas: a just and philosophical distribution of the soil amongst the people who dwelt upon it. Indeed, in the matter of land tenure, both the Incas and the Aztecs—these semi-civilised peoples of prehistoric America—employed a system which the most advanced nations of to-day—Great Britain or the United States—have not yet evolved, although in the case of Britain it seems that such is slowly appearing. The system was that of parcelling out the land among the families of the villages or country-side, and did not permit its absorption by large, individual landholders. The peasant thus had his means of support assured, and it was forbidden to dispose of the land thus allotted, which reverted to the State in the case of extinction of the family. This land system was governed by a careful code of laws, in these American communities. In Peru the individual ownership of land was a very marked feature of the social *régime*.[10] Lands were nevertheless set apart for the sovereign.

10 See my books "Peru," and the "Andes and the Amazon." These land systems are worthy of study by economists upon the land question to-day.

Taxes were paid upon agriculture and manufacture, in goods. These included most of the very varied products of the empire—varying as they did with the wide range of climate and topography, just as the products of the Mexico of to-day vary. Gold and copper utensils, pottery, arms, paper, cochineal, timber, cocoa, grains, fruits, gums, animals, and birds, and the beautiful feather-work in which the people excelled, were among these. Spacious warehouses in the capitals existed (as in Peru) for the storing of these, and any embezzlement or maladministration was rigorously punished.

Another institution of the Aztecs which calls to the traveller's mind a similar one among the coeval Incas of Peru, three thousand miles away in South America, was that of their means of communication. Such were maintained by relays of runners or postmen, who journeyed at great speed over roads which connected the distant parts of the empire; and it is stated that two hundred miles were covered in a day by these trained messengers, each of which performed the two leagues—the distance between the post-houses—within an hour. Just as the Inca Emperor of Peru, at Cuzco, beyond the great Cordillera of the Andes, was served with fish brought in *fresh* from the Pacific Ocean, so Montezuma, the Aztec monarch, also ate it, straight from the Gulf of Mexico, at his capital of Tenochtitlan beyond the maritime Cordillera of Anahuac. Striking and of marked interest to the traveller of to-day, in those vast and rugged regions of Mexico and Peru, is this matter of the native couriers, who journeyed over mountain roads, swollen rivers, desert plains, and ice-crowned summits.

The wealthier people lived in houses of stone, finished and furnished with certain barbaric luxuriance, in which tapestries woven and richly coloured, and secured with fastenings of gold, had their place. A remarkable industry and article of clothing of the early Mexicans was the beautiful feather-work, made of the plumage of the many-coloured birds, for which Mexico is famous. Surtouts of this feather-work were worn outside their military dresses, or armour, of padded cotton.

War was the great mainspring of action of the Aztecs. It is true that they had a long peaceful period after their establishing upon the lake-girt island of the Eagle and the Serpent, and that they developed their civilisation in some security within this natural fortification, but nevertheless, as previously shown, they extended their conquests on all sides. Fear, not regard, kept the subject-nations of Anahuac under their sway, however, and this was one of the elements leading to the downfall of the empire, in the course of time. Military orders were much esteemed and bestowed. The armies were well equipped and drilled, and breaches of discipline were rigorously punished. The hospitals, which were established for the treatment of the sick and wounded, called forth the praise of the Spanish chroniclers. Captives of war were made as abundantly as possible, to be reserved for the sacrificial stone of the war-god, and the Aztecs carried on this appalling practice of human sacrifice to such an extent as has not been equalled by any other nation. But the most atrocious part of the ceremony, as practised on some occasions, was that of the serving up of the body of victims at a repast, where they were eaten!—sheer cannibalism, which is vouched for as their practice as a religious rite.

How was the history of the early Mexicans handed down and perpetuated? It is probable that the ancient civilisations of America were near the dawn of a literature when their culture was destroyed. They had already some phonetic signs in use, from which, in the natural course of time, an alphabet might have evolved; but the picture-writing, or clumsy hieroglyphical representation of things in line and colour to express ideas, was their main method. Yet their laws, State accounts, history, and other matters were so recorded. When the Spaniards set foot on the coast a hieroglyphical representation of them and their ships, delineated on native paper, was in the hands of Montezuma a few hours afterwards—a species of rapid edition of a newspaper indeed! But these written records were supplemented by oral descriptions, and the two methods in conjunction formed the Aztec literature. Paper for such documents were made of skins, or cotton cloth, or of the fibrous leaves of the *maguey*, and this last, a species of "papyrus," was carefully prepared, and was of a durable nature. Aztec literature of this nature existed in considerable quantities at the beginning of the Hispanic occupation. It was thoroughly destroyed by the execrable act of the first Archbishop of Mexico—Zumarraga, who, looking upon these papers as "devilish scrolls," had them collected, piled up, and burnt! Some few, however, escaped, and were preserved and published in Europe. Some famous Maya documents of this nature, from Yucatan, have also brought to light some details of those people.

The Mexicans' scientific knowledge was simple and primitive. Some arithmetical system had been evolved, but, on the other hand, they had calculated and adopted a chronology—probably it had been inherited from the Toltecs—which displayed a remarkable precision, in that they adjusted the difference of the civil and solar year in a way superior to that of contemporary European nations.

In primitive Mexico—like primitive Peru—agriculture was far advanced as an industry. Land was apportioned, as has been shown, on a philosophical basis for the needs of the inhabitants. In that respect the system was far superior to that of the Republic of Mexico of to-day, where the whole surface of the land is mainly held by large landholders. Irrigation was an advanced art, artificial canals being made to conduct the water from the streams to the arid lands. The main article of diet among the mass of the people—then, as now—was *maiz*, which grows freely from highlands to lowlands. Bananas, chocolate—indeed, the latter, *chocolatl*, is an Aztec word—were among their numerous agricultural products. The *maguey*—the *Agave americana*—was an invaluable ally of life and civilisation. It afforded them the famous beverage of *pulque*; they made ropes, mats, paper, and other things from its fibre; and the leaves furnished an article of diet.

Mining was confined to the getting of gold from riverbeds, where it had been concentrated by Nature, and possibly on a small scale by amalgamation with quicksilver. Copper and tin were found and used, and indeed to-day the natives in certain places beat out large copper vessels[11] and offer for sale masses of rude copper *matte*,11 from their primitive earthen furnaces. The obsidian mines of Itzala furnished them with tools for the cutting of stone, sculpture, and other purposes, and for their terrible weapons of war.

11 I have used and purchased these articles in the State of Durango.

Sculpture and painting were very rudimentary, the former being confined chiefly to the representation of repugnant deities, although the carved stone edifices and temples were in some cases singularly beautiful, as elsewhere described. The sculptured figures of Mexican deities, in some cases, remind the traveller strongly of similar representations of the Incas,[12] such as exist in the fastnesses of the Andes of Peru. The famous Mexican Calendar stone, weighing about fifty tons, which was brought for many miles over broken country to the Aztec capital, is one of the most remarkable examples of their sculpture. Numerous smaller examples of prehistoric sculpture exist, some beautiful in design and execution. The feathered serpent is a frequent symbolical device upon these native works of art.

> 12 The figure of the conventionalised serpent-god on the onyx tablet found in 1895 in the Valley of Mexico and taken to the Museum of Chicago (see Holmes's "Ancient Cities of Mexico") strongly reminds me of the figure on the stone from Chavin in Peru (see "The Andes and the Amazon").

PREHISTORIC MEXICO: RUINS OF TEMPLE AT CHICHEN-YTZA, IN YUCATAN.

Pottery was made without the potter's wheel, by modelling; and painting and burning were practised. Musical instruments were also made of clay. Trade was conducted in ancient Mexico in great fairs or marketplaces, not in shops, and indeed this custom is still that preferred by the Mexican natives of the *peon* class to-day. The currency consisted of quills of gold-dust, small pieces of tin, and stamped copper, and barter was a principal mode of transaction. The merchants were an important class, carrying on extensive operations and expeditions far beyond the borders of the empire, under armed escorts, and they occupied often a position of political, and even diplomatic nature, such as was a peculiar feature of Aztec civilisation.

Social conditions showed much of quiet civilisation and tolerance. The women were never employed in the fields; and they took equal part with the men in social matters. They were modest and not unattractive, traits which remain to this day among the peasant class of Mexico. The *ménage* of Aztec homes, method of feasting, foods, napery, ablutions, and other matters, as recorded by the historians show a marked stage of refinement, except for the abominable practice of cannibalism. Chocolate and *pulque* were the favourite drinks.

Any survey of the Aztec customs shows a remarkable fact—they seem to have received their civilisation and customs from more than one source. For among the most refined habits and methods the most barbarous and disgusting acts are found. A refined and humane spirit of culture seems, by some method, or at some time, to have been grafted on to a spirit of primitive savagery, and each to have retained its character and practices. But their social system was not an unhappy one for their people. It was an epoch of handiwork, where all were employed and all were fed; and if there were few comforts and enlightenments in their life, there was, at least, little misery, such as is so freely encountered in the life of modern civilisation.

But destiny was now to compass the end of the Aztec *régime,* for from the shores of the stormy waters of the seas towards the sunrise, came rumours of strange white men. Who were they? asked the Aztec emperor and his advisers, in solemn conclave. Were they not those heralded by the long-expected Quetzalcoatl? If so, of what use was it to defy the fates, which had set forth long ago that the land should be ruled, some day, by a white race coming from the East? And when a fleet of great "water-houses," with white wings, touched at Yucatan, and the swift runners brought the tidings over nigh a thousand miles of forest and mountain in a few days, the credulous ear of Montezuma listened easily. And when the Spaniards landed at Vera Cruz, and won their way up to the fastnesses of Anahuac, it was still the hand of destiny. The time was fulfilled, the arm of civilisation had reached out towards the West, and it fell athwart the Great Plateau of unknown Mexico.

CHAPTER IV

CORTES AND THE CONQUEST

Landing of Cortes—Orizaba peak—The dawn of conquest—Discovery of Yucatan—Velasquez and Grijalva—Life and character of Cortes—Cortes selected to head the expedition—Departure from Cuba—Arrival at Yucatan—The coast of Vera Cruz—Marina—Vera Cruz established—Aztec surprise at guns and horses—Montezuma—Dazzling Aztec gifts—Messages to Montezuma—Hostility of the Aztecs—Key to the situation—The Cempoallas—Father Olmedo—Religion and hypocrisy of the Christians—March to Cempoalla—Montezuma's tax-collectors—Duplicity of Cortes—Vacillation of Montezuma—Destruction of Totonac idols—Cortes despatches presents to the King of Spain—Cortes destroys his ships—March towards the Aztec capital—Scenery upon line of march—The fortress of Tlascala—Brusque variations of climate—The Tlascalans—Severe fighting—Capitulation of Tlascala—Faithful allies—Messengers from Montezuma—March to Cholula—Massacre of Cholula—The snow-capped volcanoes—First sight of Tenochtitlan.

> "Brightly my star, new hope supplying,
> Leads on the hour shall all, all repay!"

Such, indeed, might have been the sentiment which inspired the breasts of Hernando Cortes and his Spaniards on that memorable Good Friday, April 21, 1519, as they first set foot upon the Mexican mainland, upon those sandy shores which in the act they christened Vera Cruz.

Before them, far away beyond the sandy desert and the tree-crowned slopes, stretched a high cordillera, a curtain drawn between them and the unknown world of the interior. What lay there? Matters of grave interest and preoccupation! For beyond that far, blue maritime defence of Anahuac—they had that moment learned it—there dwelt a mighty potentate and people, steeped with savage soldier-craft, rendered more terrible by the barbaric civilisation which it upheld. Here were no gentle savages such as they had hunted in the forests of Cuba and Hispaniola; and the mail-clad, helmeted Spaniards listened at first with mixed feelings to the accounts of the friendly Indians who greeted them at the shore, feelings in which the spirit of conquest rose high and dominant.

The ten caravels of Cortes are swinging at anchor in the bay, whose white-capped waters they have just passed. The Spaniards have reconnoitred the beach, and their eyes have followed the rising landscape to where, beyond the forest-clad mountains, and emerging from the clouds which girt them, a single gleaming, snowy point appeared, piercing the blue heavens like the gnomon of a mighty dial. It was Citlaltepetl, the "mountain of the star," the natives told them. It was the lofty Orizaba, the sunlight on its perpetual snow-cap bringing it to deceptive nearness.

Halting thus upon this sunny shore, who were these Spaniards, and what was their mission and character? Let us briefly sketch them. Those were stirring times in "ocean chivalry." The dream of Columbus had been accomplished for twenty-five years; Balboa had crossed the isthmus a few years since and Panama was known. The islands of Cuba and Santa Domingo had been settled and made starting-points for further discoveries, and two years before —in 1517—a Cuban *hidalgo*, Hernandez de Cordova, blown by a fierce gale, with his three ships, far from his objective point of the Bahamas, landed on an unknown land where the Indians said "*Tectecan*"—"I do not understand you." What was this land? It was the peninsula now called Yucatan —"*tectecan*"—part of the Mexico of to-day. And on Cordova's return to Cuba, the governor of that island, Don Diego de Velasquez, bestirred himself right actively, impelled by certain longings for conquest he had long nourished, and by the adventures, and curious things of laboured gold brought back by Cordova. Fitting out four vessels, Velasquez put them under the command of his nephew, Juan de Grijalva, and quickly sent them forth to win him riches and fame in those unknown lands—May, 1518. Grijalva duly touched and coasted upon the islands and shores of Yucatan, and his name remains to-day in the great Grijalva river. Thence he followed the horseshoe curve of the Gulf of Mexico, and arrived and landed at San Juan de Ulua, the same point where we left Cortes and his Spaniards halting. To Grijalva is due the prestige of first landing on the shores of Mexico, and of having intercourse with its people of the Aztecs. But, Grijalva tarrying long, Don Diego de Velasquez had despatched another expedition, commanding his nephew to return, which the latter did and was received coldly by the jealous and ungenerous Governor, as he is painted by his historians. Still bent on greater conquest, Velasquez cast about for men, money, and ships, and his eye fell on the capable Hernando Cortes, the young Spaniard who, born in Estremadura in 1485, had set out, impatient of the old world, to seek his fortunes in the new: and had amassed—"God knows by what methods," as one of his chroniclers says—a small fortune under the Governor's rule. Here was the man, and, incidentally, here was part of the money! For Cortes was popular and daring, and notwithstanding the several occasions on which he had come into collision with the Governor and the law, Velasquez held him in certain favour.

The life of Cortes up to that point—let us touch upon it before accompanying him, and know what manner of man he was—had been urged principally by selfish adventure and amorous intrigues. He had arrived in Hispaniola in 1504, and upon being offered a grant of land and *repartimiento* of Indians replied that "he had left Spain in search of gold—not to become a land-tilling peasant." In 1511, under Velasquez, who had been appointed to the conquest of Cuba, Cortes found outlet for his adventurous spirit, and in the Indian warfare of the island gave promise of the valour and activity which underlay a jocular and seemingly trivial character. At the same time he became accustomed to the barbarous methods of conquest and cruelty displayed by the Spaniards in those regions, and to the abuse of power and arbitrary jealousies and exactions displayed both to natives and colonials by the petty Imperial authorities. Cortes had soon fallen foul of Velasquez. On two occasions he had been thrown into prison by the Governor's orders, but had escaped, partly by his own activity, and partly—it is held—by connivance of his gaolers. Associated with these episodes was a beautiful Spanish girl, Catalina Juarez, whom he had refused to marry in spite of the representations of her family, due to his relations with her: Velasquez also being interested in the family, in the person of Catalina's sister. However, after a time, Cortes married and lived happily with her upon his estate. Land and Indians were granted him, and he acquired some wealth from agriculture and mining, maintaining good relations with the Governor, Velasquez.

Now it was that Pedro de Alvarado, the future conqueror of Guatemala, who had accompanied Grijalva to Mexico, returned, and now it was that Velasquez cast about for men, money and ships, to push the conquest of

Mexico. Choice fell upon Cortes. The long-nourished hopes of the young Spaniard—he was thirty-four or five—were fulfilled. He realised all his resources to subscribe towards the expense, covering indeed the major portion of the cost of ships and stores. The little port of Santiago de Cuba echoed with the bustle of preparation. The vessels, most of which were simply open brigantines, the largest not more than one hundred tons, were rapidly fitted out. Hundreds of men flocked instantly to his leadership. Away to the West their thoughts and enthusiasm carried one and all; gold, adventure, fame—who would not go!

The light and easy character of Cortes changed under the grave import and responsibility of this great mission, in which he seemed to recognise some fulfilment by Providence of his lifelong hopes. Here he was, a relatively humble subject of Spain, of relatively obscure parentage, although conscious of that powerful instinct of being a *caballero*—a gentleman—singled out for this great enterprise! There was but one fear—that its command should be snatched from him at the last moment! And, indeed, this was averted by a mere hair's breadth, say the chroniclers. For the jealous Velasquez, influenced by other jealous advisers, and fearing that the independent spirit of Cortes would arrogate to himself the glory and profit of the enterprise, once away from his influence, resolved at the last moment to quit him of his command and substitute another. Cortes heard of it. Apprehension lent him a superhuman energy. Once away from Cuba's shores—ah! then he could parley with its Governor. He visited his trusty officers. Butchers, bakers, ammunition-makers were bribed and hurried, the stores were rushed on board, commander and crew embarked at midnight, and when morning dawned the good people of Santiago de Cuba awoke to see the white sails of the squadron rising to meet the breeze, whilst the rattle of the cables of the up-getting moorings fell upon their ears. Down rushed Velasquez from his bed, and galloped to the wharf. "Stop them! Stop them!" But it was too late—who could stop them?

Before his sails filled to the breeze Cortes approached the shore in an armed boat. "Farewell! good Governor," was the burden of his words. "Time is short, and what is to be done 'twere well it were done quickly!" And so he sailed away towards the West, into a sunset-land of conquest-dreams, and left Velasquez fuming on the quay.[13]

13 This story of the departure of Cortes is doubted by some writers, but it appeals to the mind of the adventurous traveller in those regions, even to-day, with too strong a ring of probability to be ignored.

But the jealous Governor's resources were not quite exhausted. He despatched swift messengers to other Cuban ports where the expedition must touch for further supplies, ill-provisioned as it was by the hasty departure, with orders for the authorities at these points to detain Cortes at all hazards. It was useless. Far from detention, he received supplies and reinforcements. A number of well-known *hidalgos* joined him, among them Pedro de Alvarado, Cristoval de Olid, Velasquez de Leon, Gonzalo de Sandoval, Hernandez Puertocarrero, Alonzo de Avila, and others who took a valiant part afterwards in the conquest. At his last port of departure Cortes wrote a letter to Velasquez, of a conciliatory nature: reviewed his forces, which amounted to nearly nine hundred Spaniards and two hundred Indians, with ten heavy guns, several falconets, ample ammunition, and sixteen horses, in eleven vessels. Having addressed the forces in words of enthusiasm, dangling before them the glories of conquest, specially pointing out to them that they were carrying the Cross to set before savages, Cortes invoked the patronage of St. Peter, and the squadron set sail for the shores of Yucatan.

How they arrived at the island of Cozumel, fought with the Indians of the mainland, tumbled the gross idols of the savages from their pyramid-temple, and set up an altar to the Virgin; and how they recovered an unfortunate Spaniard who had sojourned eight years, after shipwreck, with the natives of Yucatan; how Alvarado antagonised the natives and Cortes pacified them; and how they sailed thence to the real shores of Mexico, where we left them halting, are fascinating matters of their voyage which we must thus lightly pass over.

PREHISTORIC MEXICO: RUINS OF "THE PALACE" AT CHICHEN-YTZA, IN YUCATAN.

Behold a level, sun-beat, wind-swept plain, the drifting sand blown into *médanos*, or sand-hills, by the hurricanes of the gulf, the perennial *norte*. Here are the *Conquistadores* grouped, Cortes and his associates. Among them is the figure of a woman, and her name is worthy to rank in the first verse and chapter of our story. It is Marina, the beautiful Indian girl who had been given to the Spaniards, among other female slaves, at Tabasco, in Yucatan, and who, Cortes had learned, spoke the language of the Mexicans, in addition to her native Yucatec. So Marina was the interpreter through whose medium understanding was had with the natives. This was in conjunction with the Spaniard Aguilar—the rescued castaway, who spoke the language of Marina. But this was only at first, for as Cortes loved her and she loved him, she soon acquired the Castilian of the *Conquistador* as his mistress.

Thus was parley opened with the natives and their caciques, and knowledge gained of Montezuma, the great Emperor of the Aztecs, and of the power and circumstances of their empire, whose rule extended to the coast whereon they stood. Cortes and his captains made presents to the caciques, and received such in return, and it was decided to establish the colony of Villa Rica de

Vera Cruz. A pretty piece of juggling—singular yet not unjustifiable—took place in the inauguration of this, Cortes establishing his captains as its municipality, resigning the commission he had received from the Governor of Cuba into the hands of the body he had called into being himself, and then accepting from it a commission as captain-general, all taking title as officials of the Crown of Spain! This proceeding, solemnly carried out on the edge of the wilderness, and in sound of the roaring waters of the Gulf, is not without a *Gilbertian* spice.

Rude habitations had been built, guns mounted, and supplies secured from the Indian population which flocked around the Spaniards. And suddenly a new sensation was sprung upon these simple people. The horses were brought on shore, and the cavalry manoeuvred upon the beach; cannons were fired and trumpets sounded, the shot from the guns, purposely directed against the trees, smashing them to splinters. Filled with awe the Aztec chief of the place—the friendly cacique Teuhtile—bade his picture-writers depict it all; and upon the native paper these terrible gachupines[14] and their great "water-houses," and thundering engines, and singular musical instruments, were drawn in lifelike form by these native "newspaper artists," to be despatched by the native postmen over the rocky fastnesses of the Cordilleras to the great Montezuma. Then Cortes announced his mission. He was the ambassador of a mighty Emperor from beyond the seas, come to greet the Emperor of the Aztecs and to carry a present from his monarch, the mightiest in the world. When could he be admitted before Montezuma? The awe in which this potentate was held by his vassals was shown in Teuhtile's reply: "Was it possible that a monarch, the equal of the Aztec king, existed elsewhere? How could the white men ask, at such short notice, to be admitted to the semi-sacred presence?" But he brought forward presents of beautiful feather-work and ornaments of gold for the Spaniards; and Cortes, not to be outdone, produced a richly-carved chair and other things admired by the simple natives, including articles of cut glass, which were held to be gems of great price, as of course the Aztecs had no knowledge of glass. All these matters were carried out with due ceremony, messengers with the presents were sent to Montezuma, and the Spaniards, pending the return of the emissaries of Teuhtile with their greeting, devoted themselves to the perfecting of their dwellings.

14 The Aztec word for centaurs, which was applied to the horsemen.

Little more than a week elapsed. In that time the swift native carriers had traversed and re-traversed the steep and rugged road from the coast to the valley of Anahuac, a distance of about two hundred miles each way. The substance of their message from Montezuma was "Come not hither; the road is long and dangerous; return to your country with our greetings to your great King." A magnificent present accompanied this somewhat chilling reply—articles of gold and silver, beautifully wrought, among them a huge gold plate, and one of silver, circular in form and "as large as carriage-wheels," twenty-eight spans in circumference, representing respectively the images of the sun and the moon and engraved with figures of animals, doubtless indicative of some chronological symbol—the value of the gold wheel was afterwards estimated at more than £50,000—other articles of clothing and armour, including a number of beautiful golden shields inlaid and decorated, necklaces of rubies and pearls, and a quantity of the intricate and beautiful feather-work.

What was the result of all this, upon the Spaniards—this wealth of treasure and this unencouraging greeting? "Go back again," was the substance of Cortes's reply to the ambassadors of Montezuma; "tell your monarch the mountain road and its dangers do not appal us—we who have sailed two thousand leagues of troubled ocean to arrive here—and we cannot return to our great sovereign without having personally greeted yours." Again the Spaniards waited the messengers' return, weary of the wind- and sand-swept plains of Vera Cruz; assailed by the *calenturas* ever encountered upon the American coasts, the bilious malarial disorders which Nature has made the scourge of the tropics, and which the science of modern man has only just begun to investigate. Again the messengers—within ten days—returned. Stripped of its diplomatic covering of ceremony and further presents, the Aztec Emperor's reply may be condensed as "Get thee hence!" And, as if to bear out some royal mandate, the natives disappeared from the vicinity, the supplies were cut off, leaving the Spaniards halting upon this debatable ground, in chagrin and indecision.

But not for long. The stern design of the Spaniards had been forced, and was growing. "I vowed to your Royal Highness that I would have Montezuma prisoner, or dead, or subject to your Majesty," wrote Cortes to Carlos V. of Spain, from Vera Cruz; and "Think you we were such Spaniards as to lie there idly?" wrote Bernal Diaz, the soldier-penman, afterwards. Yet there was some disaffection in the camp, a portion of the men, wearied of inaction and fearful of dangers, desiring to return to Cuba. Here Cortes's diplomacy came to the rescue. "On board, all of you!" he exclaimed. "Back to Cuba and its Governor, and see what happens!" The threat and sneer had the effect he expected. Scarcely a man would return, but on the contrary they clamoured for the establishment of a colony and for a march on Montezuma and his capital, whilst the few who remained disaffected were clapped in irons, among them the *hidalgo* Velasquez, a relative of the Governor of Cuba.

And now it was that the key to the situation was put into the hands of Cortes. An embassy from a semi-civilised, powerful nation to the north, upon the gulf-shores—the Totonacs, of Cempoalla, as they announced themselves—suddenly arrived in the colony of the Christians. They brought an invitation from their chief for the Spaniards to visit him, with the information—and here was the circumstance which should make conquest possible—that the Totonacs were weary of the Aztec yoke, and yearned for independence. "Ha!" thought Cortes and his *hidalgo* associates, "they are delivered into our hands! They are divided, and so they will fall." Father Olmedo, the wise and pious confessor of the forces, to whose prudence the security of the Spaniards owed much, and who was the representative of the great Church which became so potent in those lands, blessed his comrades' conclaves, and celebrated solemn Masses. Indeed, every move of the Spaniards was accomplished under such auspices, and was always referred by Cortes to the influence of the desire to carry the Cross of Christ and all it embodied, to those heathen peoples; and in a spirited address to the soldiers he declared that "without this motive their expedition was but one of oppression and robbery." The true proportions of piety and hypocrisy contained in these expressions and acts must be left to the knowledge of human nature of the reader. Suffice to say that the Spaniards did, to a large extent, look upon themselves as Crusaders, and that a militant religious fervour animated them, in conjunction with a spirit of avarice and cruelty.

And so they marched on Cempoalla, along the sandy shores of the gulf, passing through villages, with temples devoted to the abominable sacrificial rites which they had seen in Yucatan. Thence they encountered the fringe of the tropical forests, and at length entered the strange town of Cempoalla, with its numerous inhabitants, and streets, and houses, and excellent surrounding cultivation. Here they remained some days, the Spaniards delighted with the fertile region and the hospitable natives. The great Cacique had received them in his residence—a building of stone upon a pyramid, after the fashion of the structures of that country, and, the fair Marina interpreting, Cortes stated his mission—"to redress abuses and punish oppressors, and to establish the true faith." The substance of the chief's reply was that, though weary of the oppressive yoke of the Aztecs: Montezuma was a terrible monarch, who could pour down his warriors upon them. But Cortes gathered encouragement from his attitude, and in the meantime a juncture had been effected with the ships upon the coast a few leagues distant, at a port discovered by Montejo. Further deliberations took place during the ensuing days, when a momentous event occurred in the arrival of special emissaries from Montezuma to the Cacique, setting forth the anger of the Emperor, and demanding instant reparation and tribute for the disloyalty of the Totonacs in having entertained the invaders. The fearful and hesitating Totonacs—it was but natural—would have appeased their anger; but under the instigation of Cortes these Aztec tax-collectors were seized and imprisoned. Characteristic of the Spaniard of those days was the act of double-dealing then performed by Cortes. He secretly released the prisoners at night, soothed their feelings, sent them on board a ship, and bid them report his goodwill to Montezuma!

The Totonacs were now too deeply compromised to do aught but become the sworn allies of the Spaniards. The cherished dream of the return of Quetzalcoatl had not been fulfilled, but here were these valiant strangers, who had defied the omnipotent Montezuma! The Spaniards then established a colony upon the coast near at hand, aided by the natives, and a town soon arose which was a centre of operations and general point of distribution for the subsequent operations. Engaged upon the work was Cortes, when new emissaries arrived from the outraged Montezuma. The Totonacs were only to be spared out of deference for the white men who had liberated the tax-collectors! Montezuma was debating much within himself and with his advisers at this time. "Surely these terrible white strangers, who had come out of the East, were the long-expected Quetzalcoatl and his people? It was necessary to placate or temporise with them, for what destiny had written concerning the passing of his empire must come to pass." So had pondered the great Aztec chief, and it was this fear of destiny which had dictated his attitude, vacillating as it was, towards the strangers. But the emissaries returned to the lord of Anahuac with the same message as before—that the white men would visit him in person.

Presents of wives—the soft, pretty Indian damsels, daughters of the principal chiefs—were made to Cortes and his officers by the Cacique, in gratitude for assistance against a neighbouring tribe, which the Spaniards rendered. They must, however, be baptized first, said Cortes, and the opportunity was taken to enforce the Christian religion upon their allies. Protests and menace followed, but the idols of Cempoalla were torn from their pyramid sanctuaries and hurled to the ground; the foul sacrificial altars cleansed; the image of the Virgin installed there; and a solemn Mass celebrated by Father Olmedo.

Other stirring events crowded rapidly on. A swift ship was despatched to Spain with the wheel of gold; the beautiful feather-work, and the other rare presents of the Aztecs, all given over by the Spaniards as a royal gift to the young Spanish king; together with a voluminous epistle. This was sent with the design of forestalling the machinations of Velasquez; and though the vessel touched at Cuba, it escaped detention, and safely arrived in Spain. But meantime disaffection arose in the new colony, and a conspiracy was formed to seize a vessel and escape to Cuba, by some of the Spaniards who were discontented and fearful of the future. The plot was discovered and the authors seized and executed, and a dramatic sequel to this conspiracy came about. Cortes and some of his advisers resolved to prevent the recurrence of any further danger of this nature; to put it out of the power of any to desert; to place the knowledge of the inevitable before his troops, that the conquest must be undertaken or death found in the attempt. He sank his ships! Yes; the brigantines which had borne them thither, and were their only means of retreat from those savage shores, were dismantled and destroyed.

And now the Spaniards resolutely turn their faces to the mountains. Threats and entreaties are stilled; the colony is established, the base secured, the ships are sunk, save that single white-winged caravel far over the waters of the gulf, prow to the shores of Spain. The Mass is said, the books are closed. "Forward! my comrades," said Cortes; "before us lies a mountain road; and adventure, gold, and glory!"

The traveller of to-day, as he traverses by rail the desert coast zone of the Mexican littoral, and ascends the steep slopes of the eastern Cordillera of the Sierra Madre, to gain access to the Great Plateau or Valley of Mexico beyond it, reposing amid the cushions of his Pullman car, will neither endure the fatigue which the *Conquistadores* suffered nor be assailed, night and day, with the menace of savage foes on every hand. But the grand and varied setting still remains: the strange and beautiful fairyland of Nature's rapid transformation scenes, the changing landscape and successive climates of this remarkable region. The sandy wastes give place to tropical forests and fertile valleys, with their bright accompaniment of profuse flower- and bird-life. These, in turn, disappear from the changing panorama, and the traveller reaches the appalling escarpments of the Mexican Andes, looking down from time to time from dizzy ridges, where the ascending steel lines of the railroad spiral has brought him, to where distant fertile vales lie in the glimmering haze, thousands of feet below. And then the scene changes, and the dark rocky ribs and bleak plateau show that the summit is reached, ten thousand feet above the level of the ocean's ebb and flow.

THE LAND OF THE CONQUEST: STATE OF VERA CRUZ; VIEW ON THE MEXICAN RAILWAY; THE TOWN OF MALTRATA IS SEEN THOUSANDS OF FEET BELOW.

But what we shall have accomplished in a day the weary *Conquistadores* have spent many marches in overcoming. Cortes and his men are halting at the end of a broad valley. What is the cause of the delay? An extraordinary fortification confronts them; a wall, twice as high as a man, made of stone blocks, and of enormous thickness, absolutely closes the passage of the valley, and extends for several miles on either hand to where it abuts upon the rocky ramparts of the Sierra itself. Was this some enchanted castle raised up by magician hand? Certainly not; it was the outer defence of the land of the Tlascalans; the bulwark of the brave and independent mountain republic, which had ever defied the power of the Aztecs.

To reach this point the Spaniards had toiled on day after day, sleeping at night upon their arms. From the tropical lands and climate of the *tierra caliente* they had reached the frowning fastnesses of the great mountains and lofty peaks, which overhang the crest of the eastern slope of the tableland of Mexico. The rainy season was upon them, and the trails were wet and heavy, and the atmosphere and humour of the tropic lands had been debilitating, as indeed they are to the European of today. The brusque change of climate from heat to cold tried them sorely, although the latter was the more invigorating. Day by day a huge coffin-shaped mountain had overhung the horizon—the Cofre de Perote, an extinct volcano, in whose vicinity the desolating action of old lava-flows startles the traveller's eye. As they reached the summit of the range—the crests of the Eastern Sierra Madre—the rain and snow and bitter winds, the functions of Nature which she ever lets loose upon the head of the traveller who defies her in such inclement regions, assailed the Spaniards, and some of the unfortunate Indians, natives of the tropic lands of the coast, succumbed to the cold. On, on they toiled up this untrodden way—untrodden, that is, by the foot of civilised man before that day, and at length, having crossed the summit, the *divortia aquarum* of the continent, they began the descent towards the mild climate of the Valley of Mexico.

Upon the confines of this valley was a town surrounded by extensive cultivated fields of *maiz*. Stone buildings, numerous *teocallis*, and a large population attested the importance of the place; and when the Spaniards asked if it was tributary to Montezuma the chief replied with another question, asking with surprise if there existed any other lord worthy of tribute. Another chief and tribe some miles beyond, gave a good reception to the Spaniards, and there they gladly halted for some days. The house of the chief was upon a hill, "protected by a better fort than can be found in half

Spain," wrote Cortes to his Emperor at Castile. Here it was that the Spaniards received news of the existence of the people of Cholula and Tlascala, who inhabited the regions of their intended line of march. "Go by the road of the Tlascalans," the friendly chief advised; "the Cholulans are a treacherous people." Cortes despatched messengers to the chief of Tlascala, but no reply was received, and after waiting some days the Spaniards continued their march, to where we left them halting before the stone wall across the valley.

And then began the most stirring events of their march. The Tlascalans were a people who had developed a remarkable civilisation and social and military organisation, akin to that of the Aztecs. On the arrival of the messengers of Cortes much dissension had prevailed in their councils, some of the chiefs—the community was ruled by a council of four—maintaining that this was an opportunity for vengeance against their hereditary enemies, the hated Aztecs and their prince, Montezuma. "Let us ally ourselves with these terrible strangers," they urged, "and march against the Mexicans." For the doings of the Spaniards had echoed through the land already, with a tale of smitten tribes and broken idols. But the wily old Xicotencatl thought otherwise. "What do we know of their purpose?" was his counsel; so it was agreed that the army of the Tlascalans and Otomies, who were in force near the frontier, under the command of the fiery young warrior—son of old Xicotencatl, and bearing the same name—should attack them. "If we fail," the old barbarian urged, "we will disavow the act of our general; if we win—"!

The stone fortification at the valley's end had been undefended, and with Cortes at their head the Spaniards entered Tlascalan territory. Skirmishing was followed by a pitched battle between the Christians and the Tlascalans, in which the firearms and lances of the Spaniards wrought terrible havoc on their antagonists. Astounded at the sight of the horses—those extraordinary beings, whether of animal or demoniacal origin they knew not—and appalled by the thundering of the guns, which seemed to have some superhuman source, the Tlascalans at first fell back. But they overcame their fears, fell savagely upon the invaders, and were with difficulty repulsed, having managed to kill two of the horses. Greatly to Cortes's regret was this, for the noble animals were few, and—more serious still—their death removed that semi-superstitious dread regarding them, which the natives held. However, the Spaniards afterwards buried them from sight.

Night fell, a season when the Indians fought not, but on the morrow the messengers which had been sent to the Tlascalans arrived—having escaped—with the news that the enemy was approaching in great force. So indeed it befel, and upon the plain in front of the Spaniards appeared a mighty host, varyingly estimated between thirty and a hundred thousand warriors. The Spaniards with their allies numbered—fearful odds!—about three thousand. "The God of the Christians will bear us through," said the brave and beautiful Marina. A frightful battle now ensued, the issue of which hung in the scale for hours. Charging, volleying, borne this way and that by the flood of the enemy's numbers, the gallant band of the Spaniards snatched victory from almost certain defeat, their superior weapons and cavalry, together with the bad tactics of the Indians, who knew not how to employ their unwieldy army to best advantage, at length decided the day for the Christians, who inflicted terrible punishment upon their foes. The Tlascalans' policy now showed signs of weakening, but further assaults were necessary, and some treachery, under the guise of friendship, having been discovered on the part of the fifty Tlascalan envoys to the Spanish camp, Cortes barbarously cut off the hands of these and sent them back to tell the tale.

The upshot of these engagements was that the Tlascalans capitulated, apologised for their conduct, invited the strangers to take possession of their capital, and assured them that they would now be allies, not enemies, of the white men, who were undoubtedly the representatives of the great and long-expected Quetzalcoatl. The joy in the Spanish camp at this turn of affairs knew no bounds; well did the Spaniards know that the continued opposition of the Indians would have been their ruin, whilst in their alliance was salvation and the key to the Conquest.

Behold the war-worn and hungry Spaniards, lean and tattered from marching and privations in the inclement uplands, now installed in comfort in the centre of the powerful Tlascalan capital. Forth had come to greet them young Xicotencatl, who, to do him justice, took upon himself the responsibility of the war; and as the Spaniards entered the capital the streets were lined with men, women, and children, and decorated with garlands of flowers as for a triumphal procession. The old chief who had urged for opposition now changed his tactics, and as Cortes entered he embraced him, passing his hand over the face of the Spaniard to see what manner of man he was, for the aged Tlascalan was blind, having reached, it has been said—probably with exaggeration—a hundred and forty years of age! "The city is much larger than Granada," wrote Cortes to Carlos V., with a description of its markets, shops, houses, and intelligent and industrious population.

Six weeks the Spaniards sojourned there, recuperating their energies, living on the best the plentiful land afforded—Tlascala signified in the Indian tongue "the land of bread"—taking wives from among the maidens of the chiefs' daughters, and endeavouring, first with the foolish haste of Cortes and then with the slow prudence of Father Olmedo, to instil some tenets of the Christian religion into their hosts. But religious fervour had to give way to material necessities, and the Tlascalan idols remained unsmitten, although their human sacrifices were somewhat stayed.

Rested and mended, the Spaniards now set impatient gaze upon the oak- and fir-clad mountain slopes which bounded the valley. Above them loomed upward the great Malinche, snow-capped queen of the Tlascalan mountain fastnesses; and still the friendly Tlascalans, stern foes but noble allies, loaded them with every favour and bid them tarry. When, however, they would stay no longer they raised a great body of warriors to accompany them, warning Cortez against the wiles of Montezuma. "Beware of his presents and his promises; he is false and seeks your destruction," they urged, and their implacable hatred of the Aztecs showed itself in their words and mien.

Contrary to the advice of their new allies, the Spaniards decided to journey on to Mexico through Cholula, the land of the great pyramid. Embassies had arrived, both from Montezuma and from the Cholulans, the latter inviting the Spaniards to go that way; and the great Aztec monarch, swayed now by the shadow of oncoming destiny, offering the Spaniards a welcome to his capital. "Trust not the Tlascalans, those barbarous foes," was the burden of his message, "but come through friendly Cholula"—words which the Tlascalans heard with sneers and counter-advice. The purpose of the Tlascalans was not a disinterested one. An attack upon Montezuma was their desire, and preliminary to this they hoped to embroil the Spaniards with the perfidious Cholulans. Another embassy—and this was an important event—had waited upon Cortes. It was from the Ixtlilxochitl, one of the rival claimants for the throne of Texcoco, which, it will be remembered, was a powerful and advanced community in confederation with the Aztecs; and Cortes was not slow to fan the flame of disaffection which this indicated, by an encouraging message to the young prince.

THE LAND OF THE CONQUEST: A VALLEY IN THE STATE OF VERA CRUZ, ON THE LINE OF THE MEXICAN RAILWAY.

A farewell was taken of the staunch Tlascalans, the invariable Mass was celebrated by Father Olmedo, and, accompanied by a large body of Tlascalan warriors, the Spaniards set out for Cholula. What befel in this beautiful and populous place—which, Bernal Diaz wrote, reminded him, from its numerous towers, of Valladolid—was of terrible and ruthless import. Cholula, with its great *teocalli*, was the Mecca of Anahuac, and was veritably a land flowing with milk and honey. Well-built houses, numerous *teocallis*, or pyramidal temples, well-dressed people with embroidered cloaks, and numbers of censer-swinging priests formed the *ensemble* which greeted the Spaniards' eyes, whilst the intense cultivation of the ground and the fields of *maguey*, *maiz*, and other products, irrigated by canals from the mountain streams, formed the environment of this advanced community. "Not a palm's-breadth of land that is not cultivated," wrote Cortes in his despatches to Castile, "and the city, as we approached, was more beautiful than the cities of Spain." Beautiful and gay doubtless Cholula was when the Spaniards entered; drenched with the blood of its inhabitants and devastated by fire it lay before they left it! There had been signs of treachery, even on the road thither, work of the Cholulans; but, lodged in the city, the Spaniards discovered, through the agency of the intelligent Marina, a plot to annihilate them later. Taking the Cholulans unawares as they crowded the streets with—at the moment—harmless curiosity, the Spaniards, with cannon, musket, and sabre, mowed down the unfortunate and unprotected natives in one bloody massacre, aided by the ferocious Tlascalans, who fell upon the Cholulans from the rear. The appalling and unnecessary slaughter at Cholula has called down upon the heads of Cortes and the Spaniards the execration of historians. Some have endeavoured to excuse or palliate it, but it remains as one of the indelible stains of the Spanish *Conquistadores* upon the history they were making. Having accomplished this "punitive" act, an image of the Virgin was set up on the summit of the great pyramidal temple, and some order restored. "They are now your Highness's faithful vassals," wrote Cortes to the king of Spain!

After this the way seemed clear. Far on the horizon loomed the white, snow-capped cones of Popocatepetl and Ixtaccihuatl, beautiful and pure above the deserts, the canyons, and the forests beneath them—the gateway to Mexico. From the foremost, above its snow-cap, there belched forth a great column of smoke, for at that period Popocatepetl was an active volcano. Onwards the Spaniards pressed with buoyant hearts and eager feet, and when they stood upon the summit of the range their eyes beheld the beautiful valley of Mexico, the haven for which they had long toiled and fought, stretched below. There, shimmering in distance, lay the strange, unknown city of the Aztecs, like a gem upon the borders of its lakes: its towers and buildings gleaming white in the brilliant sun of the tropic upland beneath the azure firmament and brought to deceptive nearness by the clear atmosphere of that high environment. There at last was their longed-for goal, the mysterious Tenochtitlan.

CHAPTER V

THE FALL OF THE LAKE CITY

The Valley of Mexico—The City and the Causeways—The *Conquistadores* enter Mexico City—Meeting of Cortes and Montezuma—Greeting of the Aztec emperor to the Spaniards—Tradition of Quetzalcoatl—Splendid reception—The Teocalli—Spanish duplicity—Capture of Montezuma—Spanish gambling—News from Vera Cruz—Forced march to the coast—Cortes defeats Narvaez—Bad news from Mexico—Back to the capital—Alvarado's folly—Barbarous acts of the Spaniards—The fight on the pyramid—Destruction of Aztec idols—Death of Montezuma—Spaniards flee from the city—Frightful struggle on the Causeway—Alvarado's leap—The *Noche Triste*—Battle of Otumba—Marvellous victory—Spanish recuperation—Cuitlahuac and Guatemoc—Fresh operations against the capital—Building of the brigantines—Aztec tenacity—Expedition to Cuernavaca—Xochimilco—Attack upon the city—Struggles and reverses—Sacrifice of Spaniards—Desertion of the Allies—Return of the Allies—Renewed attacks—Fortitude of the Aztecs—The famous catapult—Sufferings of the Aztecs—Final attack—Appalling slaughter—Ferocious Tlascalans—Fall of Mexico.

The Valley of Mexico is a region of somewhat remarkable topographical character. It consists of a plain or inter-montane basin, enclosed on all sides by ranges of hills, forming a hydrographic entity whose waters have no natural outlet.[15] A group of lakes occupy the central part of this valley, very much reduced, however, in size since the time of the Conquest.

15 See p. 17.

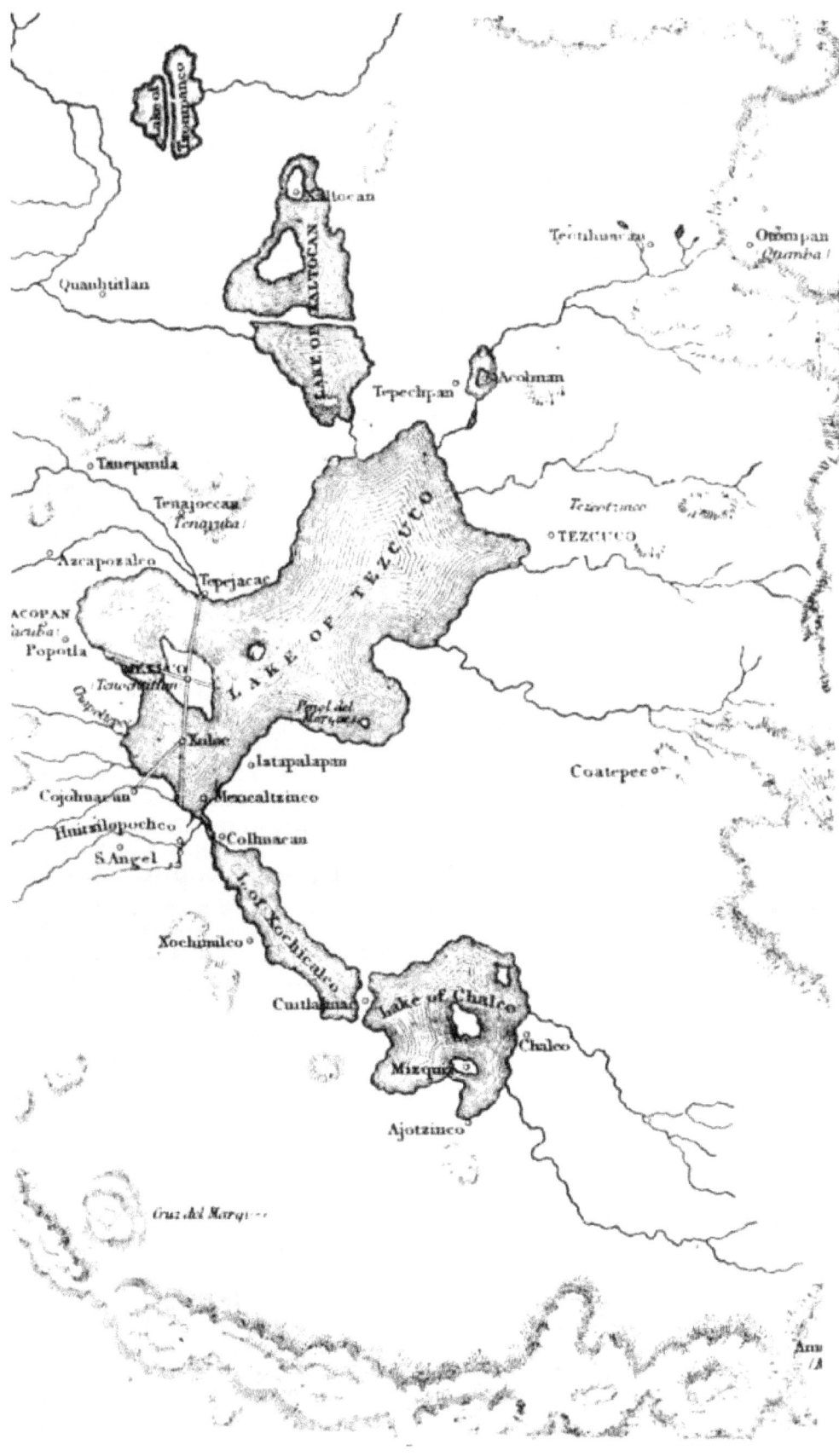

THE LAKES OF THE VALLEY OF MEXICO AT THE TIME OF THE CONQUEST, SHOWING
THE CAUSEWAYS TO THE AZTEC ISLAND-CITY OF TENOCHTITLAN.
(From Prescott's "Conquest of Mexico.")

It was the 8th of November, 1519. Across the southern end of the great Lake Texcoco stretched a singular dyke or causeway, several miles in length and a few yards in width—a road or pathway built up of stone and mortar above the surrounding water, connecting the shores of that inland sea with an island and three other similar causeways. Upon this island arose a beautiful city with streets of strange buildings, above which rose great pyramids with sanctuaries upon their summits; and upon the bosom of the lake numerous canoes were plying, laden with men and merchandise. So rose those towers, and lived and moved the dwellers of this lake city, unknowing and unknown of European man, living their life as if no other world than theirs held sway beneath the firmament of the "unknown God." But the spell is broken. A trumpet sound is ringing through the morning air. Across the causeway comes a troop of strange men-animals—fearful things which snort and tramp, making the causeway rumble, whilst the notes of that strange music echo away among the towers and pyramids of the city, and are borne far over the waters of the lake, to smite the ears of wondering Indians.

Cortes and his Spaniards rode steadily along the causeway, their hearts beating—as well they might—with astonishment, admiration, apprehension, and all those emotions to which their unique and romantic position gave impulse. Guided by the messengers of Montezuma, the white men rode beneath a fortification in mid-causeway, where another similar structure joined it from another shore of the lake, passed the drawbridge and the city walls, and clattered up the stone-paved avenue of Tenochtitlan to where, in pomp and splendour, surrounded by his lords and vassals, the great Aztec chief awaited them, in a royal litter gleaming with polished gold.

Cortes and his men dropped foot to earth, and Montezuma descended from his litter. The Spaniard *Conquistador,* after the custom of his race, advanced to embrace the chief, "but," wrote Cortes to Charles V., "the two lords in attendance prevented me with their hands that I might not touch him, and both Montezuma and they performed instead their ceremony of kissing the ground."

The meeting of these two chiefs—one the autocrat of a strange, unknown civilisation there in the heart of the mountains, the other the representative of an equally strange and unknown power from an outside world, both, to the other, undreamt of—is of dramatic memory. But the address of Montezuma was singularly dignified, prophetic, or philosophical. After the presents and greetings were exchanged, and the monarch and the invader sate at their ease, he spake in this wise: "You who have come from the direction of the sunrise, from a great lord of some far regions, shall not lack power here to command, for well we know as to our ancestry that we are not of the aborigines of this land where we now dwell, but of that of a great lord—which must be that you represent—who brought us here in ages past, departed, and promised to return. Rest here, therefore, and rejoice; take what you will, my house is yours; but believe not the slanders of my enemies through whose countries you have journeyed."

So strong was the remarkable tradition of Quetzalcoatl, that it had held this powerful chief and his warlike people in check before the invasion of a band of adventurers from abroad. A word of command from him, and the Spaniards, with all their advantages of firearms and horses, could never have passed the causeway or set foot within that impregnable city of Tenochtitlan—that fatal causeway, as indeed it afterwards became.

Barbaric splendour, blended with the arts and industries of a civilised and practical people, formed the environment of this long-striven-for goal, where the men of Spain now lay at ease. A great pile of low stone buildings gave them commodious quarters. Rich gifts of gold and clothing, and ample food supplies, were given and provided for the white men; and their hearts, whether of the high-mettled and scornful cavaliers, or of the rude boors who formed the common soldiery, were won by the gentle courtesy and the generosity of Montezuma and the respect of the Aztecs who obeyed him. Even the savage and hated Tlascalan allies were lodged and provided for—their detested presence tolerated from consideration for the Spaniards. Here was an unhoped-for and magnificent reception. Here was a way and a time where the civilisation and religion of the Christian world might have been implanted—it would seem—by the philosophy of natural methods, by forbearance, example, and sagacity. So, at least, have thought some of the old chroniclers—so the student of to-day cannot but think.

But it was not to be so. The heart of the thinker bleeds to-day for the things of history which might have been; and the story of Montezuma is strong to give us philosophical regret. Some six days elapsed in this peaceful occupation of the city. Cortes and his Spaniards admired the huge market-place, where products from all quarters of the country were brought together: food, clothing, weapons, manufactured articles of rich material and colour, objects of gold, and a wealth of flowers which the inhabitants loved, stone buildings which lined the streets, the canals and streets which gave access thereto, and, in brief, the whole detail and substance of that remarkable centre of a semi-civilisation which the Spaniards commonly pronounced the equal of anything in their own native land. In company with Montezuma Cortes ascended the great *teocalli*, or pyramidal temple, and he and his companion, from this high point, beheld with amazement the panorama of the city below—with the lakes, the causeways giving access to the mainland, the towns on the farther side, and the intense cultivation of the valley. "Only the murmur of the people below reached our ears, as we gazed upon this panorama," wrote Bernal Diaz, who was there. To the chiefs who had been ordered to carry Cortes up the fatiguing stairway-ascent of the pyramid, and to the polite inquiries of Montezuma, the *Conquistador* replied, "that a Spaniard was never weary!" "But this abode of the devil," he said, with less politic words, which somewhat offended Montezuma—indicating the blood-stained sanctuary of the summit where they stood—"should rather be the home of the Cross"; and, indeed, the abominable place might well arouse the indignation of a Christian man: even one of that race and religion which later, in the same place, burned its own brethren at the stake for the good of their souls!

A few days wrought a change. Montezuma became a prisoner in the Spanish camp! In the heart of his own city, surrounded by his powerful chiefs and armies, the Aztec languished in vile, if seemingly voluntary, durance; and, an instrument in the invaders' hands, he governed his realm from their quarters. How was this astonishing transformation brought about? Cortes and his companions were in a singular position. Living in friendly harmony with their powerful host, shielded by his strange, superstitious reverence for a tradition, they yet could not but fear some change of circumstance which might, at any moment, plunge them into insecurity or threaten them with destruction. Moreover, Cortes knew not in what condition he stood with the dreaded powers of Castile. What favour or disfavour had he incurred in Spain for his irregular proceedings?—adverse representation of which, he well knew, would have been made by Velasquez and others, jealous of the conquest. Also—and this was a more poignant consideration than any other—Mexico was not conquered; it was only discovered. Action was necessary—to go or stay. "Listen," said Cortes to his captains, as they held solemn conclave. "This is my plan. We will seize and hold Montezuma. What say you?" It was done. For a pretext for this unworthy act the murder of two Spaniards upon an expedition at Vera Cruz was assigned. Visiting Montezuma's residence under pretence of asking redress for this—which was fully granted by the Aztec king, with absolute proofs of his non-participation in the occurrence—the Spaniards demanded that he should accompany them to their camp and take up his residence there.

This remarkable request was acceded to by the weak Montezuma—let us not say weak, but rather fatalist—and, accompanied by his weeping vassals, he allowed himself to be conducted to the stone fortress which had been assigned to the Spaniards as their habitation. The circumstance is perhaps unique in history.

And then the barbarous abuse of power, so strong a trait in the Spanish character, was exercised by Cortes and his captains. The chiefs who had been responsible for the killing of the two Spaniards arrived in the capital in accordance with Montezuma's summons. The Spaniards seized them, bound them to stakes in the courtyard, and burned them alive, an abominable act and stain upon their name, for which they paid dearly afterwards. Montezuma had been put in chains, the prisoners having confessed, although falsely, it is held, that they had acted in accordance with the Emperor's instructions. Afterwards Montezuma's shackles were taken off, but the indignity remained, although the Spaniards treated him well and endeavoured to render his captivity light, not so much out of regard for him, as that the safe keeping of his person was a valuable hostage for them.

The days went on in the Spanish camp. There was gaming with the huge treasure which, after his captivity, Montezuma gave the Spaniards; a treasure of which the gold, in three great heaps upon the floor of the habitation, was of value so prodigious as to dazzle even them, and of which a fifth was set apart for the Spanish king. Not content with these matters, or, rather, urged by their religious fervour, the Spaniards obtained permission to erect an altar and crucifix in one of the sanctuaries of the great *teocalli*. There Father Olmedo celebrated Mass, and the *Te Deum* was chanted by the soldiers, side by side with the sacrificial stone; the abominable war-god's image, and all the attendant machinery of its savage priestcraft.

But a time of change looms up. Six months have elapsed since the Spaniards entered the city. The unnatural condition of these things bears its fruit. The Aztec king has sounded the knell of his own authority and prestige, and the Spaniards' religious work has incurred the hatred of the seething multitude, scarcely held in check by the commands of Montezuma. Cortes and most of his captains at this critical time are called to Vera Cruz by Sandoval, the captain in charge; and go they must, for life or death. For hostile ships, sent by the jealous Velasquez and commanded by one Narvaez, menace the base of operations on the coast. Leaving Alvarado in charge of Montezuma and Spanish prestige in Tenochtitlan, Cortes by forced marches gained the coast, journeying with great speed, and under grave apprehension.

Fortune on this occasion favoured the *Conquistador* in a remarkable way. With only a third of his small force—140 men had remained in the capital—Cortes, under cover of a fearful storm at night, attacked Narvaez and the Spaniards of his command, routing them and taking the leader prisoner. The defeated soldiers soon enrolled themselves under Cortes's successful banner, stimulated by tales of gold and glory in the interior. But whilst the *Conquistadores* were resting and congratulating themselves upon the addition of men, horses, and ammunition to their forces, grave tidings came from Mexico. The Indians of Tenochtitlan had arisen, assaulted the fortifications of the Spaniards on all sides, and unless Cortes desired to see all his work undone, his people massacred, and his hard-won prestige ruined, he must make his way as fast as God would let him again to the city on the lakes of Anahuac.

Up, up they went once more. Up through the tropical forests and among the appalling escarpments of the Sierra. Again they descended the valley slopes, approached the lakes—round which an ominous abandonment prevailed—and crossing the long causeway, entered the Spanish camp. The fault of the insurrection, Cortes learned now, lay with the commander in charge—the foolish and cruel Alvarado, whose barbarous acts on other occasions had needlessly embroiled the Spaniards with the natives. A great celebration and religious festival was being held—Cortes learned—and whilst the Aztec nobles and people were occupied, unsuspecting any hostile act of their guests, Alvarado and the Spaniards, armed to the teeth, had mingled with the crowd with their purpose all planned, fallen upon the unarmed worshippers, and perpetrated a frightful massacre—"without pity or Christian mercy, so that the gutters ran with blood as in a rain-storm," say the chroniclers.

The result of this barbarous act was a vengeance and punishment which cost the *Conquistadores* dear, and stripped them in a few days of all they had won. For the maddened people, roused by sorrow and hate, and urged on by the priests, assailed the Spanish dwelling with frenzied attack. A rain of darts and missiles descended day after day upon the quarters of the Christians, so numerous that they had to be gathered in heaps and burnt in the courtyard. The main point of attack by the Mexicans was the great *teocalli* of the war-god, which overlooked the Spaniards' quarters, and so fierce was the hail of arrows and stones from this that a sortie was made. Cortes, with Sandoval and Alvarado, and a number of the Spaniards, led a gallant attack on the pyramid, fought their way up its precipitous steps and terraces, and after a frightful hand-to-hand struggle on its giddy summit, forced the Aztecs and their priests over the edge, and rolled the infernal idol of Huitzilopotchli, the war-god, down among the people in the streets below.

Impressed as they were by the destruction of their temple and god—an event which was rapidly circulated about the country by hieroglyphical paintings—the Aztecs abated nothing of their attack and siege of the hated white men. All superstitious fear had gone, and the true character of these people the Spaniards had now to learn. Day after day the barbarians came on. Sortie after sortie, sometimes with success, sometimes with severe loss, was made by the Christians, Cortes more than once barely escaping with his life, while numerous Spaniards and horses fell. The labyrinth of streets and cross-canals and bridges much hampered the Spaniards' movements, and houses and walls were torn down to fill these fatal ditches. Distress and famine fell upon the garrison, mutiny arose, and some of the Spaniards cursed themselves and their leader as fools for having left their comfortable homes in Cuba to embark on this mad enterprise, whose termination seemed as if it might be—as indeed it was for many of them—the sacrificial stone of the heathen god.

But Cortes, intrepid and serene in the face of disaster, called them to order. The unfortunate Montezuma, who, buried in a profound melancholy, took no part in the struggle, was urged to address his frenzied people from the tower of the fortification. He consented, and the Aztec warriors without the walls gazed with astonishment on their captured chief, and heard with still greater amazement his commands that strife against the white man should cease. But the power of his name and presence was gone; howls and execration arose from the mob; a stone from a sling struck Montezuma upon the forehead, and he sank back into the arms of the Spaniards and was borne to his quarters. For a space, the mob, horror-struck at its sacrilegious act, fled from the place, and not a man was seen within the square that day. Montezuma, sorely stricken, declined rapidly, and refusing the attentions of Father Olmedo, who knelt at his bedside with uplifted crucifix, sank to his end. "Half an hour of life alone remains me; at least I will die in the faith of my forefathers," he said, adding in expiring tones to Cortes, his last words: "To your care and your Emperor's I commend my daughters, my precious jewels. You, for whose sake I have been brought to indignity and death, will not refuse me this last request." So perished the noble Montezuma.[16]

> 16 It is stated by some historians that the death of Montezuma was really brought about by Cortes and the Spaniards, who, considering the unfortunate monarch an incumbrance, killed him in captivity; and there are grounds for suspecting that this is true.

The bridges broken, the savages screaming outside the walls, hope of victory gone, there was now no counsel of war for the Spaniards save that of escape. But how? At night and along the great causeway was the only plan. A weird scene it was on the beginning of that *Noche Triste*—the sorrowful night—which stands forth so unforgetably in the history of the Conquest. Disorder everywhere; piles of gold and valuables upon the floor, each Spaniard, whether cavalier or boor, loading himself with what he thought he could carry. "Pocket what you can," Cortes said, "but recollect that gold is heavy and we have to travel swiftly"—grave advice, the neglect of which cost some their lives upon that awful night.

And then began the retreat along the fatal causeway. It was known that there were three openings in this, and a portable bridge had been made and was borne along to enable passage to be effected. Hurrying on in the hope of passing the breaches before alarm might be given, the Spaniards entered upon the causeway and placed their portable bridge upon the first breach. Was safety to be theirs? No! What was that appalling sound, sonorous and melancholy, which rang over the city and the waters amid the darkness? It was the great drum on the *teocalli*; the *tambor* of the war-god, sounded by vigilant priests, calling the people to vengeance and battle. And in their myriads the Aztecs poured forth and fell upon the Christians, raining darts and stones upon them, and making the night hideous with their war-cries. Meanwhile Cortes and the advance guard had passed over, and reached the second breach. "Bring up the bridge!" was, the repeated order, as those behind crowded on. Useless; the bridge was stuck fast in the first breach, wedged down by the weight of guns and horses which had passed over it, and as these dread tidings were heard the mass of men upon the narrow causeway lost their presence of mind. Those behind crowded on those in front; men and horses rolled into the lake; Spaniards and Tlascalans fell victims to the Aztecs, who crowded the water in their canoes and leapt upon the causeway; the shouts of vengeance and triumph of the savages resounded all along the dyke, silencing the muttered oath or prayer of the Christians huddled at the breach. Down went horse and man, artillery and treasure, until with the bodies of Christians and Indians and horses, and bales of merchandise and chests of ammunition the breach was almost filled, and a portion of the fugitives passed over. And now the third breach yawns before them—deep and wide. The morning is dawning upon the fatal scene; the salt waters of the lake have closed over many a gallant Christian head; the frightful causeway is strewn with wreck of man and merchandise. "The rear guard perishes!" and "back and save them!" were the words which rang out then; and Cortes and his remaining cavaliers, who were in the lead, rode back, even in that frightful hour—be it recorded to their honour—and, swimming the breach once more, strove to support their comrades. There stood Alvarado unhorsed and battling, with the savages pressing upon his rear. Escape there seemed none. Canoes and spears teemed on every side, and Cortes and his companions were forced onward. The heroic figure of Alvarado stood up against the grey sky alone—a moment—and then he measured the breach with his eye, whilst—

> "Friends and foes in dumb surprise
> With parted lips and straining eyes
>   Stood gazing,"—

but not "where he sank," for sink he did not.[17] Planting his lance on the wreckage in the waters of the breach, after the manner of a leaping-pole, the heroic Spaniard collected his energies, leapt forward, and passed the chasm at a bound. To this day, in the City of Mexico, the spot exists, and is known as the *puente de Alvarado*.

> 17 It is stated that the Aztecs paused in admiration of this feat, whilst "the Son of the Sun," as they termed Alvarado, from his fair hair and rubicund visage, performed this extraordinary leap; considering it miraculous.

Away off the causeway into the grey dawn of morning passed the remnant of the routed army, wounded, bleeding, starving, their comrades gone, some to death, some to the sacrifice, and annihilation threatening all. Baggage and artillery were gone, not a carbine was left, and Cortes, seating himself upon the steps of a ruined temple on the shore, wept bitter tears of sorrow and vanished fortune. So passed the *Noche Triste*.

The next great event of this remarkable campaign was the battle of Otumba. The wretched soldiers, having obtained what rest and nourishment were possible, continued their retreat around the northern part of the lake valley; passed beneath the shadow of the pyramids of Teotihuacan—standing ever there ruined and wrapped in the mystery of their prehistoric builders—and seven days after the events of that awful night crossed the summit of the range which bounds the plain of Anahuac. Thence they set their gaze eastwards towards the coast. What was it that greeted their eyes on the plain below? A mighty army of warriors whose hosts absolutely covered the plain with glowing lance and waving plumes—the forces of the warlike Otomies. So numerous were they that, dressed in their armour of white quilted cotton, it "looked as if the land was covered with snow," as the historians put it. There was nothing for it but to face these fearful odds, and, weakened as they were, the remnant of the Spanish force, encouraged by their leader and exhorted by their priest, fell valiantly on. They were soon wrapped in the enfolding masses of the savages, who attacked them with the utmost ferocity. The cavalry fell back; the Spaniards were stricken on every side, and absolute disaster hung over them. "We believed it to be our last day," Cortes wrote to Spain afterwards. But the tide of battle changed miraculously. In a last furious charge Cortes, followed by the few officers who remained, leaped upon the foe, reached the litter of their chief, and, running him through the body with a lance, tore down the standard. This act saved the day. Stricken with panic at the loss of their leader, the Indians fell into disorder, threw down their arms, and turned and fled. Hot upon them, and thirsting for revenge, poured the Spaniards and Tlascalans—it is to be recollected that the

Christians had no firearms nor artillery—and utterly routed them. The victory of Otumba is considered one of the most remarkable in the history of the New World.

THE CONQUEST OF MEXICO: CORTES AT THE BATTLE OF OTUMBA.
(From the painting by Ramirez.)

Their fortunes thus somewhat ameliorated, the Spaniards continued onward to Tlascala, where they were received with the utmost hospitality, and there they recuperated their shattered energies. Further alliance was entered into with these people, despite embassies from the Aztecs. Further operations were successfully conducted against the powerful Tepeacans—allies of the Aztecs—who were beaten, and transferred their allegiance to the men of Castile. These successes were followed by others; the Tlascalans in a severe battle defeated a large force of the Aztecs; numerous other tribes, influenced by these matters, sent to offer their allegiance, and a vast part of the country was soon under the authority of the Spaniards. The intrepid and persistent spirit of Cortes, undismayed by the reverses which the attempted conquest of Mexico had cost him and his followers, now laid his plans for a further campaign against the lake-city of Anahuac. Over Tenochtitlan there had reigned a master-enemy, to whose work had been due the frightful reverses of the "sorrowful night" and the battle of Otumba. This was Cuitlahuac, brother of Montezuma. But having saved his capital from falling before the detested white men, this capable prince expired from smallpox—a disease introduced into the country by the invaders—after a few months' reign. In his stead now arose the famous Guatemoc, Montezuma's nephew, and he also had sworn a deep hatred against the ravishers of his country.

Up, up once more, away over the rocky fastnesses of the sierra, followed by his allies, the flower of the armies of Tlascala, Tepeaca, and Cholula, Cortes and his Spaniards pressed. But his measures this time had been taken with care and forethought. The resources of the country furnished sinews of war. Twelve brigantines were put under construction by the Spanish shipbuilder who was among the forces, timber and pitch being obtained from the mountains near at hand, and the ironwork and rigging of the destroyed navy of Vera Cruz used for their outfitting. This astonishing piece of work was performed by the Tlascalans, and the ships, carried from Tlascala to the shore of Texcoco, were floated thereon by means of a canal dug by these magnificent allies of the Spanish Crown. The building of ships in a forest and carrying them in pieces for sixty miles over mountains and plains to the water, is a feat which may well command our admiration even to-day!

The subjugation of the Aztec city proved to be a protracted and bloody task. The only method by which it could be compassed was that of laying waste the surrounding places on the lake and the holding of the environs of the city in a state of siege. Cortes established his centre of operations in the city of Texcoco, capital of the nation of the same name, on the eastern extremity of the lake, and the young Prince Ixtlilxochitl, whom he installed upon the throne of that kingdom, was his powerful ally. Indeed, it was only the disaffections of the outlying peoples, who generally abhorred the Aztec hegemony, that enabled the Spaniards to carry on their operations, or, indeed, to set foot in the country at all.

A series of severe struggles began then, both by land and water—burning, slaughter, and the destruction of the lake towns. The Aztecs, with their great number, raining darts and stones upon the invaders at every engagement, attacked them with unparalleled ferocity both by forces on shore and their canoes on the lake. The Spaniards took heavy toll of the enemy at every turn, assisted by their allies the Tlascalans, as savage and implacable as the Aztecs, whom they attacked with a singular and persistent spirit of hatred, the result of long years of oppression by the dominant power of Anahuac. Cortes, on every occasion when it seemed that the last chance of success might attend it, offered terms to the Aztec capital, by no means dishonourable, assuring them their liberty and self-government in return for allegiance to the Crown of Spain and the renouncing of their abominable system of sacrificial religion. These advances were invariably met by the most implacable negatives. The Aztecs, far from offering to yield, swore they would sacrifice, when the day was theirs, every Spaniard and Tlascalan on the bloody altars of their gods; and as for entering into any treaty, the last man, woman, and child would resist the hated invaders until the last drop of blood was shed and the last stone of their city thrown down. This vaunt, as regards the latter part, was almost literally carried out, and to some extent as regards the former.

During the earlier part of the siege a welcome addition was made to the Spanish forces. Three vessels from Hispaniola arrived at Vera Cruz, and the two hundred men, artillery, gunpowder, and quantity of horses they brought placed the Spaniards again in possession of superior arms. Previous to this the brigantines had arrived, transported by the Tlascalans, eight thousand bearers loaded with timbers and appliances, "a marvellous sight to see," wrote Cortes to the king. "I assure your Majesty that the train of bearers was six miles long." It is related by a subsequent historian, in 1626, that tallow being scarce for the shipwrights' purposes, it was obtained from the dead bodies of Indians who had fallen in the fights; presumably by boiling them down.[18]

> 18 This obtaining of *sebo humano*, or "human tallow," by the Spaniards seems to have been practised in Peru also, according to stories told me by the natives of the Andes, and recorded in my book, "The Andes and the Amazon."

Plans were then laid for an attack upon the island-city. But before this it was necessary to subjugate some troublesome Indians to the west, and the expedition to Cuernavaca was successfully carried out. A remarkable incident of this was the surprise attack upon the enemy in an impregnable position, by the crossing of a profound chasm by means of two overhanging trees, which were utilised as a natural bridge by some Tlascalans and the Spaniards, who passed the dangerous spot by this method. Return was then made to Xochimilco on the fresh-water lake of that name, adjoining at that time that of Texcoco on the south. The name of this place in the Aztec tongue signifies "The Field of Flowers," for there were numbers of the singular *chinampas*, or floating-gardens, which were a feature of the aquatic life of the Mexicans, existing upon this lake.

The siege operations were conducted vigorously both by land and water. Again before the eyes of the Spaniards stretched that fatal causeway—path of death amid the salt waters of Texcoco for so many of their brave comrades upon the *Noche Triste* of their terrible flight from Tenochtitlan. And there loomed once more that dreaded *teocalli*, whence the war-drum's mournful notes were heard. Guarded now by the capable and persistent Guatemoc, the city refused an offer of treaty, and invited the destruction which was to fall upon it. From the *azoteas*, or roofs of their buildings and temples, the undaunted Mexicans beheld the white-winged brigantines, armed with those belching engines of thunder and death whose sting they well knew: and saw the ruthless hand of devastation laying waste their fair town of the lake shore, and cutting off their means of life.

But the Spaniards had yet to learn to their cost the lengths of Aztec tenacity and ferocity. It will be recollected that the city was connected to the lake shores by means of four causeways, built above the surface of the water; engineering structures of stone and mortar and earth, which had from the first aroused the admiration of the Spaniards. These causeways, whilst they rendered the city almost impregnable from attack, were a source of weakness in the easy cutting-off of food supplies, which they afforded to the enemy. A simultaneous assault on all these approaches was organised by the Spaniards, under Sandoval, Alvarado, and Cortes himself, respectively, whilst the brigantines, with their raking artillery, were to support the attack by water, aided by the canoes of the Tlascalan and Texcocan allies. A series of attacks was made by this method, and at last the various bodies of Spaniards advanced along the causeways and gained the city walls. But frightful disaster befel them. The comparative ease with which they entered the city aroused Cortes's suspicions; and at that moment, from the summit of the great *teocalli*, rang out a fearful note—the horn of Guatemoc, calling for vengeance and a concerted attack. The notes of the horn struck some ominous sense of chill in the Spaniards' breasts, and the soldier-penman, Bernal Diaz, who was fighting valiantly there, says that the noise echoed and re-echoed, and rang in his ears for days afterwards. The Spaniards on this, as on other occasions, had foolishly neglected to secure the breaches in the causeways as they passed, or at least the rash Alvarado had not done so with his command, his earlier lesson unheeded; and when the Christians were hurled backwards —for their easy entrance into the great square of the city had been in the nature of a decoy—disaster befel them, which at one moment seemed as if it would be a repetition of that of the *Noche Triste.* "The moment I reached that fearful bridge," Cortes wrote in his despatches, "I saw the Spaniards returning in full flight." Remaining to hold the breach, if possible, and cover the retreat, the chivalrous Cortes almost lost his life from a furious attack by the barbarians in their canoes, and was only saved by the devotion of his own men and Indian allies, who gave their lives in his rescue. Word, nevertheless, had gone forth among the men that Cortes had fallen; and the savages, throwing before the faces of Alvarado and Sandoval the bloody heads of decapitated Spaniards, cried tauntingly the name "Malintzin," which was that by which Cortes was known among the Mexicans. Men and horses rolled into the lake; dead bodies filled the breaches; the Christians and their allies were beaten back, and "as we were all wounded it was only the help of God which saved us from destruction," wrote Bernal Diaz. Indeed, both Cortes and the Spaniards only escaped, on these and other occasions, from the Aztecs' desire to take them alive for sacrifice.

Once more, after disastrous retreats and heavy loss, the bleeding and discouraged Spaniards lay in their camp, as evening fell. Of dead, wounded, and captured the Spaniards missed more than a hundred and twenty of their comrades, and the Tlascalans a thousand, whilst valuable artillery, guns, and horses were lost. But listen! what is that mournful, penetrating sound which smites the Christians' ears? It is the war-god's drum, and even from where the Spaniards stand there is visible a procession ascending the steps of the *teocalli,* and, to their horror, the forms of their lost comrades are seen within it: whose hearts are doomed to be torn out living from their breasts to smoke before the shrine of Huitzilopochtli, the war-devil of their enemies. From that high and fearful place their comrades' eyes must be gazing with despairing look towards the impotent Spanish camp, glazing soon in death as the obsidian knives of the priests performed their fiendish work. The disastrous situation of the Spaniards was made worse by the desertion, at this juncture, of the Tlascalan and other allies. Awed by a prophecy sent out confidently by the Aztec priests, that both Christians and allies should be delivered into their hands before eight days had passed (prophecy or doom, which the priests said, was from the mouth of the war-god, appeased by the late victory), the superstitious Indians of Cortes's forces sneaked off in the night.

Continued reverses, in the face of long-continued action and desire for the attaining a given end, forges in the finer calibre of mind a spirit of unremitting purpose. Blow after blow, which would turn away the ordinary individual from his endeavour, serves to steel the real hero to a dispassionate and persistent patience, and the purpose from its very intensity becomes almost a sacred cause, and seems to obtain from the unseen powers of circumstance success at last. So with Cortes and others of the Spaniards. The period prescribed by the somewhat rash prophecy of the Aztec priests and their infernal oracle having passed without anything remarkable having taken place, the Tlascalan and Texcocan allies, upbraided and warned by the Spaniards' messengers, now sneaked back to resume the attack against the city. The Aztecs had sought to cause disaffection in outlying places by sending round the bloody heads of decapitated Spaniards and horses, but with little effect. Cortes then prepared for a final effort. The plan adopted was to be slower but surer than the former one of simple slaughter. It was determined to raze the city to the ground; to destroy the buildings step by step, fill up the canals, and so lay waste the whole area from the outside, so that unobstructed advance might be maintained.

The execution of this plan was begun. The city ends of the causeways were captured and held; street after street was demolished, and canal after canal filled up amid scenes of incessant fighting and slaughter. Day after day the Spaniards returned to their work; day after day with admirable tenacity the inhabitants of Tenochtitlan disputed the ground inch by inch, watered with the blood of themselves, their women and their children. Their supplies cut off, famine and pestilence wrought more terrible havoc among them—crowded as they gradually became into one quarter of the city—than the arms of the Spaniards and the Tlascalans. At the termination of each day's work the Spanish prepared an ambuscade for the enemy, drawing them on by seeming to retire, and massacring them with the artillery and gun-fire and lances, to say nothing of the weapons of their savage allies. On one of these occasions "the enemy rushed out yelling as if they had gained the greatest victory in the world," Cortes wrote in his despatches, and "more than five hundred, all of the bravest and principal men, were killed in this ambush." He added, and it was a common occurrence, "our allies"—the Indians—"supped well that night, cutting up and eating their captives!" During the days of this terrible siege the famous catapult was made, an extraordinary engine to discharge great stones upon the enemy. This was to enable the Spaniards to husband their powder, which was getting low, and the Aztecs watched the construction of this machine with certain fear. It was completed and set to work, but the builder, a Spanish soldier of inventive faculty, nearly played the part of the engineer hoist with his own petard, for the great stone fired rose, it is true, but went straight up and descended again upon the machine, which was ever afterwards the laughing-stock of the army.

Further severe losses were now inflicted upon the beleaguered inhabitants, as more ammunition had been obtained. Peace had again been offered by the Spaniards, and again refused by the Aztecs. An Aztec chief of high rank had been captured, and then returned to Guatemoc as a peace envoy. The Mexicans' reply was to execute and sacrifice the unfortunate emissary, and then collecting their forces they poured out upon the causeways like a furious tide, which seemed as if it would sweep all before it. But the Spaniards were prepared. The narrow causeways were commanded by the artillery, which poured such a deadly hail upon the enemy's numbers that they returned fleeing to the city.

And soon the end approaches. The division led by Cortes made a fierce assault; and whilst the battle raged the Spaniards observed that the summit of one of the *teocallis* was in flames. It was the work of Alvarado's men, who had penetrated already to the plaza. Forces were joined, and the inhabitants of the city, driven into one quarter thereof, still made their stubborn and—now—suicidal stand. For the streets were piled up with corpses, the Aztecs refraining from throwing the bodies of their slain into the lake, or outside the city, in order not to show their weakness. Pestilence and famine had made terrible inroads upon the population. Miserable wretches, men, women, and children, were encountered wandering about careless of the enemy, only bent upon finding some roots, bark, or offal which might appease the hunger at their vitals. The salt waters of the lake, which they had been obliged to drink, for the Spaniards had cut the aqueduct which brought the fresh water from Chapultepec, had caused many to sicken and die. Mothers had devoured their dead children; the bodies of the slain had been eaten, and the bark gnawed from the trunks of trees. In their dire extremity some of the chiefs of the beleaguered city called Cortes to the barricade. He went, trusting that capitulation was at hand, for, as both he and his historians record, the slaughter was far from their choosing. "Do but finish your work quickly," was the burden of their parley. "Let us go and rest in the heaven of our war-god; we are weary of life and suffering. How is it that you, a son of the Sun, tarry so long in finishing, when the Sun himself makes circuit of the earth in a day, and so accomplishes his work speedily?"

This remarkable appeal struck renewed pity to the heart of Cortes, and once more he begged them to surrender and avoid further suffering, and the Spaniards drew off their forces for a space. But the inexorable Guatemoc, although he sent an embassy to say he would hold parley, and the Spaniards waited for him, did not fulfil the promise at the last moment. Incensed at this behaviour, the Spaniards and the Tlascalans renewed the attack with overpowering energy on the one part and barbaric savagery on the other. Contrary to the orders of the Spaniards, their savage allies gave no quarter, but murdered men, women, and children in fiendish exultation. The stench of the dead in the beleaguered city was overpowering; the soil was soaked with blood; the gutters ran as in a rain-storm, say the chroniclers, and, wrote Cortes to the King of Spain: "Such slaughter was done that day on land and water that killed and prisoners numbered forty thousand; and such were the shrieks and weeping of women and children that there were none of us whose hearts did not break." He adds that it was impossible to contain the savage killing and torturing by their allies the Tlascalans, who practised such cruelty as had never been seen, and "out of all order of nature."

At nightfall the attacking forces drew off, leaving the remainder of the inhabitants of the stricken city to consider their position. It is stated that the Tlascalans made a great banquet of the flesh of the fallen Aztecs, and that on this and other occasions they fished up the bloated bodies of their enemies from the lake and devoured them! At sunrise on the following day Cortes and a few followers entered the city, hoping to have a supplication for terms from Guatemoc. The army was stationed outside the walls, ready, in the event of a refusal—the signal of which should be a musket-shot—to pour in and strike the final blow. A parley was entered into as before, which lasted several hours. "Do you surrender?" Cortes demanded. The final reply of Guatemoc was, "I will not come: I prefer to die where I am: do your worst."

A musket-shot rang out upon the air; the Spaniards and their allies fell on to merciless slaughter: cannons, muskets, arrows, slings, lances—all told their tale upon the huddled mass of panic-stricken people, who, after presenting a feeble and momentary front, poured forth upon the fatal causeways to escape. Drowned and suffocated in the waters of the lake, mowed down by the fire from the brigantines, and butchered by the brutal Tlascalans, women, children, and men struggled and shrieked among that frightful carnage; upon which it were almost impious to dwell further. Guatemoc, with his wife and children, strove to escape, and the canoe containing them was already out upon the lake, when a brigantine ran it down and captured him. All resistance was at an end. No sign of life or authority remained among the ruined walls; the fair city by the lake was broken and tenantless, its idols fallen, and its people fled. The Homeric struggle was over; the conquest of Mexico was accomplished.

CHAPTER VI

MEXICO AND THE VICEROYS

General considerations—Character of Viceroy rule—Spanish civilisation—Administration of Cortes—Torture of Guatemoc—Conquests of Guatemala and Honduras—Murder of Guatemoc—Fall of Cortes—First viceroy Mendoza—His good administration—Misrule of the *Audiencias*—Slavery and abuse of the Indians—The Philippine islands—Progress under the Viceroys—Plans for draining the Valley of Mexico—British buccaneers—Priestly excesses—Raid of Agramonte—Exploration of California—Spain and England at war—Improvements and progress in the eighteenth century—Waning of Spanish power—Decrepitude of Spain—Summary of Spanish rule—Spanish gifts to Mexico—The rising of Hidalgo—Spanish oppression of the colonists—Oppression by the colonists of the Indians—Republicanism and liberty—Operations and death of Hidalgo—The revolution of Morelos—Mier—The dawn of Independence—The birth of Spanish-American nations.

The history of Mexico, like its topography, shows a series of intense and varied pictures. Indeed, it ever occurs to the student of the Spanish-American past, and observer of Spanish-American hills and valleys, that the diverse physical changes seem to have had some analogy with or to have exercised some influence upon the acts of mankind there. Whether in Mexico, Peru, or other parts of North, Central, and South America, formed by the rugged ranges of the Andes, the accompaniments of prehistoric civilisation, daring conquest, bloody and picturesque revolution, and social turmoil are found. Amid these great mountain peaks and profound valleys strange semi-civilised barbarians raised their temples, and European men, arriving thither in armed bands, have torn both themselves and their predecessors to pieces, as if some dictate of Nature had said, "Fight; for here is no peace."

Yet what was really destined to take place in Mexico was the evolution of a distinct civilisation. Three hundred years of the implanting of the seed of Spanish culture and ideals, and fifty years of drastic revolutionary tilling of the social soil, wrought a nation at length.

Transplanted from the Old World, the methods and character of Spanish life, with all its virtues and defects, rapidly took root in Mexico. The long rule of the Viceroys is steeped in an atmosphere often brilliant and attractive, often dark and sinister, always romantic and impressive. The grandees of Spain came out to rule this new country, and gave it of their best, nor disdained to spend their years therein, and a stream of capable legislators and erudite professors and devout ecclesiastics hurried to the new field which lay open to their services and powers. The patriotism and fervency of their work, whatever defects they showed from time to time, cannot fail to arouse the applause of the student of those times. The colonial *régime* gave solid and enduring character to the Mexican people. It gave them traditions, history, refinement, which are a priceless heritage for them, and it builded beautiful cities and raised up valuable institutions which are the substratum of their civilisation. The wonderful vitality and extent of Spanish influence and character which flowed from these centres—Mexico, Peru, and others—over thousands of miles of rugged Cordillera and through impassable forests, was, in some respects, the most notable condition within the shores of all the New World. The stamp of the great civilisation which Spain, herself the result of a human blend of undying character, implanted within these continents is great and imperishable, and holds something for the world at large which is, as yet, scarcely suspected.

But, to return to history. In 1522 Cortes was appointed Governor and Captain-General of the great territory which Spain acquired as a result of the Conquest, and to which the name of "New Spain" was given—a designation, however, which was never able to usurp its ancient and natural one of "Mexico." The charges which had been brought against Cortes by his jealous enemies had been inquired into by an impartial group of statesmen appointed by the young King of Spain, Charles V., and set aside; and thus began the rule of Spain in Mexico. The Conquistador thus reached the summit of fame and power—the reward of his indomitable spirit of persistence in the path and project which his imagination had fired.

The *régime* of Cortes was not without benefit to the colony. A fine city arose upon the ruins of Tenochtitlan. Settlement of the country was carried on; valuable products of the Old World—among them the sugar-cane and orange and grape-vines—were introduced and cultivated; exploration of the country was pushed on a considerable scale, resulting in the discovery of the Pacific coast of Mexico. The conquest of Guatemala was carried out by Pedro de Alvarado, sent thither by Cortes, and that of Honduras by Olid. Cortes personally carried an expedition to Honduras, but disturbances in Mexico obliged him to return.

Guatemoc, the brave young Aztec defender of Tenochtitlan, fared ill at the hands of the Spaniards. To their shame it is that, after the fall of the city, they tortured him—by permission of Cortes—in order to extract information as to the whereabouts of the Aztec treasure; for the invaders had obtained disappointingly little gold. In company with one of his chiefs the Spaniards roasted the feet of Guatemoc before a fire: "Think you that I am upon some bed of delight?" was the reply of the stoic Aztec to his groaning companion in torture, who asked if he did not suffer. Guatemoc remained crippled for life by this barbarous act, but he accompanied Cortes to Honduras, and upon this expedition it was that the Spaniards executed—or murdered—him. He was accused of treachery in having endeavoured to incite a rebellion against the Spaniards, and they hanged him head downwards from a tree. "Ah!

Malintzin,"[19] the unfortunate Aztec said to Cortes after his mock trial, "vain I ever knew it to trust in your promises!"

19 The Aztec name for Cortes.

And now the time arrives when the star of the Conquistador is to wane and set. The execution of Guatemoc had brought about a reprimand from Spain; for it is to be recollected that the Spanish sovereigns never sought the actual destruction of the American princes, and Pizarro, also, was reprimanded after his murder of Atahualpa, in Peru. Cortes, upon his return to Mexico from the Honduras expedition, found that Spain was not pleased with his administration. Enemies had been at work, and gratitude for his great services was easily set aside in the fickle favour of the monarch. A special commissioner, in the person of the licentiate Ponce de Leon, was awaiting him, appointed by Carlos V. to impeach him, as a result of grave charges of maladministration—true or untrue—which had been brought against him in Spain. In this connection it is to be recollected that Cortes, faithful to his country, had twice refused to be made King of Mexico by his own followers. Cortes, finding his enemies too strong, went to Spain to lay his case before the Emperor personally, but was denied the civil governorship of Mexico, although military control was given him, and the title of Marqués del Valle. But although he returned to Mexico, he was no longer in the dominant position of former years. Cortes returned to Spain in 1540 from Mexico, once more to lay the plaint of his unjust treatment before Carlos V., a result of his disputes with the first viceroy, Mendoza. He was treated with indifference and coldness; his life terminated in disappointment and regrets, and he died in Spain in December, 1547. So pass the actors in the drama of the Conquest. As to Guatemoc, his memory is perpetuated in the handsome statue in the *paseo de Colon* of modern Mexico, whilst—strange sentiment of the race which Cortes founded—no monument to the bold Conquistador exists throughout the land.

From the time of the fall of the fortunes of Cortes in 1535 to the first cry for independence by Hidalgo in 1810, New Spain was administered by viceroys and *Audiencias*—the latter being a species of administrative councils consisting of a president and four members, nominated by royal decree. The first viceroy, Mendoza, and many of the subsequent officials of this rank governed Mexico for a period, and were transferred thence to the viceregency of Peru, which latter country had been brought into Spain's colonial possessions by the conquest under Pizarro, in 1532. Indeed, Pizarro a short time after that date had made his second entry into Cuzco, the Inca capital of Peru, wearing an ermine robe which Cortes had sent him. During Mendoza's period, printing was first introduced into Mexico—or, indeed, into the New World—the Mint and the University were founded, and exploration of the northern part of the country was undertaken. The rule of the first viceroy, Mendoza, was good; he was upright and capable, and his methods were in marked contrast to the excesses and cruelties practised by the first *Audiencia*, which had preceded his and the second *Audiencia's régime*. Bishops and priests took active part in the affairs of Mexico from the beginning, and the first *Audiencia* had been involved in grave conflict with the clergy. One of the main features of the period was the system of *repartmientos* and *encomiendas* under which the Indians were portioned out as serfs to the Spanish colonists. Exceeding brutality marked this system of slavery; and at an early date it became necessary to abolish the practice of branding the unfortunate serfs with hot irons, like cattle! Thus began the system of cruelty and abuse of the natives under Spanish rule—not from Spain, however, but by the colonists—whose counterpart was enacted in the South American countries contemporaneously. It is to the credit of Churchmen that they often took the part of the Indians; and a venerated name to this day among the natives of Michoacan is that of Quiroga, the first Bishop of that province, who penetrated there to endeavour to counteract the effect of the marked abuses of Guzman, president of the first *Audiencia*, who in 1527 burned to death their chief, because he would not, or could not, give up his gold. Velasquez, the second viceroy, succeeding Mendoza, also had grave questions with the *Audiencia*. He also was an upright man, and his death was hastened by these matters. Indeed, the *Audiencias* were singularly unfortunate in their proceedings, and their rule was almost always marked by a mistaken policy exaggerated by acts of cruelty and oppression. During the time of Velasco an expedition sent by him sailed from Mexico westward, and took possession in 1564 of the Philippine Islands, which were so named after the reigning King of Spain, Philip II.

Viceroy succeeded viceroy then in the history of Mexico, and tyranny and benevolence followed each other alternately in the governing of the people. Under the cruel Muñoz, a member of the *Audiencia,* the son of Cortes was tortured, and gaols were filled and blood was freely shed on political and other charges. In 1571 another sinister event took place—the establishing of the Inquisition. A few years later the foundation of the Cathedral of Mexico was laid, the beautiful structure which to-day dominates the capital. A matter which was early forced upon the attention of the viceroys and city councils was the occurrence of flooding of the city and attendant epidemics and disaster; for the peculiar hydrographic conditions of the Valley of Mexico rendered it liable to floods, the first of which had occurred 1553. In 1580 plans were formulated for drainage by means of a canal which should give outlet through the surrounding hills. In 1603 this project was again brought forward and again abandoned; and in 1607 work was actually begun, with a force of nearly half a million Indians, upon the great cut of Nochistongo, which still exists and lies open to the view of the traveller upon the Mexican railway to-day.

Towards the close of the sixteenth century the ports of New Spain, especially Vera Cruz, were visited by those enterprising and unscrupulous sea-rovers of Britain, Drake, Cavendish, Hawkins, and others, who took toll of coast towns and plate-ships throughout the regions which Spain claimed as her own, but which pretensions were not respected by others of the maritime nations of Europe. A memorable period was this in the history of the New World, as of the Old, for this flood-tide of staunch buccaneers from Britain and Holland did but swell onward and culminate in the defeat of the Invincible Armada off the Elizabethan coast, 1588. The student of the history of Spanish America at this period will not spare much sympathy for Spain and Spanish misrule. Under Philip II. a constant drain of treasure from Mexico and Peru for the needy Mother Country had given rise to serious abuses in the mines, and silver was extracted to fabulous values and sent to Spain under the system of forced labour.

GUANAJUATO AS SEEN FROM THE HILLS: THE HISTORIC TREASURE-HOUSE OF MEXICO.

In 1622 acute questions arose between the Court and ecclesiastical authorities, as ever inevitably took place in Spain's colonial dominions. Bishops excommunicated viceroys, and viceroys fulminated banishment against bishops: riotings and beheadings followed, and royal interpositions were constantly necessary to uphold or condemn the action of one or the other side. In 1629 an appalling inundation of the City of Mexico took place, following a similar occurrence in 1622, due to the discontinuance of the drainage works which had earlier been begun; and it is stated that thirty thousand of the poor inhabitants of the valley perished as a result. Two years later acute dissatisfaction began to arise at the great acquisition of wealth and power by the clergy, and a memorial sent to Philip IV. by the municipality of Mexico begged that no more religious institutions or communities might be established, asserting that more than half the wealth of the country was in the hands of these, and that there were more than six thousand priests—most of them idle—in the country.

From the middle to the close of the seventeenth century the social life of the people developed but slowly. The main events were the conspiracy of the Irishman Lampart to secure independence for the country, the dedication of the cathedral of Mexico, the founding of the town of Albuquerque in the territory of New Mexico—to-day part of the United States, the enactment against the violation of private correspondence, the fortification of the ports on the Gulf coast against the operations of sea-rovers—among them the famous British buccaneer Morgan, the eruption of Popocatepetl (1665), the sacking of the town of Campeche by British ships (1680), the insurrection and murders by the Indians of Chihuahua and New Mexico, the piratical exploit of Agramonte and his band, who disembarked at and looted the port of Vera Cruz, imprisoning the greater part of the population in a church, the exploration of California, and the operations against the French and English settlers upon the Mexican Gulf coast. The last years of the century were disturbed by serious rioting and tumult in the capital, due to scarcity of food and the inundation of the city.

The first years of 1700 opened with some alarm for the Spaniards of Mexico, for England and Spain were at war, and it was feared that British naval operations might be undertaken against the country. The loss of a plate-ship's treasure, due to the war, caused heavier taxes to fall upon the colonists, for continued exactions marked this century, from Spain, for treasure for the prosecution of her wars. The Gulf coast was placed in a position of defence against the British, who, however, after the capture of Habana, in 1762, concluded peace with Spain in the following year. Previous to that the English Admiral Anson had captured a galleon on its way from Acapulco to Manilla, with two and a half million dollars on board. The main events of this century, in addition to the foregoing, were the explorations of the Jesuits in California (1700), the severe earthquake of 1711, the distress among the common people, due to famine and oppression, which the Viceroy, the Duke of Linares, strove to remedy. In 1734 the first *creole* Viceroy, the Marquis of Casa Fuerte, born in Lima, was appointed, and during his *régime* the first Mexican newspaper was published. During the war between England and Spain the Viceroy Figueroa, Marquis of Gracia Real, was almost captured by the British, who gave chase to the ship in which he came from Spain. Further events were the singular phenomenon of the forming of the volcano of Jorullo in Michoacan in 1759, the celebration of peace between England and Spain in 1763, the suppression of the Jesuits and their expulsion from the country in 1767, under the Marquis de Croix; the continued exactions of the Council of the Indies for treasure from the colonists, the clearing of the Gulf of Mexico of buccaneers in 1785, the reorganisation and improvement of the city of Mexico under Padilla, Count of Revillagigedo (1789-94); the encouragement of agriculture, mining, manufacturing, road-building, exploration, improvement of sanitary conditions, and amelioration of those concerning the administration of justice, which this good viceroy carried out. But at the close of the century, under his effete successor, Branciforte (1799), a conspiracy was inaugurated, but frustrated, for the massacre of Spaniards, and the establishing of the independence of the country.

At the beginning of the great nineteenth century, the long array of viceroys, governors, and priests nears its close. The imperial authority of the Spanish sovereign, unquestioned since Cortes won the country for it, reached its natural waning, urged on and influenced by world-happenings in European lands reacting upon these remote shores of New Spain. Not only was this the case in Mexico. The decrepitude of the Mother Country, the old age and infirmity which had been creeping upon Castile through the excesses of her rulers, who learnt nothing from time or circumstance, was laid bare to the people of America throughout the vast regions held by Spain. Mexico, Peru, Chile, Colombia, Argentina—for the voice of Bolivar was ringing through the Andes—all in the first and second decades of the progressive nineteenth century were bent upon one stern task, the throwing off of the yoke of Spain and the establishing of native administrations. The flower of the earth, the vast and rich tropics and sub-tropics of North and South America, from California, Texas, and the Rocky Mountains, Mexico, Central America, down through the great Andes of Peru and Chile to Cape Horn, was in the hands of Spain, and it slipped from the grasp of a foolish and moribund nation.

But before entering upon these events let us take a final glance and draw a summary of the three long centuries—1521 to 1821—of this great array of Imperial Governors and their rule. Since that day of August 13, 1521, when Cortes unfurled the standard of Spain over the castle of Montezuma: to the consummation of Mexican independence, the entry of Iturbide into the city of Mexico on September 27, 1821: five Governors, two *Audiencias*, or Royal Commissions, and sixty-two Viceroys had guided the destiny of colonial Mexico. Many of the names of these authorities stand out in lustre as good and humane, tolerant and energetic for the advancement of the colony; merciful to the Indian population, and worthy of the approbation of the history of their time. Others were rapacious and cruel, using their power for their own ends, and showing that ruthless cruelty and indifference to bloodshed and suffering—holding the lives of natives as cheap as that of animals—which has been characteristic of Spaniards of all time. Counts, marquises, Churchmen—all have passed upon the scroll of those three hundred years; some left indelible marks for good, some for evil; whilst others, effete and useless, are buried in forgetfulness. The Spanish character, architecture, institutions, and class distinctions were now indelibly stamped upon the people of Mexico. The Aztec *régime* had passed for ever; the Indian race was outclassed and subordinate; and the *mestizos*, the people of mixed native and Hispanic blood, were rapidly becoming the most numerous part of the civilised population of the country. Whatever of good had existed in the Aztec semi-civilisation—and there was much of use in their land laws and other social measures—was entirely stamped out, and the sentiment and practice of European civilisation established. It is to be recollected that Spain adopted nothing, whether in Mexico or in Peru, of the ancient civilisation. Both the Aztecs and Incas lived under a set of laws which in some cases were superior to those of the conquerors, especially those relating to landholding and the payment of taxes and distribution of wealth. Under these primitive civilisations of America poverty or starvation was impossible, as every citizen was provided for. The Spaniards, however, would have none of it, and the land and the Indians, body and soul, were the property of their taskmasters. They might starve or not, as circumstances might dictate, after the fashion of European and American civilisation even of to-day, which denies any inherent right to ownership and enjoyment of the land and its resources on the part of its citizens. But Spain stamped many institutions in Mexico with the beauty and utility of her own civilisation. She endowed it with traditions and culture; she gave it the spirit of Western ambition which bids every citizen assert his right. The Mexican of to-day owes all he has—law, literature, art, and social system, and refinement and religion—to Spain.

But let us now take our stand with Hidalgo, the warrior-priest of Mexico. The hand of Spain is still pressing on the country. The year 1810 has arrived and the father of Mexico's independence is uttering his famous cry, "*Viva America! viva* religion! death to bad government!" After the native place of Hidalgo this message—for such it rapidly became—was known as *el grito de Dolores*—"the call of Dolores." The time was ripe for the assertion of independence. Spain was invaded by Napoleon; the King had abdicated. Who was the authority who should carry on the government—or misgovernment—of the colony? asked the city Council of Mexico as they urged the Viceroy to retain his authority against all comers. Unfortunately, the Spaniards, residents of the capital, precipitated lawlessness by rising and seizing the persons of the Viceroy Iturrigaray and high ecclesiastics, and some political murders followed. But the predisposing causes for the assertion of independence were nearer home. The British colonies, away to the north-east on the same continent, had severed the link which bound them to the Mother Country. The embryo of the great republic of the United States—poor and weak then—was established, and the spirit of independence was in the air. Most poignant of all, however, was the feeling caused by Spain's treatment of the Mexicans. Instead of fomenting the industries and trade of her colonies, Spain established amazing monopolies and unjust measures of repression. The trade which had grown between Mexico and China, and the great galleons which came and went from Acapulco—a more important seaport then than now even—was considered detrimental to Spain's own commerce. It was prohibited! The culture of grapes in Mexico, where they had been introduced and flourished exceedingly well, seemed antagonistic to the wine-making industry of Iberia; Hidalgo's vineyard, upon which he had lavished enterprise and care, was forthwith destroyed by the Spanish authorities! Thus industry and commerce were purposely stunted in Mexico, as they had been in Peru, by Imperial policy, and this went hand in hand with the restriction or denial of any political rights, and the oppression of the native population in the mines and plantations. "Learn to be silent and to obey, for which you were born, and not to discuss politics or have opinions," ran the proclamation of a viceroy in the latter half of the eighteenth century, addressed to the Mexicans! Other contributory causes to the revolution were the sentiments of the great French philosophers of the eighteenth century, which had sunk into the Mexican character.

STATUE OF HIDALGO AT MONTERREY.

But it would not be just to proclaim that life under Spain's rule was hard or oppressive, or marked by continued ferocity and bloodshed. The Mexicans lived in relative comfort and even luxury, and amassed wealth. Enormous fortunes were made in the mines, and titles of nobility were constantly granted from Spain to fortunate mine-owners who, by means of suddenly-acquired wealth, were enabled to render services to the Crown. Nor can the abuses of the natives be cast at Spain's door altogether. The colonists of Mexico, like those of Peru or, indeed, of any of the communities of the New World themselves, were the greatest oppressors of the natives in extortion, confiscation, forced labour, and the like, and it was the "interference" of the Imperial authorities, viceroy or Archbishop, against the oppression of the *encomiendas*, which, even in early days, often gave rise to discontent. The sovereigns of Spain enacted laws for the protection of the natives, in many cases, and strove to better their position. Indeed, it may be said that, to the present day, the regulation of affairs between colonists and natives—whether in America, Asia, or Africa—requires the justice of an imperial home Government, however far off from the scene of its "interference." Independence in America, whether in the United States or in the Spanish States, did not necessarily spell liberty, toleration, and brotherhood, whether in civil or religious matters.

From Spain's unlawful king—the brother of Napoleon—or, rather, from the various *juntas* or bodies formed in Spain to oppose the French domination, came claims for jurisdiction over Mexico, causing confusion in the minds of the colonists, which culminated in the conspiracies of Queretero and Hidalgo's cry, and the proclamation of Independence on September 15, 1810. Under Hidalgo an insurgent band seized various places in the central part of the country, including the great silver-producing town and mines of Guanajuato, where, unfortunately, these first exponents of liberty committed serious excesses. Thence, taking the capital of the State of Michoacan—Morelia—they advanced upon the city of Mexico. They engaged and defeated the royalist forces which had been sent against them by the viceroy Venegas, who had succeeded the *Audiencia* and the deported Iturrigaray, at Monte de las Cruces, some twenty miles from the capital, after a well-contested battle. To the generalship of Allende was mainly due this great victory, and had Hidalgo followed it up by an attack upon the capital city, subsequent operations might have been favourable to the insurgents. As it was, the royalists under Calleja attacked and captured Guanajuato, taking a terrible revenge upon its people—ruthless cruelties such as, perpetrated by both sides in these struggles, have repeatedly written the history of Mexico's revolution in blood. Finally Hidalgo and his associates, at Guadalajara and elsewhere, were after valiant fighting, discomfited entirely; disaster overtook them, and the warrior-priest, with Allende, Aldama, and Jimenez—valiant generals all—was shot at Chihuahua in July, 1811. There, in the small chapel of San Francisco, his decapitated body was laid, and afterwards removed to Mexico.

Was the spark of liberty extinguished by these reverses? The answer was furnished by yet another militant ecclesiastic—the famous Morelos of Michoacan. Stoutly did he and his insurgents maintain the city of Cuantla against the royalist forces under Calleja, until famine compelled them to evacuate the place under cover of darkness. The defence of Cuantla has covered the name of Morelos with glory in his country's history, and at the time it was watched even from Europe with interest, by the eagle eye of the great Wellington. This remarkable soldier-priest captured various important places—Orizaba, Oaxaca, and Acapulco, and established the first Mexican Congress at the town of Chilpancingo, in the State of Guerrero, in September, 1813. But the star of Mexico's national independence had yet to reach its zenith. Disaster overtook the insurgent forces; all fortune abandoned them and Morelos was captured, court-martialled, judged by the Inquisition, and shot, in December, 1815.

The tyranny of Ferdinand VII. of Spain gave birth to yet another scourge for Spanish rule in Mexico. Mina was a Spaniard, a celebrated *guerilla* chief in the mountains of Navarre, where he waged war against Napoleon and the French, and that *casus belli* being terminated, strove to raise a revolution against the Spanish sovereign at Madrid. Frustrated there he fled to London, and Mexican refugees in that city—among them the *padre* Mier—enlisted his sympathy for Mexican independence; and, having obtained adherents both in England and the United States, Mier landed on the Mexican shores of Tamaulipas and won a series of brilliant victories with his small force against the Spanish royalists. But again history records, as it has ever recorded in the story of freedom throughout the world, that baptism of failure which must ever precede success; and this young adventurer for Mexico's independence —he was but twenty-eight—suffered disaster, was captured, and shot in November, 1817.

Thus it was that the heroic efforts of all these who had given their lives for the political dream of an independent Mexico laid them down—not fruitlessly—upon the morning of its consummation. To the credit of the Church it is that the spirit of freedom first took material form in men nourished in the shadow of the aisles. In Mexico's history eternal laurels have crowned the brows of Hidalgo and Morelos; their names are perpetuated in the great tracts of land which bear them, and their memory is indelibly enshrined in their countrymen's hearts. At this period the feathers of Spain's colonial wing were being plucked one by one. In all the countries of Latin America the irresistible spirit of change, development, and independence was sweeping over the New World, bred of the world-march of new thought which the French Revolution had set in motion. The great nineteenth century had dawned, and the effects of the convulsions of social life had been felt, and had furnished springs of action even in remote towns of the South American Andes and of the Mexican plateau. Caracas and Chile in 1810, Buenos Ayres in 1813, Mexico in 1821, Peru in 1824—all showed that the hour of destiny had arrived and that new nations were being launched upon the world.

CHAPTER VII

THE EVOLUTION OF MODERN MEXICO

Monarchical *régime* of Iturbide—Great area of Mexican Empire—Santa Anna—The Holy Alliance—Execution of Iturbide—The Monroe Doctrine—British friendship—The United States—Masonic institutions —Political parties—Expulsion of Spaniards—Revolution and crime— Clerical antagonism—Foreign complications—The "pie-war"—The Texan war—The slavery question—Mexican valour—American invasion of Mexico—Fall of Mexico—Treaty of Guadalupe—Cession of California—Gold in California—Benito Juarez appears— Conservatives and Liberals—Massacre of Tacubaya—The Reform laws —Disestablishment of the Church—Dishonest Mexican finance— Advent of Maximilian—The English, Spanish, and French expedition— Perfidy of the French—Capture of Mexico City by the French— Crowning of Maximilian—Porfirio Diaz—Rule of Maximilian—Fall of his empire—Death of Maximilian—The tragedy of Querétaro—Diaz takes Mexico City—Presidency of Juarez—Lerdo—Career and character of Diaz—First railways built—Successful administration of Diaz—Political stability—Forward policy.

Mexico began her independent history with a monarch, a prominent figure which now stands forth in the history of the country, Iturbide—royalist, soldier-general, candidate for viceroy, insurgent chief, and Emperor by turns. Despatched at the head of the Spanish Royalist army from the capital to crush the insurgent forces under Guerrero, who maintained defiance in the south, Iturbide, after conference with the enemy, announced to his officers and army that he espoused and would support the cause of independence. Whether this was a result of conviction of its justice, or whether it obeyed dictates of personal ambition to whose success a surer road seemed to open by his defection, remained best known to himself; but, be it as it were, his eloquence and enthusiasm inspired all who lent ear to him.

Events followed rapidly. The "plan of Iguala," a document proclaiming the independence of Mexico, with a suggestion of royal rule, was drawn up and promulgated on March 2, 1821, and the change of side by its author, Iturbide, called many other persons to the insurgent cause, and city after city fell to their arms or capitulated at their advance. At the moment the last Spanish Viceroy, Don Juan O'Donojú, was landing at Vera Cruz, but, sagely taking in the situation, he saw that Mexico was lost for Spain, proposed a conference, accepted the plan of Iguala, joined forces with Iturbide, and, all obstacles having been overcome, the insurgent army made its way to the capital, entering it, with Iturbide at its head, on September 27, 1821. The triumph of the independent cause was assured and the birth of the new Empire of Mexico was heralded at that moment.

The geographical extent of Mexico at that date was very considerable. It embraced all that enormous area of territory of Texas, New Mexico, California, the whole of modern Mexico and Yucatan, and the present south-bounding republic of Guatemala. This great area of the Empire of Mexico was, indeed, the third largest country in the world, coming next after the Russian and Chinese empires. Such was the great political entity over which Iturbide's brief royal sway extended—brief, for, crowned Emperor Augustine I. on July 21, 1822, he abdicated on March 19, 1823—a brief kingship of a few months—left the country, returned, hoping to benefit it, and was "executed" on July 19, 1824! Thus passed the Empire—the first attempt for royal rule in the Americas, although not the last.

It is not to be supposed that the birth of independence in Mexico had brought forth peace and order among the Mexicans. Far from it. If the *grito* of Hidalgo had heralded political liberty it was also the signal for the almost continual internecine wars and bloody struggles which made the name of Mexico a synonym for revolution and bloodshed for more than half a century, and which it only began to lose at the close of the nineteenth century. The execution of Iturbide showed the rise of that spirit of ferocity and remorseless ingratitude which has always characterised the political history and strife of Latin America, whether Mexico, Peru, Venezuela, Chile, or any other of the Hispanic self-governing countries. Immediately after the formation of Iturbide's regency, which included O'Donojú, whose acts had been repudiated by Spain, dissensions arose, and the first Constitutional Congress, of February 24, 1822, soon formed itself into political sections, some of which regarded Iturbide with disfavour. From his position as Emperor he threw various Congressmen into prison for opposition to the empire (a sentiment which grew rapidly), and finally dissolved Congress. At this time the somewhat sinister figure of Santa-Anna arose, with a *pronunciamiento* at Vera Cruz in favour of a republican form of government; and although supported by Bravo, Guerrero, and others, the insurgents fell before the forces of the Emperor. Iturbide, however, did not desire to disrupt the nation. He had been crowned and anointed with great pomp and ceremony in the beautiful Cathedral of Mexico, but he abdicated, and sailed on an English ship for Italy, and the Congress passed an Act pronouncing him an outlaw and traitor. This Act, as before stated, showed the spirit of singular remorselessness and ferocious ingratitude characterising the Spanish-Americans' political methods. These were the days of the "Holy Alliance," which strove to bring about Spain's re-domination of America, and Iturbide, in London, learning of the plan, and ignorant of the iniquitous Act launched against him, embarked for Mexico, thinking to lend his sword on behalf of his native country if she were threatened by the Alliance. He was captured and illegally sentenced by the Congress of a petty Mexican province—Tamaulipas—and shot. Serene and disdainful, he fell, a figure which compels more respect than censure in the mind of the student of to-day.

These were portentous times in the history of the New World. It must not be forgotten that the independence of Mexico took place in what was a reactionary time in Europe, and the spirit of the Holy Alliance was rendered evident by the attitude of France. But there was Britain to be reckoned with. Britain did not hesitate to declare for the emancipation of the Spanish colonies, and the "Monroe Doctrine" was conceived by the famous words of Canning in "calling into being the New World to redress the balance of the

Old." In August, 1823, Canning sounded the American Government as to whether they "would act in concert with Britain against any aggression against the independence of the Spanish-American Republics," which brought forth the famous enunciation of President Monroe in Washington "that any such aggression would be hostile to themselves and dangerous to their peace and safety"—the basis of the now well-known Monroe Doctrine. Nevertheless, the United States regarded Mexico at that period with little favour or sympathy, and indeed this fact has been noted with some resentment by Mexican historians. But it is to be recollected that the United States itself was weak, and could not be expected to antagonise Europe too deeply. As it was, Mexico entered into the concert of nations without a friend in the world, save as the not necessarily disinterested or altruistic declaration of Britain and the United States might be construed as friendship. But the recognition of Mexico's independence by Britain in 1825 and treaty of friendship brought the first foreign capital to the land's resources, whilst the war between Mexico and the United States in a territorial dispute, showed that a spirit of equity was yet foreign to the Anglo-Saxon Republic.

On the ruins of the transient empire of Iturbide the building of the Mexican Republic was begun. The National Constitution was proclaimed in October, 1824, by the Federal Congress, and the famous insurgent leader, Guadalupe Victoria, named President, with Bravo as Vice-President. Great Britain and the United States recognised the new Republic in the first year—1825—of its existence, and the latter country sent its Minister in representation. Two political parties came into existence—the Centralists, principally Spanish, and the Federalists—and to the dissensions of these the continual revolutions and disturbances from that date to the middle of the century were due. Another disturbing factor was the introduction of Masonic lodges—the Scotch rite and the York rite, the latter introduced by the American Minister, which, becoming adopted by various partisans, were respectively opposed by others—and these Masonic institutions were the cause of disturbance in the politics of Mexico for many years. Among religious people the word "Mason" became a term of reproach. Due to the work of the York Masons, a great expulsion of Spaniards took place in 1827, the Spaniards having been finally ousted from the country, losing their last stronghold of the Castle of San Juan de Ulua at Vera Cruz in 1825.

It might have been supposed that Mexico, having gained its heart's desire of freedom from the dominion of Spain, with its own independent Government, would have established itself in peace, and continued on along the lines of national development. But it was not so. Insistent and sanguinary revolution reared its sinister head, to destroy all peace and security, and hold the country in barbaric strife for many years. It would be tedious to follow the causes and incidents of these *pronunciamientos*, imprisonings, seizings, shootings, executions, treachery, cruelty, and bloodshed of which this half-century of Mexican history is largely built up. The profession of arms became almost the only one which ambitious men would follow, and ambition and unscrupulousness went hand in hand. A condition of chronic disorder grew which paralysed the civil development of the country, made bankrupt the national treasury, and prostituted the people to becoming mere levies of insurgents, to be drawn upon by this or that revolutionary leader whose sinister star for the moment happened to be in the ascendant. Armed highwaymen infested the roads and inhabited the mountains, and travel was impossible without an escort. A terrible disregard of human life resulted, and became so strong a characteristic of the Mexicans as has even to-day not become eradicated.

In 1833 the beginning of a serious cause of civil trouble made its appearance, and one which has profoundly influenced the Mexicans and their life. This was the antagonism between the people and the politicians, and the clergy. Intensely religious, in the Romish faith, the Mexicans, like the South Americans, were subject to periods of bitter and relentless feeling against clerical domination, the result mainly of the extortions of the Church and its insidious acquiring of temporal power and amassing of wealth. Speaking generally, the Church brought about its own disestablishment by its own fault. Enactments were passed at this date to curtail the power and privileges of the clergy, declaring that tithes should not be collectable by civil law, nor the fulfilment of monastic vows enforced, and prohibiting the Church from meddling with public instruction. The political parties which then grew to being for or against these measures respectively were the Liberals and Conservatives, and to their dissensions were mainly due the subsequent disorders; and up to the present day they form the party divisions of Mexican politics. These measures were the precursor of the famous Reform Laws of 1859, under Juarez, which disestablished the Church and appropriated its property.

The incessant turbulence at home was varied from time to time by acute questions with foreign Powers. In 1829 Spain made a determined attempt to regain Mexico, with an expedition of 4,000 men, which, however, was absolutely repulsed by the Federal army under Santa-Anna and Mier: the Spanish general, Barradas, surrendering his armament and flags, at the news of which immense rejoicing took possession of Mexico. The independence of the Republic was recognised by Spain in 1836. Two years later—1838—a complication arose with France, and the war known as the *Guerra de los Pasteles*, or "Pie-War," came about, its singular designation resulting from the claim of a French pastry-cook for sixty thousand dollars as indemnity for the theft of some pies! Expensive confections these proved to be, for under the Prince de Joinville the French landed and surprised Vera Cruz, attacked the house of Santa-Anna—this famous general losing a leg by a cannon-shot—whilst, on peace being concluded soon afterwards, Mexico agreed to pay $600,000 to settle all questions against her.

Following upon these incidents revolutions and *pronunciamientos* succeeded each other like autumn leaves, and rights and obligations were trampled underfoot almost as ruthlessly as these. In 1837 the Federal system had been supplanted by "Centralism," and the marchings of armies and the rise and fall of generals and Presidents come thick and fast throughout the country. A party was formed for the restitution of a monarchical form of government following upon the publication of a pamphlet by Gutierrez Estrada to the effect—and the student of history will scarcely contradict it—that the Mexican people were not fitted to live under a Republican *régime*.

But the greatest event of this period of Mexican history now looms up—the war with the United States. The origin of this was the question concerning the great State of Texas. Much earlier, in 1821, some colonisation of that territory had been initiated by the Austins, father and son, who founded the city of that name. The Austins were Americans, and had obtained permission from the Government of Mexico to establish a colony, but disagreements soon came about. American filibusters of lawless character began to settle up the country, as well as peaceful colonists, and questions soon arose as to political representation and influence. A decree had been made by the Mexican Government forbidding slavery, and this became a poignant cause of discontent to the Texans, who, partaking of the character of the Americans of that period, saw nothing incompatible in holding their fellow-creatures in bondage under the ægis of "Liberty"! Whatever may have been the faults displayed—and there were faults, both on the Mexican and the Texan side—the fact remains to the honour of Mexico that she forbade slavery, which showed her civilisation certainly not inferior to her Anglo-Saxon neighbours. The lawlessness and system of slavery established in Texas at that period bore afterwards a terrible fruit, which the "race-war" and "colour-line" of to-day show are not yet eradicated. Santa-Anna had been sent against Texas, and he played a far from creditable part. The war for Texan independence began in 1835, and its fortunes varied at first, the Mexican general treating the Texans with barbaric cruelty upon winning a first engagement. But Sam Houston arose—his name is greeted with acclamation in Texas to-day—and Santa-Anna, beaten and captured, took a discreditable and craven part, signing, in return for his release and safety, an agreement to recognise Texan independence. Mexico, however, did not recognise this, notwithstanding that a Texan Constitution was set up in 1836. Returning now to Santa-Anna's Presidency, his erratic acts disgusted his countrymen, and *pronunciamientos* followed. Hoping to divert popular opinion from himself, Santa-Anna proposed the prosecution of a war with Texas, for its recovery, notwithstanding his personal previous agreements.

The assertion of hegemony by the United States brought on the beginnings of war between the two dominating peoples of the North American continent. The Republic of Texas, the United States declared, must remain untouched; any hostile act against it would be considered directed against the States itself, with which Texas was now to be incorporated. Mexico, torn by dissensions of its own, was not in a good position to oppose the policy of its neighbour at the moment. The revolutions against Santa-Anna culminated in his defeat and departure from the country under an act of banishment.

It is not to be supposed that the Mexicans, oppressed as they were by the revolutions and disasters arising from their own character, were without any good and noble traits which might redeem the lawlessness from which they suffered. Many deeds of Mexican arms, of self-abnegation in times of peril, and of heroic acts in the face of deadly odds, have left glorious episodes in their history. It is to be recollected that the struggles in which they were engaged arose often from an excess of zeal for liberty, and a strong spirit of individualism which could not support political oppression or affront. An instance of their heroic spirit is afforded by an incident in the American War.

The storming of the Castle of Chapultepec was being carried on by the United States troops, who, after severe hand-to-hand fighting, penetrated to the fortress and made their way to the turret, to haul down the banner upon which the colours of Mexico, and the eagle, serpent and cactus were displayed. But the turret was disputed hotly by a few young Mexicans—boys almost—military cadets there. Seeing their beloved flag about to fall into the hands of the—to them—hated *Yankees*,[20] they fought to the last drop, and, rather than the standard should be captured, one of them, wrapping it round his body, leaped from the turret and was dashed to pieces on the stones below!

20 The designation of Yankee is very generally used in Spanish-American, for the Americans—not, however, in an offensive sense.

THE CASTLE OF CHAPULTEPEC.

But we anticipate. The first battle between the forces of Mexico and the United States was fought at Palo Alto in the north, in May, 1846; the command of the former being under General Arista, and the latter under

General Zachary Taylor, but the Mexicans were defeated. Texas had been declared a part of the American Union in the previous year (December, 1845), and the military occupation by the Americans of Mexican territory—for the boundaries were ill-defined—formed the culminating *casus belli*. Torn by dissensions at home, and betrayed by the treachery of her own generals—among them the traitorous Paredes—Mexico was in no position to face a war with her powerful neighbour. Following on the battle of Palo Alto, Santa-Anna, who had returned, had been elected President, but had declared he could serve his country best by leading its army, and he advanced against the Americans under Taylor. Previous to this, the Americans, with a force of 6,700 men, had taken the city of Monterrey—a pretty, Spanish-built town far within the border of Mexico, which had been established by one of the viceroys—notwithstanding that the Mexicans, 10,000 strong, under General Ampudea, had defended it. The engagement under Santa-Anna lasted for two days—the battle of Buena Vista, February, 1847. Its issue long hung in the balance, and although the Americans gained the victory, it was a doubtful and indecisive one.

The American Government now decided to push the war to the end. But serious obstacles discouraged the attempt to march upon the capital of Mexico. The vast stretches of appalling desert which at that time formed that part of the continent of North America—now included in Texas, Chihuahua, and Coahuila—were waterless, and without resources, and beaten by a fiery sun; conditions which to-day, in some parts of the regions, are scarcely altered. The bravery and ferocity of the Mexicans, who were—and are—among the most expert horsemen in the world, would have rendered the advance over the intervening topographical wastes between Mexico's frontier and her capital of extremely doubtful issue. Attack was made, therefore, by sea, and an army of 12,000 men under General Winfield Scott landed at Vera Cruz on March 9, 1847. By September of the same year Vera Cruz, Puebla Contreras, Molino del Rey, Chapultepec, had all been the scene of strenuous engagements; but Mexico was to lose, and the invading Anglo-Saxons, having eaten their way to the heart of the Latin Republic, against considerable odds, occupied the capital on September 14, 1847.

Split into factions by political strife, which even the hammering at their gates of a common enemy had not sufficed to heal, Mexico received a terrible lesson. The history of Mexico had repeated itself. Just as Cortes and his

Spaniards had penetrated from Vera Cruz to Tenochtitlan, thanks to dissensions among the Aztec inhabitants of the country, so had the Americans ascended over the same route to a similar victory by analogous circumstances. Even whilst the victorious forces of the Anglo-Saxons were marching onwards, the mad political generals and transient Presidents of Mexico were launching *pronunciamientos*, fighting among themselves, and shedding the blood of their own countrymen; and not until February 2, 1848, was peace entered into with the Americans, and the treaty of Guadalupe Hildalgo signed. Mexico ceded to the United States under this agreement the area of an empire! Texas had already been lost; California and New Mexico[21] were given up now, rich and extensive regions, although little known at the time, as indemnity for which the United States Government paid the sum of fifteen million dollars.

21 The English reader may ask, Where is New Mexico? It is that territory lying between Arizona and Texas, forming part of the American Union.

So was concluded what the Mexicans have termed "the unjust war," and the historian will probably not feel called upon to dispute the designation. Great bitterness of feeling between the two nations was aroused on account of this conquest and cession of territory, which, among the Mexicans of the great plateau, is, even at the present day, far from being forgotten. It was but a short time after the cession of California that gold was discovered—the famous days of 1849—and Mexico did not know what she was losing. Perhaps in the interests of the development of the fine State of California and its progressive people, circumstances were for the best as they were. Santa-Anna disappears from the scene in 1855. After the war he had assumed semi-regal titles and pretensions, and had brought about or permitted a further cession in the unpopular treaty with the United States. Further revolutions and *pronunciamientos* followed, and civil war divided the country.

The figure of Juarez, famous in his country's history, was appearing, and this remarkable man became President in January, 1858. In the previous year a new Constitution had been adopted, and is that which has remained in force to the present day. It was duly subjected to a futile *pronunciamiento*! Further legal enactments were made by the Liberals against the clergy, as well as the anti-mortmain statute, framed by Lerdo with the object of releasing the great properties held by civil and religious corporations; and it was mainly aimed at the power and wealth of the Church—a foretaste of the Reform Laws.

Benito Juarez was a Mexican in whom no strain of Spanish blood existed, his parents having been pure-blooded Indians of the Zapotecas of Oaxaca. Shepherd, student of divinity, Governor of Oaxaca, Minister of Justice, and President by turns, the name and fame of this remarkable example of aboriginal intelligence stands strongly out in the history of his country. The Conservative party were not slow in launching *pronunciamientos*, and disaster befel the Liberal Government of Juarez, who was compelled to flee for the time being. The whole of the Republic again became the scene of desolating civil warfare, due to the bitter struggles of the Liberal and Conservative parties. Generals, calling themselves Presidents, set up Governments in various parts of the country, and *pronunciamientos* and bloodshed were the order of the day. But chief among the sanguinary scenes of this appalling drama, carried out with the religion of Christ as its mainspring, was the Tacubaya massacre. This place, a beautiful residential suburb of the City of Mexico, became the field of a strenuous engagement, the victorious forces of the Conservatives, under General Marquez, signalling their triumph by an abominable massacre, in which the medical attendants, including an English physician, all of whom had voluntarily given their services for succour of the wounded, were taken out and deliberately put to death in cold blood, by order of the ferocious Marquez. Another murder lies to the account of Marquez—that of Ocampo, one of the best of the Liberal statesmen. But the Liberal cause gained ground. Juarez landed at Vera Cruz; and the famous Reform Laws of July 12, 1859, were made, forming part of the basis of the administration set up at Vera Cruz. This code was directed against clericalism. The property of the Church was confiscated and nationalised; the clergy were severely arraigned as the authors of the sanguinary and fratricidal wars which had devastated the country; accused of abusing their power in a scandalous manner, with baleful control of their wealth; and, in short, the Church was disestablished and religious freedom proclaimed, together with the abolishing of religious orders and institutions, whilst marriage was later declared a civil contract.

Torn by their unceasing dissensions at home, the unfortunate Mexican nation now brought upon themselves complications from abroad. The Government of Juarez, having triumphed over the Conservatives, had been installed in the capital amid popular enthusiasm. But what was the state of the country over which it ruled? Sources of public revenue were paralysed or hypothecated; there was not a dollar in the treasury; and private enterprise and the activities of ordinary wealth were ruined. Funds must be obtained in some way; and an Act of Congress was passed in July, 1861, suspending the payment of Mexico's foreign debts. This grave step laid Mexico open to the most serious charges in European capitals, and her action was stigmatised as repudiation and robbery, especially in London, where the first Mexican loan had been contracted in 1823. This act of the Mexican Liberal Congress was naturally painted in its worst colours by the reactionary representatives of the Conservative party in Europe, who, desirous of bringing back a priestly and monarchical *régime*, thought this an opportunity and motive for compassing it by means of European intervention. In justice to Mexico at that period it must be chronicled that repudiation of her debts was not intended; only suspension in her temporary distress. But the reprehensible Act of President Miramon, in violating the British Legation and seizing $660,000 belonging to the British bondholders, in November, 1860, had not been forgotten.

Maximilian—the picturesque and melancholy-appearing figure: the ill-fated monarch of an unnatural New World empire—was the culminating figure of Mexico's internecine warfare and questionable financial acts. The story of Maximilian stands out from the pages of Mexico's history in pathetic colours, wringing a sigh from us as we scan its pages, or halt a space in the museum of Mexico's capital before the gilded tawdry coach of the ill-fated Austrian, which is preserved there in musty ruin. For up rose Napoleon III., pricking up his ears at this suggestion of a monarchy in America; and, urged by him, the tripartite convention by France, Spain, and England was brought to being in London, October, 1861, whose purpose was—or, at any rate by the British and Spanish—intervention and the enforcement of the just claims of their bondholders against the defaulting Mexicans. Sailing from Europe, the fleets of the three Powers arrived at Vera Cruz at the end of the year. No idea of conquest of, or interposition in, Mexican territory was intended in this action, only enforcement of just claims, and so it was proclaimed; and a conference having been celebrated with the Mexican representatives, and a preliminary agreement entered into, the Spanish and British ships in all sincerity withdrew and sailed for home. Not so the French—and the charge of perfidy is recorded against France for her act—for the troops of Napoleon repudiated the agreement and entered upon a war of conquest or subjugation. Severe reverses marked their campaign at first, the Mexicans obstinately defending the integrity of the country, under the administration of Juarez, with able generals at the front. Among these was Diaz—later the famous President

Diaz—who won some early laurels in the defence of Puebla. But Puebla fell, Juarez abandoned the capital, and the French, under General Forey, entered the City of Mexico without opposition and set up a *junta* of prominent Mexicans to decide on the form of government to be adopted. The decision of the *junta* was for a limited monarchy, whose sovereign should be designated Emperor of Mexico, and whose crown should be offered to Maximilian, Archduke of Austria, or, failing him, to some other Catholic prince who might be nominated by "the kindness of his Majesty Napoleon III. of France!" So it befel; a deputation of Mexicans was sent to the Hapsburg prince in his castle upon the far-off Adriatic Sea. Maximiliano accepted under certain conditions; arrived in Mexico, and in company with his wife Carlota, daughter of Leopold, King of the Belgians, was crowned with great solemnity in the Cathedral of Mexico in June, 1864.

Meantime the Liberal party, thus ousted from the seat of Government, was not idle. Juarez established his administration in successive northern towns, approaching the United States border. War to the death against the monarchical system, which had been crammed down the Liberal throat, was their slogan and source of inspiration. The doughty Porfirio Diaz, nominated to a high command, was despatched to Oaxaca; besieged there by the French under Bazaine, making a most determined stand; surrendered at length through lack of food, ammunition, and disaffection among his own people; was captured, imprisoned; escaped; turned against the pursuing enemy and overcame them, re-capturing again his native city, and once more turned the tables upon the Conservatives and the Monarchy.

CITY OF OAXACA: SPANISH-COLONIAL ARCHITECTURE; THE PORTALES OF THE MUNICIPAL PALACE AND PLAZA.

The star of Empire, which shone for less than three years under Maximilian, now sets with dramatic suddenness. From the first it was seen that the Emperor was no bigoted Churchman, and his refusal to rescind the clauses of the Reform Laws involved the Imperial Government in grave questions and antagonisms with the disappointed clericals; and the Emperor, indeed, showed himself much in sympathy with the Liberals. These, however, bent upon their own absolute way, would hold no parley with him, notwithstanding that overtures had been made to Diaz after the recapture of Oaxaca.

The end approaches rapidly. The city of Puebla, a Conservative stronghold, falls before Diaz and three thousand of the Republican army, and siege is laid to the City of Mexico in April, 1867. Maximilian had seen the trend towards the inevitable, but had striven, during the previous year, to consolidate the clerical party, whilst the Empress Carlota—brave and pathetic figure of these dramatic events—had gone to France to implore Napoleon to countermand his perfidious withdrawal of the French troops, and to endeavour to secure a settlement of the matters at issue with the clericals with Pope Pius IX. It was useless. The French army left the shores of the country they had wantonly outraged, abandoning the unfortunate figure-head placed there as a result of French machinations, with only the Belgians and Austrians of Maximilian's immediate following. The ill-fated Austrian wavered between his advisers—whether to abandon the thankless task upon which he was engaged, or whether to stay with it to the bitter end. He ultimately chose the latter course; reversing a first intention of abdicating, returned to Mexico city; left thence for Querétaro, and intrenched himself, with an effective force of some nine thousand Imperialists, in that town. The Republicans, twenty-one thousand strong, laid strenuous siege to and attacked the place, suffering several repulses; but the treachery of Lopez, of the Imperialist army, afforded them the entrance to the town, and Querétaro fell.

The fate of the Emperor Maximilian was now in the hands of Juarez. A court-martial was called, and Maximilian was permitted to select counsel for his defence. The deliberations resulted in a sentence of death against Maximilian and his two chiefs and faithful generals, Miramon and Mejia. Juarez took his pen to sign the death-warrant, when before him—the Indian President, son of a despised race—there appeared and kneeled the figure of the Austrian princess, Carlota, supplicating for clemency for her husband. It is said that Juarez wavered, but at that fateful moment the stern Lerdo appeared at the door of the apartment, and shaking a warning finger, uttered those words which sealed the doom of Maximilian, and which have come down ever since in Mexico's history as a species of national axiom—"Ahora ó nunca se salva la patria!"[22] Juarez signed; the condemned Emperor took his stand upon the Cerro de las Campanas outside Querétaro, and faced the file of carbines pointed at his breast, serene and dignified. "Take you the place of honour in the centre," he said in turn to Miramon and Mejia—the latter a full-blooded Indian general who had been privately offered, and had refused, a pardon by Juarez. But both declined, and the three brave men faced forward. A volley rang out upon the early morning air, and with it passed the life of Maximilian and his chiefs, and the last Imperial *régime* of Mexico.

22 "Now or never for our country's salvation."

This execution—or murder—of Maximilian—for the student is at liberty to term it which he will, according to the trend of his sympathies—took place on June 19, 1867. The wife of the ill-fated member of the unfortunate House of Hapsburg went mad, and in that state lived long in Europe. To the commander of the Austrian warship, who, arriving at Vera Cruz, demanded the remains of the "Emperor of Mexico," answer was returned by the Mexicans that no such person was known; when he then requested the body of "Maximilian of Austria" it was delivered to him. "Savages and barbarians" was the verdict of Europe against the Mexicans for the termination of this drama, and only of recent years—1901—have diplomatic relations been reopened between Mexico and Austria. The impartial historian sees in the *dénouement* the dictates of fate for a Republican *régime* throughout the New World, and acknowledges the philosophical right for this form of government; although it may well be open to question if the republicanism of the Americans has yet brought much of advancement to mankind in general or to their own civilisation in particular. The figure of Maximilian, weak though it may have been, was not without nobility; nor did his brief rule lack possibilities for the nation—one party of which had invited his advent and the other consummated his destruction.

The City of Mexico capitulated to Diaz. President Juarez returned thither and assumed the reins of government amid general approval and that popular enthusiasm which usually acclaims a change of *régime* in any time or country, and which was followed a few years later by renewed dissensions. But the figure and name of Juarez are engraved on the history of his country among its greatest, and furnish an example of the possibilities of intellect and power to be encountered in the aboriginal races of Mexico, stifled but not destroyed by the advent of the white race. Juarez is the only President of Mexico who has died in the occupancy of his office! He was followed by Lerdo, against whose government a *pronunciamiento* and revolution was launched, with a result that Lerdo fled to the United States. An event of much industrial importance to the country took place during Lerdo's term—the completion and opening of the railway from Vera Cruz to the capital, in January, 1873, thus placing in connection with the seaboard and the outside world the much-contested City of Mexico, with its chequered history.

The fall of Lerdo was the signal for, or rather the result of, the coming forward of the most prominent figure of Mexico's modern history—a figure, moreover, which links the turbulent past with progressive Mexico of to-day. This is the figure of Porfirio Diaz, the son of an innkeeper: student for priesthood, law student, revolutionist, soldier, statesman, and President by turns. Diaz has also Indian blood in his veins, upon the maternal side. After the events connected with the fall of the Empire the ambitions of Diaz found outlet in the disaffections against Lerdo's government. It was hardly to be expected that the ambitions and jealousies of the times could yet give way to consolidation for national interests and desire for peace and development; and the only hope for the country was in the advent of a strong man and a strong system, such as, under better auspices, the monarchical *régime* might have afforded. The strong man appeared in the very antithesis of monarchy— Porfirio Diaz; and the autocratic *régime*—almost monarchical except in name —in the military-civil government which followed. Good, indeed, seemed to proceed out of evil, and the autocratic President of Mexico came through chaos to power as a revolutionist himself, by the edge of the sword, shedding his own countrymen's blood, and borne on the crest of an insurrectionary wave. Yet there was more behind the fortunes and character of Diaz than mere selfish ambition or the habit of a disorderly soldier-spirit. He had early conceived Liberal views against clerical domination, and his earlier career showed loftier aspirations than those of the ordinary tawdry revolutionist of the times, who, under the name of liberty, indulged too often personal or party licence against law, decency, and humanity. Diaz, after the revolution, assumed executive power in November, 1876, and after a brief interval took the oath and Presidential chair on May 5, 1877. The term of President Gonzalez followed, and during this measures of civil progress were inaugurated. Diplomatic relations were reopened with Great Britain, and a beginning made to adjust the debt with the foreign bond-holders. The Mexican Central Railway, linking the Republic with its neighbour the United States, was inaugurated, and was an important factor in the political settling-down of the country.

Diaz was re-elected to the Presidency for December 1, 1884. From that period until the present day he has held the office continuously—seven Presidential terms—a *régime* which has partaken more of the nature of a hereditary sovereignty than of an elective post. It is to be recollected, however, that in all Spanish-American countries—and Mexico has been no exception—intimidation and bribery at the polls and breaches of constitutional law have been potent factors in election matters. It would not be correct, however, to ascribe these influences to the latter terms of office of President Diaz, who, there can be little doubt, has enjoyed the confidence of his fellow-citizens and a majority of their votes.[23] His enemies, the inevitable enemies of a political chief, have been few and silent; and, moreover, in these years of Mexican history sudden and silent retribution has been visited upon the least whisper or suspicion of *pronunciamientos*, whether near the capital or whether in the remote towns of the great plateau!

23 The character of President Diaz has been drawn in the various books recently written on Mexico. It is not the intention of this work to indulge in the flattery which in some cases has been given to him, especially in Mexican books. I had the pleasure of meeting the President on a brief occasion some years ago. Diaz completes the 80th year of his strenuous life in 1910. (See also [page 165](#).)

THE PRESIDENT OF MEXICO, GENERAL PORFIRIO DIAZ.

A certain main and important condition presented itself to the comprehension of Diaz early in his administration, and compliance with it has been one of the principal contributing causes to his success. This was the necessity for the bettering of the means of communication of the country. Roads, railways, and telegraph multiplied accordingly under the fostering work of the Diaz Governments, mainly by inducements held out to foreign capitalists; partly by the expenditure of national funds. When troops and messages can be moved and flashed about rapidly *pronunciamientos* tend to diminish. The credit of the country abroad was firmly re-established in 1886 by a proper adjustment of the foreign debt with Mexico's European creditors; and as a result further loans were secured. The Mexican National Railway, traversing the country from the capital to the United States frontier, was opened in November, 1888, as well as a line southwards to Oaxaca, later; and thus the nineteenth century closed with an era of growing stability and prosperity at home and a creditable reputation abroad. The old elements of unscrupulous ambition had been outlived, and the best men the country produced were directing its governing and development. The fiscal policy of the administration had been wisely thought out and applied, and had proved a success, and difficulties due to the depreciation of the silver coinage had been weathered.

The twentieth century opened for Mexico with a continuance of the same governing elements, policy, and general development, Diaz being re-elected for the term beginning in December, 1900, and again for the term 1904-1910: this being his seventh tenure of office. Important public works have been carried to completion during these last periods, chief among them being the drainage of the Valley of Mexico—that historical scheme begun by the viceroys—and the harbour works of Vera Cruz; rendering shipping safe from the great "northers" which since the time of Cortes have harassed vessels lying in the bay. These works were performed by British firms; and yet another, under similar auspices, was the completion of the Tehuantepec Railway—a trans-Continental line from the Atlantic (Gulf) to the Pacific; all of which works are of really historical importance. The present time—1909—finds Mexico an established power on her continent, with considerable opportunities for good or evil in the influence of international matters in North and Central America, and with her own future well mapped out in so much as the ingenuity of her public men may devise.

What this future will really be must depend upon the temper of her people and the prudence of political changes. The staunch leader who, thanks to the species of limited Presidential Monarchy which circumstances have required and permitted, has successfully carried on the leadership must, in the natural course of events, yield this up. This will afford an opportunity for ambition and possible strife on the part of those elements which have been overawed in the past, and which it is too much to expect have been altogether eliminated. Then will be the real test of Mexican self-control and prudence, and it seems probable that these will be exercised.

CHAPTER VIII

PHYSICAL CONDITIONS: MOUNTAINS, TABLELANDS, AND FLORA AND FAUNA

Geographical conditions—Tehuantepec—Yucatan—Boundaries and area—Population—Vera Cruz—Elevations above sea-level—Latitude—General topography—The Great Plateau—The Sierra Madres—The Mexican Andes—General structure—The coasts—Highest peaks—Snow-cap and volcanoes—Geological formation—Geological scenery—Hydrographic systems—Rivers—Navigation—Water-power—Lakes—Climate and temperatures—The three climatic zones—Rainfall—Snowfall—Flora and fauna—Soil—Singular cactus forms—The desert flora—The tropical flora—Forest regions—Wild animals—Serpents, monkeys, and felidæ—Sporting conditions—Birds.

We have traced the evolution of the Mexican people through the phases of their chequered history: let us now examine more closely their habitat, the country and its physical structure, and natural clothing; its mountains and plains and accompanying vegetation, no less interesting and picturesque in their respective fields.

The geographical conditions of Mexico and its geology and accompanying topography are peculiar, and indeed in some respects unique. Mexico has been termed "the bridge of the world's commerce,"[24] and, in fact, its geographical position between the two great oceans of the world—the Atlantic and the Pacific, and between, or joining, two great continents, North and South America—would seem to warrant such a description, especially having regard to the coming development of that part of the world and the rise of the Pacific Ocean in commercial importance. It is indeed a favourite theory of some writers that the commercial and civilised centre of the world is destined to shift from the Atlantic to the Pacific Ocean. This theory, which must be characterised, however, as open to much conjecture, has been lightly discussed elsewhere in these pages. But be it as it may, the situation of the cornucopia-shaped land of Mexico is of great and growing importance. Among the geographical features of almost international importance is the remarkable isthmus of Tehuantepec—now traversed by a railway—which separates by only 120 miles the deep waters of the Atlantic and Pacific Ocean systems. It is an isthmus of Panama of greater width, and certainly may form a "bridge of commerce."

24 Humboldt.

Mexico—apart from the Yucatan peninsula—consists of a great triangular-shaped area, forming the tapering end of the North American Continent. It is bounded on the north and north-east by the United States; on the east by the Atlantic waters of the Gulf of Mexico, Gulf of Campeche, and Caribbean Sea; on the west and south by the Pacific Ocean; and on the south-east by Guatemala and British Honduras. Mexico is, therefore, a close neighbour of a part of the British Empire! The greatest length of the country is 2,000 miles nearly, its greatest width 760 miles, and its area 767,000 square miles. Thus it is nearly nine times the size of Great Britain, or as large as Great Britain, France, Germany, and Austria-Hungary all joined together; and this enormous area is inhabited at present by only fourteen or fifteen million people.

Although Mexico lies half within and half without the tropics, it is generally known as a tropical country; and, indeed, the main gateway to it, Vera Cruz, is a tropical seaport, which may well give rise to such a general impression upon the part of the European traveller. A different impression, however, is acquired upon entering the country from the United States to the north. No tropic forests and bright-plumaged birds are encountered there as at Vera Cruz; instead are vast stretches of desert lying within the temperate zone, alternating with cultivated plains and interspersed with large towns. The traveller, roused by the shriek of the locomotive, looks forth into the clear dawn of the chill Mexican morning from the window of his sleeping-berth upon the Pullman car, as the train speeds over the plateau.

MEXICO'S ARTIFICIAL HARBOURS: THE NEW PORT WORKS AT VERA CRUZ, A SOLID AND COSTLY ENTERPRISE.

No fact is more strongly borne upon the traveller in Andine and Cordillera-formed countries than that latitude forms but an unreliable guide to climate and temperature. Nearness to the Equator, with its accompanying torridity, is often counterbalanced by high elevations above sea-level, with consequent rarefied air and low temperature—a combination which embodies considerable advantages, as well as some drawbacks. These conditions are very marked in Mexico. Entering the country from Vera Cruz, we rise rapidly from sea-level to 7,410 feet at the City of Mexico; entering from the United States, we rise imperceptibly from 4,000 feet to the same elevation. As to its geographical position, the country extends over 18° of latitude, from 32½° north to 14½° north, and it lies between the 86th and 118th meridian west of Greenwich.

Topographically the country offers a very varied surface, the main features of which are the Great Plateau, the extensive, lofty tableland known as the *mesa central*; and the Pacific and Atlantic slopes, formed by the flanks of the Sierra Madres mountains towards these oceans respectively. At the base of these ranges are the lowlands of the coasts; whilst the eastern extremity of the country is formed by the singular plains of the peninsula of Yucatan.

A large part of the country's area is taken up by this great plateau of Anahuac, as it is sometimes termed. The tableland is bounded both on the east and the west by ranges of mountains, known as the Eastern Sierra Madre and the Western Sierra Madre respectively. These mountains close in towards the south, enclosing the tableland in a tapering form, and the Valley of Mexico which forms its extremity. On the north the *mesa central* is intersected by the Rio Grande, which forms the boundary of Mexico with the United States; and the plateau continues thence into the territory of that country. The length of this plateau, from north-west to south-east, or, roughly, upon its longitudinal axis, is approximately 800 miles, and its greatest width between the summits of the enclosing mountains about 500 miles. The tableland is, however, intersected by various lesser ranges of hills, and is not by any means a flat, unbroken expanse. Nevertheless, its formation is such that a vehicle might be driven from the City of Mexico for vast distances without having resort to roads. It may be looked upon physically as a great plane, inclined or tipped from south to north, or from the City of Mexico to the United States border. The general elevation above sea-level of the inclined plane at its southern end is 8,000 feet, and that at its northern 4,000 feet—a slope of 4,000 feet in a direction away from the Equator; and a fact which greatly influences its climate. The Mexican plateau is the result of after-formation from the mountain system of the country. The Sierra Madres are the Mexican Andes, part of the chain-formation of those vast Cordilleras which are most developed in South America, on the one hand, and are encountered in the Rocky Mountains of North America on the other. In South America the Andes consist of huge parallel chains with river and lake-basins of profound depth between them. In Mexico the same formation must have existed, but the basins have been filled up by material discharged from volcanoes and from the erosion of the mountains themselves, doubtless caused by the severe and sudden rain-storms and rapid changes of temperature characteristic of these regions. Thus the great plateau may be likened to a number of filled-up troughs, through whose general surface the tops of mountain ranges still protrude in "islands" or groups, whose crests form the intersecting hills of the plateau. Some of the plains of the plateau between these crests are hydrographic entities, with no outlet for their waters, as in the case of the *Bolson* of Mapimi—a vast rock-wilderness of 50,000 square miles in area, with great swamps and lake bottoms—and the Valley of Mexico. These great depressions, indeed, in a measure bear out the analogy or relationship with the South American Andes, as in the case of the hydrographic entity of Lake Titicaca in Peru and Bolivia, the great inland sea whose waters have no outlet save by evaporation. The enormous depth of alluvial soil found in the *bolsones* or depressions of the Mexican plateau, formed from rock-decay, or of volcanic material accumulated by the great lakes of recent times which covered them in the central part of the great *mesa central*, bear striking evidence to the filling-up process of the past. In the neighbourhood of the River Nazas wells have been sunk to great depths in this material without a single stone or rock of any description being encountered. Indeed, on some of the cotton lands of this region I have looked in vain to find even a pebble, so fine is the alluvial soil. The stratified rocks, which are scarce upon the southern part of the plateau, become much more prevalent in the north, and the vast sandy, arid plains, which cover enormous areas of land in Chihuahua and Coahuila extending thence past the valley of the Rio Grande into the great American deserts of Texas and New Mexico, are doubtless formed from the disintegration of the sandstone and chalk horizons of that region.

Leaving for a moment our examination of the great plateau, let us observe the coast. On both sides of the country—the Gulf of Mexico or the Pacific Ocean—we observe that the littoral is composed of sandy lowlands. On the eastern or Gulf side these coastal plains vary in width from a few miles up to a hundred miles; for the Cordillera approaches near to the sea at Vera Cruz, and recedes far from it in Tamaulipas. Upon the Pacific side, however, the coastal plains are more restricted in width, as the Cordillera runs nearer the sea-coast, but leaving a wider strip at the north. Indeed, in the State of Guerrero the Sierras rise almost abruptly from salt water, and the waves bathe the roots of the trees which cover the mountain slopes. The country rises rapidly from both oceans—more rapidly from the Pacific side—and forms a succession of terraces upon the slopes of the Sierra Madres, traversed by profound transversal cañons and culminating in the crests of these mountains which enclose the great plateau on both sides.

ASCENDING THE MEXICAN CORDILLERA, OR EASTERN SIERRA MADRE: THE RAILWAY IS SEEN IN THE VALLEY FAR BELOW.

The Sierra Madres, or Mexican Andes, have the general Andine direction of north-north-west. They are divided into two systems—the western and the eastern—whose respective crests in the north are from 400 to 500 miles apart, enclosing the *mesa central*, and which approach towards the south. The Pacific range has some important ramifications from its main system, but the general Andine structure is maintained. The range is again encountered in the long peninsula of North-Western Mexico—known as Lower California—where it parallels the eastern side of this great tongue of land for more than 700 miles. Indeed, a study of Mexico's orography and the delineation upon the map shows the series of parallel features formed by alternate mountain-folds and intervening basins—the peninsula of Lower California; the Gulf of the same name; the Western Sierra Madre; the intersecting crests of the great plateau; the Eastern Sierra Madre, and the Gulf Coast. Thus these huge "earth-wrinkles" of the Andine system of South America show their characteristics in Mexico, modified, however, by cross-agencies of volcanic nature. The map of Mexico shows strikingly how the country is formed upon its rocky framework, the ribs of these vast folds.

THE STATE OF VERA CRUZ: THE PEAK OF ORIZABA; PLAZA OF THE CITY OF CORDOVA.

The passes over these mountain ranges, giving access to the plateau-interior of Mexico from the oceans, vary from 8,500 feet to 10,000 feet, the range upon the Pacific side being generally the higher. But the highest peaks rise much above these altitudes, in some few cases reaching beyond the perpetual snow-line, although ever much lower than the Andes of South America. Three culminating peaks only pass the snow-line in Mexico, although others of the crests and summits are frequently snow-covered. The first of these three peaks is Orizaba, or Citlaltepetl—the "Star Mountain" of the native— the beautiful and symmetrically formed cone whose gleaming snow-cap is seen by the approaching traveller far over the stormy waters of the Gulf as he approaches the shores of Vera Cruz. So Grijalva and Cortes saw it; so the voyager of to-day sees it, as its snowy point seems to hang in mid-sky, its base buried in clouds and its gleaming summit surrounded by the azure of the tropic firmament. The summit of Orizaba is 18,250 feet above the level of the sea—the highest point in Mexico. Next in point of altitude is the famous Popocatepetl—the "Smoking Mountain," so called by the natives for its eruptions in centuries past, for it is no longer active. Some of the adventurous

Spaniards of the band of Cortes reached the rim of the crater on its summit, and, indeed, later the Spaniards extracted sulphur therefrom, and various ascents have been made recently. Its last eruption was in 1665. The summit of Popocatepetl is 17,250 feet above sea-level, and it is of characteristic conical form. The third perpetually snow-capped peak is Ixtaccihuatl—the "Sleeping Woman," so named by the natives from the fanciful suggestiveness of a reclining woman—and its summit is 16,960 feet above the sea. The Indian names of these striking monuments of nature serve to show the poetical nomenclature which the natives of the Americas ever gave to topographical features. Especially was this the case among the Aztecs of Mexico and the Incas of Peru. The last-named mountain is not of the characteristic conical form which volcanoes generally have, its outline—beautiful as it is—forming a serrated edge, and it appeared singularly striking from Tacubaya, where I first beheld it. Nevertheless, all these three mountains—the highest points in the country—are of volcanic origin. The majestic and poetic peaks of the "Smoking Mountain" and the "Sleeping Woman" form part of the Sierra Nevada, or Cordillera of Anahuac, in company with Malinche, another of the highest culminating peaks, 14,630 feet above sea-level. This chain is a cross ridge of volcanic and more recent formation than that of the general system of the Mexican Cordilleras, and forms, as it were, a line of volcanic action at right angles to the general Andine trend, associated perhaps with Orizaba on the east and the volcano of Colima (12,990 feet elevation) on the west. This latter mountain is the only active crater in Mexico at the present time. The great Malinche, or Malintzin—possibly named after the fair interpreter of Cortes—is a mountain of striking form, with its brow often snow-covered, upon the borders of the plateau of Tlaxcala, whilst the singular Cofre de Perote, with its box or coffin-like summit (13,400 feet above sea-level), is a prominent landmark of the eastern slope of Mexico's road from Vera Cruz, overhanging the summit of the Sierra Madre at the limit of the lowlands. Other high peaks are the Nevedo de Toluca, often snow-crowned, 14,950 feet; and Tancitaro, 12,660 feet.

The Mexican mountains are mainly of underlying granite formation. The Jurassic, Cretaceous, and Tertiary Ages rocks are much in evidence throughout the country, whilst the highest ranges, as we have seen, are of volcanic origin. The singular plains of Yucatan are largely of calcareous formation, probably a Tertiary limestone. One of the most plentiful rocks over vast areas of Mexico, and that which forms the striking variation of scenery, is the mountain limestone, the excessively hard stratified crystalline rock of the Lower Cretaceous period. This rock formation extends right across Mexico—although isolated in places—from sea to sea, and its existence possibly goes to show that the Pacific and the Gulf were one, in earlier geological times. The predominating shades of these extensive strata are blue and grey; occasionally there are black bands alternating, and they lie upheaved at such angles as remind the traveller of the still more pronounced strata of the high summits of the Peruvian Andes.[25] The mountain limestone is of very hard texture; white and crystalline, it wears away but slowly under the action of the elements, although on the steep mountain tracks over which we are journeying we shall observe it broken into cubes like sugar, beneath the incessant trampling of hoofs, or worn away to silver-sand and borne down by the streamlets into the river valleys.

25 See my book, "The Andes and the Amazon."

The rock-formations of the tablelands are those to which Mexico owes her fame as a silver-producing country, and it is in the high region, from 5,000 to 9,500 feet above sea-level, that her historical mines are encountered; and the zone of territory embraced by these well-known centres, from Pachuca to Guanajuato and onwards to Chihuahua, may be described without exaggeration as the richest argentiferous region on the surface of the globe. It is to the metamorphic formation that the abundance of mineral ores is due, and the igneous rocks which have given rise thereto—the granites, basalts, diorites, porphyries, and others. This metalliferous zone is more than 1,500 miles long, extending from the State of Chihuahua and Sonora in the north to Oaxaca and Chiapas in the south.

As we cross the coast-zone from Vera Cruz we are enabled to observe something of the orographical structure of the country and the agencies that have been at work. The coastal plains are sedimentaries of Tertiary formation. The *médanos*, or sand-dunes, of the coast, blown into singular forms by the prevailing *norte* from the Gulf, give place, as we proceed inland, to the foothills of the Eastern Sierra. Here the Cretaceous formation is shown—the hard crystalline limestone—and this, from its durable nature, has furnished material for the new breakwater at Vera Cruz. Again, as we proceed, the lower rocks are sheeted with the lava of former eruptions of volcanoes, worn away at times by the ravines, and showing the points of Cretaceous rocks protruding; and volcanic dust from the same source drifts hither and thither, and at times has been compressed by the elements into a soft tufa. The great sheets of lava, as in certain places in the Valley of Mexico, are of remarkable appearance on the face of the country, the scorified aspect seemingly little changed since the moment when the fiery sheet must have poured devastatingly down the countryside.

The rock-formation of Mexican landscape gives rise to exceedingly picturesque and romantic scenery in places, and to diverse configurations of striking beauty, among which we shall often draw rein as we journey, or which will attract us continually to the observation-point of our Pullman car as the train winds along. Upon the Gulf of Mexico or the Pacific slopes the territory is grand and broken in the extreme, and presents curious and beautiful examples of rock-scenery. The natural monoliths of the *barrancas* of the State of Hidalgo are strange examples of scenic geology; monumental caprice of Nature in megalithic structure, as shown by the remarkable basalt columns of the profound Gorge of Itzala. Vari-coloured lichens cover these basalt pillars, affording singular contrast of light and shade. Through the gorge a torrential stream flows, and the floor of the valley is covered with fragments of obsidian, or volcanic glass, gleaming black and brilliant, which has been brought down by the waters from the Cerro de Navajas. This obsidian, or Itzli, was the material from which the Aztecs made their knives and weapons, and this was their prehistoric quarry. The red lava deserts of Sonora are weird and remarkable.

Mexico is divided hydrographically into three systems: the Atlantic, or Gulf of Mexico watershed; that of the Pacific; and the hydrographic entities of the great plateau. In the first of these is the vast region of the northern part of Mexico, which, with Texas and New Mexico, drains into the Rio Grande and thence into the Gulf; the long littoral of the Gulf Coast, whose *divortia aquarum*, or water-parting, is formed by the Eastern Sierra Madre; and the peninsula of Yucatan. In the second is the vast stretch of the Pacific slope, whose *divortia aquarum* is the Western Sierra Madre; the peninsula of Lower California, and the southern side of the region south of the Isthmus of Tehuantepec. In the third are the intra-montane portions of the great plateau, whose waters have no outlet or natural source of exhaustion except that by evaporation, such as the great plains known as the Bolson of Mapimi; and the Valley of Mexico. Topographically, however—apart from the three climatic zones of hot, temperate, and cold lands—the country is divided orographically into two portions by the Isthmus of Tehuantepec, the former consisting of the characteristic mountain-chains and great plateau, and the latter of the immense plains of Yucatan, with a low elevation of not more than 300 feet above sea-level.

The formation of Mexico has not given rise to the existence of great or navigable rivers nor, indeed, of harbours. With few exceptions rivers are torrential in character, although some are of considerable length. The Rio Grande, which forms the northern boundary of the United States, and is therefore international in character, is 1,500 miles in length; rising in Colorado and passing through New Mexico in the United States, and thence entering between Texas and Chihuahua, it is joined by two large tributaries—the Pecos on the American and the Conchos river on the Mexican side. Thence it flows south-eastwardly to the Gulf of Mexico. The waters which enter Mexican territory are scarce, as they have been taken out for irrigation purposes in American territory. The Lerma, or Santiago, river is the next in point of length, and is a stream of considerable importance, dividing the main portion of Mexico topographically into two subdivisions. It flows for 540 miles from its source in the mountains near Toluca, passing through the beautiful Lake Chapala—the largest in Mexico—and forms the great cascade of Juanacatlan, the Niagara of Mexico; traverses the State of Jalisco, where it is joined by numerous affluents, and discharges into the Pacific Ocean near San Blas.

FALLS OF JUANACATLAN: THE NIAGARA OF MEXICO.

Southwardly from the above, beyond the intervening Cordillera, is the River Balsas, or Mescala, 430 miles in length. This important stream has its rise in the watershed of the central plateau, or rather the extensive slopes of the Valley of Mexico, and running with a general westerly direction between the Sierras, empties into the Pacific at Zacatula. It is navigable for a short distance. The Yaqui, discharging into Pacific waters, is 390 miles long, flowing through the Sierras of Sonora to the Gulf of California. On the littoral of the Mexican Gulf is the Panuco, which rises to the north of the Valley of Mexico, flowing thence in a great curve; and being joined by various affluents from the eastern watershed of the Sierra Madres, it discharges at the port of Tampico. The Papaloapam, also draining part of the State of Vera Cruz, empties into the Gulf near the port of the same name. From the region of the peninsula of Yucatan flow two main streams—the Usamacinta and the Grijalva—which are partly navigable. All these rivers are further described in the chapter treating of the various States to which they correspond. Another characteristic stream of Mexico is the River Nazas, whose waters, nearly all absorbed by the irrigation canals of the Laguna region, where the famous cotton plantations are, fall in times of flood into the

Lagoon of Parras, where they evaporate, the system forming a hydrographic entity, without outlet either to the Pacific or Atlantic watershed. Thus it is seen that most Mexican rivers simply rise in and descend on one or the other slopes of the country; and as the fall is rapid their courses are interrupted by numerous cascades. Except in few cases, these rivers are of no service for navigation, but the elements of water-power and irrigation facilities which they possess are more than compensating circumstances. In addition, their scenic value is very marked in many cases.

Lakes of Andine character, and others, exist throughout Mexico, the remnants of much larger lake systems, which occupied the filled-up "troughs" of the mountains, before described. Some of these sheets of water are exceedingly beautiful in their disposition and environment. Foremost among them is Chapala, in the State of Jalisco, near the handsome city of Guadalajara; and equally picturesque those smaller sheets of water in Michoacan—Lakes Cuitzeo and Patzcuaro. The remarkable groups of lakes in the Valley of Mexico, around which the Aztec civilisation flourished, comprise six salt-water and one (that of Chalco) fresh-water lake. The two maps given in these pages, of the disposition of these lakes at the time of the Conquest[26] and at the present day, respectively, show how remarkably their waters have shrunk during the intervening centuries. Indeed, this may have followed a certain drying-up process which seems to have been going on throughout the whole Andine region of the Americas, and which is evidenced by retiring snow-caps in Peru, and the receding of Lake Titicaca.

26 See page 76.

The climate and temperature of Mexico follow certain marked zones, depending upon elevation, as already indicated in the opening chapter. Both on the Atlantic and Pacific slopes these zones are encountered—the *tierra caliente* up to 3,000 feet elevation above sea-level; the *tierra templada* to 5,000 or 6,000; and the *tierra fria* above that altitude. On the tropical lowlands the heat of the torrid zone is experienced, but is not necessarily oppressive, although the European or American traveller who prefers a less enervating climate hastens to exchange that region for the more bracing air of the uplands. The night breezes, however, compensate largely for the heat of the sun, and render bearable, and indeed agreeable, the Vera Cruz littoral and the Yucatan peninsula, by the lowered temperature they afford. The rains also, which have their season from June to November, do much to refresh the atmosphere. Indeed, the year is divided mainly by the matter of rainfall into a wet and dry period, the summer and winter of other countries being unknown; or, rather, one might say, that the daytime is the summer and the night-time the winter, so marked are the diurnal changes of temperature.

In the *tierra caliente* the mean temperature varies from 77° to 80° F., but often rises to 100°, and in some of the hottest coast regions to 105° F. In the *tierra templada* the mean is from 62° to 70° F., and this is the climatic region which the Mexicans love to term "perpetual spring." In point of fact, it is a zone not unworthy of the designation, being equable, healthy, and with a beautiful and varied *flora*. It is to be recollected that the greater part of the area of the country lies in this temperate zone, although there is included in it a part of the great plateau, with its great range of heat and cold from day to night. It is, however, with reference to the Atlantic and Pacific slopes that these changes are ascribed, and this fine and enjoyable climate is encountered from Ameca in Jalisco to Chilpancingo in Guerrero on the western side; and from Jalapa northwards upon the Gulf—vast belts of territory of which any country might well be proud. Upwards from this zone is that of the *tierra fria*, with a mean temperature of 59° or 60° F., which varies little throughout the year, although the maximum and minimum from day to night is very marked.

THE PACIFIC COAST ZONE: GENERAL VIEW OF THE CITY AND ENVIRONS OF COLIMA.

As regards the climate of Mexico generally, it might have been supposed that it would be oppressively hot, the country lying, as it does, towards the

Equator. But this is far from being the case; and the New Yorker may well leave the stifling heat of his own city in summer for the tonic breezes of the Mexican uplands, just as he may winter there to avoid the bitter winter of New York. And, as to the European, we may recollect that the northernmost point of Mexico is two degrees nearer the Equator than the southernmost point of Europe, whilst the mean annual temperature of the City of Mexico— 61° F.—bears excellent comparison with such places as Algiers, 63°; Barcelona, 61°; Naples, 61°; Rome, 60°; Bordeaux, 57° F. The diurnal change in the City of Mexico, however, is very marked, rising to 89° F. during the day and falling to 35° F. at night, when the foreigner gladly dons his overcoat and the native his *capa,* or *serape*. On the whole, it is natural to describe the climate of Mexico as pleasing and invigorating, whilst bearing in mind the variation above described, due to elevation, latitude, rainfall, and wind agencies. The effects of these changes are so marked upon the vegetation of the country that all the vegetable products from the Equator to the Polar Circle can be found among them.

The rainfall throughout the country is mainly confined to the rainy season, from May or June to October or November. During the middle of this season the rains are, at times, exceedingly heavy, the dry stream beds of the plateau filling up in a few hours with a torrential flood which sweeps everything before it. The desert plains in some places are traversed by deep *barrancas,* or gullies, worn down perpendicularly through the soil; and woebetide the unlucky horseman who may be journeying along the bottom of one of these when the wave of water comes down from some sudden cloud-burst in the mountains, which happens not infrequently. Incautious Indians and *peones,* also, who have taken up their lodging in some cave or dug-out of the banks of the torrential rivers of the plateau, or who have laid drunk upon the sun-baked river-bed, are often surprised by the waters, and their bodies are recovered miles away, stranded upon some sand-bar. This serves as giving an idea of the sudden and rapid flow of water from the mountains under the torrential rains; and a good example of a river subject to such a regimen is that of the Nazas. I have crossed the dry bed of this river at Torreon on various occasions on horseback, but on the return journey an hour afterwards the horse was swimming, or, when the current was too fierce, it was necessary to make a long detour to the bridge, for the torrent was raging 300 feet wide from bank to bank.

The average rainfall varies greatly for different parts of the country. For example, in the City of Mexico a year's mean fall may be 25 inches, whilst in Monterrey, some 500 miles to the north, it would reach 130 inches. In the dry season, however, no rain falls in any of the three zones of hot, temperate, or cold lands. Snowfall is very rare as far south as the City of Mexico, but is not unknown. In the cities of the great plateau, to the north, it is almost equally rare, occurring perhaps once or twice in a lifetime. When such does take place it affords an unwonted spectacle for the *peones*, and causes them to wrap themselves in their *serapes* and muffle up their mouths as if they were in the polar regions, rather than experiencing a momentary fall of temperature! A scene of this nature occurred during my stay in Lerdo, one of the towns of this region, and is well depicted in the accompanying view. The low rainfall of the extreme north of Mexico, of two to three inches, on the border of Arizona, and the excessive fall, reaching 156 inches, on the Isthmus of Tehuantepec, with the high rate for Monterrey and the moderate fall for the capital, show how remarkable are the hygrometric conditions due to topography. The maximum rainfall is only exceeded in very few regions of the globe.

A RARE OCCURRENCE: SNOWFALL IN A MEXICAN TOWN; VIEW OF THE PLAZA OF LERDO, ON THE GREAT PLATEAU.

If the geology and topography of Mexico are marked and peculiar, the organic world also presents its own remarkable conditions; for, as to its *flora* and *fauna*, Mexico is a land of transition, between North America on the one hand and Central and South America on the other, and contains the species of both regions, in the animal and vegetable kingdoms.

As may well be imagined from such peculiar conditions, Mexico is a country whose *flora* and *fauna* are diverse and extensive. Indeed, as regards the former, every vegetable product found from the Equator to the Polar Circle exist in the country. The soil, in the tropical regions, as a result of high temperature and excessive moisture, is deep and fertile, both from the rock-decay consequent upon such conditions, and the deposit of organic matter from the profuse vegetation. In the region of the high plateau the product of rock-disintegration added to that caused by volcanic matter, and the sediment of dried-up lagoons of very recent time, have produced a great depth of soil in places, as before described, covering vast expanses, and this soil is found to be of exceeding fertility under irrigation. The conditions regarding irrigation are very marked in the region of the Nazas. On the one hand we encounter dry, bare, and uncultivated wastes; on the other verdant fields of cotton. Why is this? Both the lands are of a similar character of soil, but one is above the line of the irrigation canal, and the other below.

No description of Mexico can be complete which does not sound the praises of her varied *flora*. The most striking characteristic of the flowers of this land, as has often been remarked, is the richness and brilliance of their colour. The floating gardens, and the canoe-loads of flowers and altar adornments of such which the Aztecs used and trafficked in, bore witness to aboriginal appreciation of these. To-day the flower-market of the capital is one of its attractions, whilst in the valley of Mexico not a day in the year lacks roses, lilies, camellias, strawberries, *et hoc genus omne*.

A varied and indeed, at times, eccentric field of study is laid open for the botanist in Mexico, for not only is there a remarkable variety of species, but their distribution is often singular. Thus the pine-tree is often found at low elevations upon the tropic slopes, much below its proper *habitat* upon the mountain ranges; whilst palms flourish in certain places as high as 8,000 feet above sea-level; and the extraordinary cactus forms, which in Mexico are found in their greatest development, grow both on the high mountain slopes and the tropic lowland plains. Especially will the traveller in Mexico be struck by the imposing *organo* cactus. This extraordinary growth, in form like a series of organ pipes, from which it takes its name, or like a huge branching candelabra, arising from a single stem, is a marked feature of the landscape. A few strokes of a machete, severing the stem of one of these great succulent plants, will bring down the whole structure, weighing many tons. The cactus, especially upon the high, arid deserts of the plateau, is a striking example of a plant contending with the conditions of its environment in the struggle for life. Cacti are veritable cisterns of water, stored up against long periods of absolute drought, so that they may be able to perform their function of flowering. The *organo* and other cacti consist of great masses of juicy green cells; and to protect the scarce commodity of water which they have collected for their own use from predatory desert beasts and birds, Nature has armed them at every point with an appalling armour of thorns, or spikes, sharp as steel, and due to these matters of offence and defence the cactus is enabled to flourish in sterile places where absolutely no other vegetation could exist. Nowhere are these conditions so marked as upon the upper reaches of the high plateau of Mexico, and the variety of the cacti is most interesting. Among the cactus species are some which are of value—great value—to the human inhabitants. Chief of these is the *maguey* (*Agave americana*), which is indeed one of the staple resources of the country, with a varied use, as described in the pages dealing with agriculture. The *nopat*, or prickly-pear, is a useful plant, yielding a succulent fruit—the *tunas*—and is also the habitat of the cochineal.

A ROAD IN THE TEMPERATE ZONE, WITH PALMS AND VEGETATION.

The tropical region—the *tierra caliente*—is generally covered, as before described, with a profuse floral and arboreal vegetation, whilst the other climatic belts display their own peculiar plant and tree life. Throughout the country generally, a large number of species of timber and plants exist in an uncultivated state, of commercial value, and these are enumerated in the chapter corresponding to the natural products. Among the 115 or more species of timber and wood for constructional purposes are oak, pine, mahogany, cedar, and others, whilst the list of fibrous and medicinal plants, gum-bearing trees, as india-rubber, *chicle*, &c., tinctorial and resinous trees, edible plants and fruits, is of much interest and value. In the tropical lowlands the country is so thickly wooded as in places to be impassable, except by clearing trails and felling trees. There are virgin forests of great extent in these sparsely populated regions, both of the Pacific and Atlantic slopes. Upon the great plateau, however, and the mountain slopes immediately adjoining it conditions are very different. Great tracts of country are, as elsewhere described, absolutely bare of vegetation, both naturally and by reason of the inroads made upon the forests by civilised man. The great desert tracts never had tree or plant life in profusion, but the hilly regions bounding these, and the inward slopes of the Sierra Madres were formerly covered with thick forests, and in some regions are still so covered. But they have been denuded in certain regions of their timber, principally for fuel, as native coal has been unknown until recently, and is difficult of transport. This denudation has had an undoubted effect upon the rainfall, and has served to change the climatic conditions in these regions. In other upland regions, however, the splendid and extensive forests of oak and pine form marked features of the landscape, and are of much industrial value.

VEGETATION IN THE TROPICAL FORESTS.

The diversity of climatic and botanical conditions of Mexico gives as a natural corollary a variety of animal life, and the *fauna* is an extensive one, including, with small exception, all the species of North America on the one hand, and of South America on the other. Those of the former, naturally, are found upon the great plateau; those of the latter in the tropical lowlands.

Among the main exceptions are the llama and alpaca, the domestic wool-bearing animals of the camel family, and kindred varieties, which do not exist in Mexico, nor are found anywhere in the world outside the highlands of Peru and Bolivia. Indeed, native Mexico, before the introduction of the equine race from Europe, had no beast of burden whatever, such as the llama afforded to the South American aboriginal peoples.

The *fauna* of the country embraces fifty-two varieties of mammal quadrupeds, including three species of large felidæ—the jaguar, the puma, or cougar, and the ocelot, a carnivorous cat-like animal, whose name is derived from the native Mexican word *ocelotl*. There are five varieties of monkeys in the tropical forests, as well as a sloth. There are forty-three classes of reptiles, including alligators and turtles, and several kinds of venomous serpents, and the great boa-constrictor. Upon the plateau and mountain ranges wolves and wild-cats abound, and the coyote is the wild inhabitant of the desert plains most in evidence. There are several kinds of bears, and the wolf, skunk, bison, and tapir are found.

Mexico cannot be said to offer a field for hunters of big game, and the term "a sportsman's paradise" which is sometimes applied to it, is something of an exaggeration. Nevertheless, there is considerable sport to be had, and certain kinds of game abound. Among animals may be enumerated the peccaries, or *javilines*, deer, rabbits, hares; of reptiles, alligators, turtles, and iguanas; whilst whales, seals, and sea-lions are encountered upon the Pacific coast. Alligators are numerous in the estuaries of the rivers of both the Gulf and the Pacific sides, as well as turtles and tortoises. Of birds for the sportsman may be mentioned the wild turkey—which, indeed, was introduced to Europe from Mexico—partridges, quail, and wild pigeons. The armadillo, beaver, martin, otter, and others are among the Mexican *fauna*. Of noxious reptiles and insects the rattlesnake is much in evidence, as well as the tarantula, centipede, *alacran*, or scorpion, and varieties of ants. Of birds of beautiful plumage the Mexican tropics abound with life, and they are famed for their fine feathers, and as songsters. They are an example of Nature's compensating circumstances; for in the hot lowlands they are more distinguished for their bright plumage than their voice; whilst in the uplands they are of much more modest dress, but higher singing capacities. More than 350 species of birds have been enumerated throughout the country, and among these are fifty varieties of humming-birds, which range throughout the whole colour-scale, from blue and green to scarlet. The *zenzontle*, or mocking-bird, is a well-known bird in Mexico.

Such are, in brief, the natural conditions of geological structure, climatic conditions, and the organic world consequent thereon, of this varied and interesting land; and having thus observed them we must turn our attention to the human family whose *habitat* they form—the men and women of Mexico of to-day.

CHAPTER IX

THE MEXICAN PEOPLE

Ethnic conditions—Spanish, Mestizos, Indians—Colour-line—Foreign element—The *peones*—Land tenure—The Spanish people—The native tribes—The Apaches—The Mexican constitution—Class distinctions—Mexican upper class—Courtesy and hospitality—Quixotism of the Mexicans—Idealism and eloquence—General characteristics—Ideas of progress—American anomalies—*Haciendas*—Sport—Military distinctions—Comparison with Anglo-Saxons—Republicanism—Language—Life in the cities—Warlike instincts—The women of Mexico—Mexican youths—Religious observance—Romantic Mexican damsels—The bull-fights.

The Mexican people are divided for sociological or ethnological purposes into three divisions—the people of purely white European or Spanish descent, those of combined European and native races, and the pure-blooded Indians. The first have been technically termed *Criollas*, or Creoles, although the designation has, of recent years, been used in a different sense; the second *Mestizos*, or mixed race; whilst the third, the *Indios*, are the direct descendants of the peoples who occupied the country in pre-Hispanic times.

The total population is estimated at fifteen million souls, or possibly slightly under. Of this, according to the census of 1900, the people of purely white descent numbered about 19 per cent.; the Mestizos, who may be looked upon as the typical Mexicans of to-day, 43 per cent.; whilst the remaining 38 per cent. were assigned as the proportion for the Indians. The figures and divisions cannot be looked upon, however, as arbitrary or exact. At the present time it is considered that the Mestizo class probably embraces more than half of the total, whilst the real proportion of people of absolutely pure white race is probably much less than described, possibly not more than 10 per cent., as the mixture permeates all classes.

The white and mixed races, especially the former, constitute the property-owning and administrative classes, and naturally the Mexican upper class is drawn from these. The six million Indians, more or less, constitute some fifty aboriginal tribes in various stages of semi-civilisation or savagery, distributed all over the country from Sonora to Yucatan, and these are described elsewhere. It is not to be supposed that they are savages as a whole; for, on the contrary, they are remarkably gifted in some cases, assimilating the civilisation and intellect of the white man and furnishing excellent material for the country's citizens. The upper-class Mexicans, like the Peruvians or other Spanish-Americans when they are of unmixed white descent, naturally pride themselves upon the fact, and to a certain extent aim to preserve this condition. This is the "colour-line" of the race, and the term "Indio" is still a term expressing something of contempt, notwithstanding the fact that some of the prominent, and even intellectual, men of Mexico's history have been drawn from the Mestizo class, and—in the case of Juarez—from pure aboriginal stock. Of course, the Indian is, as yet, an inferior being.

Included in Mexico's population is a foreign element numbering some 60,000 people, more or less, Spaniards predominating, with more than 16,000, and Americans of the United States with somewhat over 15,000. This is according to the census of 1900, and it is probable that both these elements have increased considerably since then. Of British there are only some 3,000 in the country; of French about 4,000; and of Germans 2,600, approximately. The vast area of Mexican territory contains only about twenty persons to the square mile; were it populated in the same ratio as parts of Europe it might support a population of 180,000,000, it has been calculated.

As has been shown, but a small percentage of the Mexican people are of purely white descent. As for the characteristic type of Mexican—those of mixed white and aboriginal race—they form the principal human element of the country, and shade off indefinably into the *peon* class. This class, drawn both from Mestizos and Indians, forms the great working population, in the fields and the mines, and without them the national industries would be non-existent. They are a picturesque, poor and generally ignorant class, although possessed of excellent natural elements and traits which must develop as time goes on. They form a strong, virile backbone to the country, but the conditions of their life are at present but little removed from serfdom, due to their general poverty as a class and to the monopolisation of the ownership of land by the upper classes. In this connection it is to be recollected that the natives of the civilised pre-Hispanic States of the Americas—as Mexico and Peru—enjoyed an excellent system of individual land-tenure, or rather, of free land-use, which gave being to a strong, independent peasantry; and this, in Peru, still obtains to a certain degree, due principally to the inaccessibility of the Andine regions. But in Mexico such a class no longer exists, and the *peon* lives by sufferance upon the soil which was wrested from his forbears by the white man, who adopted there the singular land customs of Europe, which arrogate to the enjoyment of a few the soil which philosophy points to as belonging to the community.[27] Enormous landed estates are held in Mexico—indeed, in the State of Chihuahua the largest single estate in the world exists—and a semi-feudal *régime* of the land and its inhabitants marks the character of this modern American civilisation. The population on the soil scarcely reaches twenty persons to the square mile—principally rural or inhabiting small towns—and there is ample room, therefore, for expansion. It must, however, be stated that excellent new land laws have been promulgated of recent years in the Republic. National lands have been set aside in vast areas, and any inhabitant of the Republic may "denounce" or acquire a piece of such land, and retain it by annual tax-payment at prices varying from two *pesos*—a peso is about two shillings—in the remote regions, to twenty or thirty *pesos* per hectare—equal to 2½ acres—in the more settled States. The Mexican peasantry is not debarred absolutely from the enjoyment of the land if he has the knowledge and means to perform the simple requirements necessary to its acquisition—which generally he has not. I have dealt in detail with the matters of land acquisition elsewhere in this work, and with the conditions of life of and the character of the *peon* class familiarly.

27 In certain regions there are, of course, numerous Indian squatters and landholders.

To cast, now, a glance at ethnic conditions, it is sufficient to say that a wide range of peoples have mingled their blood in the race which now forms the people of Mexico. No other American nation constitutes so varied a blending of races. The invading Conquistadores and their followers from Spain—which itself has formed from the beginning of history a veritable crucible or mixing-ground of the world's peoples, languages and creeds—brought Iberian, Roman, Celtic, Semite, Vandal, Goth, and Moorish blood to Mexico, and mingled it with the aboriginal Aztecs and others. As to the origin of the Mexican aboriginals, this is unknown or only conjectured, but they embrace an enormous range of tribes, some 230 names of which appear in the list compiled by Mexican ethnologists. These, however, are grouped into some twelve or more linguistic families, among whom may be mentioned in order of their numerical importance the Nahuatlan, Otomian, Zapotecan, Mayan, Tarascan, Totonacan, Piman, Zoquean, and others, including the Serian and the Athapascan, or Apache. These families embody people of very varying degrees of native culture; from the low type of the abject Seri Indians, inhabiting part of Sonora; the treacherous and bloodthirsty Apaches, who formerly roved over the vast deserts of the north, up to the cultured peoples who formed the prehistoric civilisation of the country; the Nahuatl- and Maya-speaking races, who, in the peninsula of Yucatan and the Valley of Mexico, were the foremost peoples in point of culture of the whole of the New World, and who have left the remarkable chapters in stone of their history which are scattered about Mexico, and which have been described in a former chapter.

To-day the vast area and different peoples of Mexico are combined politically into one community—a Federation of States or Federal Republic; and the blending of the peoples, carnally, goes on day by day, as there are not inseparable distinctions of colour or creed to keep them asunder. Politically Mexico may be considered as the foremost of the Spanish-American Republics, her population being the greatest, and her civilisation more broadly developed than any of her sister-nations. The form of government, as stated, is that known as a Federal Republic—a definition of which is that the numerous States composing the whole are free and sovereign as regards their internal *régime*, but united under their representative, democratic Constitution as a political entity.

The Constitution is fashioned upon the model of the United States to a certain extent, and as a Federation differs from most of the other Spanish-American republics. The supreme authority of the Republic is held and exercised by three bodies—the Legislative, the Executive, and the Judiciary. The Legislative embodies the Congress, or Parliament, consisting of the Chamber of Deputies and the Senate, the members of which are elected, the first in the proportion of one for every 60,000 inhabitants, every two years: and the second of two Senators for each State every four years. The Judiciary consists of the Supreme and other courts, the judges of the first being elected, and the business of the body relates to law and justice concerning Federal, political, and international matters. The Executive in Mexico consists of a single depositary of authority—the President, who, with the vice-president, is elected, and who enter upon office on the 1st of December, for terms of six years. The Constitution which all these officials swear to uphold is that first brought to being on February 5, 1857, with various modifications. By the Reform Laws of 1859, and their additions of 1873, the Church and State are absolutely independent of each other, and the power and functions of the ecclesiastical authority are rigidly defined. The Federation consists of thirty-one States and "territories," which latter are subject to Federal control and regulation of their internal *régime*, unlike the former. The States are governed by Governors.

Mexico has, therefore, well established all the machinery of a republic, wherein equal rights of man and the sovereignty of the people are well set forth. How do these excellent methods and theories work out in practice as regards the social system and inhabitants? A republic in name, Mexico shares with Spanish-American countries generally, social conditions which are far from being embodied in the real meaning of that designation. It is not necessary to dwell much upon this palpable fact, and its reason is not far to seek. The communities of the New World which Spain conquered were inhabited by inferior peoples who were easily enslaved, or who were already subject to autocratic forms of government. Every Spaniard who arrived there —were he a noble of Castile or a common boor from his native Iberian province—was full of the arrogance and superiority, sometimes fancied, generally real, of the civilised European, and this spirit burst into full bloom amid the environment of such countries as Mexico and Peru. Thus an autocratic race was established whose class distinctions are as strong and enduring as those of the most class-ridden countries of Europe. It would be impossible to expect other conditions yet, with a great mass of the people being of Indian race, and coming on almost imperceptibly towards civic knowledge and intellectual advancement. Scarcely 13 per cent. of the total population can read and write, whilst as to the labouring classes they are only just beginning to show any advancement along lines of modern civilisation. Nevertheless the Government of the country has their welfare at heart, and in the last quarter of a century has regarded the working classes and Indians as citizens with rights rather than mere material for revolutionary struggle, as was formerly the case. The Mexican people having always been sharply divided into two classes, an upper and a lower; a middle-class, such as in Europe or the United States forms the great bulk of intelligent citizens, tends but slowly to appear, and it is this which must be encouraged to arise and to absorb the aboriginal element.

THE MEXICAN PEONES: STREET SCENE AT CORDOVA.

The upper class Mexican is often a well-educated and well-informed man of the world, and in appearance and habit differs little from the European. His wealth has permitted him to be educated in the best establishments his country affords, or often abroad, in France, England, and in a less degree the United States, and to spend years in Europe and live a life of ease, preferably in Paris—that true Mecca of the Spanish-American people. The Mexican gentleman is generally courteous and punctilious, and gives much attention to dress and matters of ceremony, after the general manner of the Spanish-American, and the frock-coat and silk hat form his indispensable exterior whenever possible. His courtesy pervades his business relations generally, as well as social affairs. And, indeed, this pleasing quality permeates the whole social *régime* from the highest official or wealthy citizen down to the poorest *peon* or to the Indian labourer. The matter of courtesy, in addition to being native both with the Spanish progenitor and the native race, is, it might be said, part of the political Constitution. The republics of Spanish-America at least regard all men as equal in this sense, a condition which is far from existing in the Anglo-Saxon Republic of the United States, where brusque assertion of even the meanest authority is evident, in the present development of that country. Nor is it to be supposed that Mexican politeness is a mere veneer, or mask, to be put on and off as occasion dictates, for it arises from native kindliness—a species of Quixotism of a laudable nature.

The Mexican largely shares the spirit of hospitality of the Spanish-American race, and this, besides being a native characteristic, was strongly implanted in colonial days by the very exigencies and circumstances of the times. In some parts of the country, until recent years, hotels or inns were unknown; and it was sufficient for the traveller to knock at almost any door to ask and receive food and shelter for himself and his retainers and beasts, even though the people of the place might be ignorant of his name or business: and the best that was forthcoming was put at his service. Something of practical patriarchal simplicity governed life in regions more remote from main routes of travel, which held, and indeed still hold, much of charm for the traveller from lands whose hospitality—as Britain or the United States—is the result often of ostentation or social necessity rather than that of native kindliness. This amiable trait of more or less pastoral communities, as Mexico and South America, tends naturally to disappear before the influence of the commercial element which is invading the country, and it is not to be expected that it will survive always.

The Spanish-American possesses an ineradicable element of *Quijotismo*—he will tell us so himself—and this element seems to have become stronger in the New World than in Spain, which gave it origin. The Mexican has it to the full, like the Peruvian; doubtless it arises largely from the conditions of caste brought about by the existence of the Mestizo and the Indian. Trembling on the verge of two races, his eyes looking towards the land of his progenitors, the enshrined Spain of his dreams, with something of *race-nostalgia*—if we may be permitted to coin the term—yearning for the distinction of the white skin and traditions of European civilisation, yet bound to the life of and race of his own *patria* by reason of the native blood within his veins, the Hispanic Mexican has cultivated a sensitive social spirit which tinges his character and action in every-day life. From this largely arise his courtesy and spirit of hospitality—although these are undeniably innate—and principally his love of pomp and externals, the keeping up of appearances, and his profound eloquence. The Mexican is intensely eloquent. His speakings and writings are profuse in their use of the fulness of the Spanish language, and teem with rich words and phrases to express abstract ideas. Indeed, judged by Anglo-Saxon habit, they would be termed grandiloquent and verbose. He indulges in similes and expressions as rich and varied as the vegetation of his own tropical lands. The most profound analogies are called up to prove the simplest fact, not only in the realm of poetry, or description, but in scientific or business matters at times, and whether he is writing upon some deep social problem or reporting upon the condition of the parish pump he will preface his account with an essay! This, whilst it betrays often an attractive idealism, is prone at times to lead to the sacrificing of exact information to elegance of style or diction. The Mexican is never at a loss for words; his eloquence is native, and whether it be the impassioned oratory of a political speaker or the society small-talk of a young man in the presence of ladies, he is never shy, and his flow of language and gesture is as natural to him as reserve and brevity to the Englishman. Indeed, the Anglo-Saxon, especially the Briton, seems repellant in comparison with the Spanish-American, and to cultivate selfishness rather than ceremony in his own social dealings.

This tendency towards idealism becomes exaggeration often, though not intended for such, and the prefixing of superlatives is very noticeable in ordinary language. Thus glory is generally "immortal glory"; knowledge "profound knowledge"; every person partaking in public affairs, if a friend of the speaker, is ever "enlightened and patriotic," and his intelligence becomes "vast intelligence." "Our distinguished and universally beloved Governor" would be the customary reference to such a functionary; and "an era of glorious progress" would be the only way of characterising his administration. Indeed, a glance over a Mexican book or article or speech seems to show that the writer has made use of every elegant and abstruse word in the dictionary. In a dissertation upon any subject he seems called upon to begin from the very beginning of things, *desde la creacion del mundo* —"from the beginning of the world," as the Spanish-American himself sarcastically says at times. Perhaps this is a habit acquired from the early Spanish chroniclers, who often began their literary works with an account of the Creation! The love of linking together the material and the poetic is, of course, at the basis of this striving after effect, and no philosophical observer would pretend to hold it up to ridicule. Anglo-Saxon civilisation grows material and commercial; the Spanish-American preserves and cultivates some poetic and cultured imagery; and perhaps Nature intends the one to affect the other in the future amalgamation of the world's races.

Less lovable a characteristic of the Spanish-American is the tendency to fulsome adulation of public or powerful personages in the hope of winning patronage. The tendency to pander to each other's vanity, however, shows up in marked contrast to the harshness and abuse of authority often employed in political matters. The Spanish character, amiable and courteous in friendship or equality, tends to become arbitrary when vested with some brief authority, and this has been at the bottom of much of the political disturbance and bloodshed of the past. It is characteristic of this race to show a certain "Oriental" trait—that which gives rise to an acquiescence in successful guile, rather than an admiration and self-sacrifice for abstract truth. This is, of course, a characteristic both of individuals and nations before they reach a certain standard of civilisation. The readiness to follow the successful cause among the upper class, and the easy regard of the unpunished criminal, are the outcome of these qualities. In business matters the Spanish-American, the Mexican, Peruvian, Chilean, Brazilian, or other has a much less sense of rigid observance of agreements, and a far greater latitude of expediency and mental juggling than the Anglo-Saxon. And this insinuation embodies one of the main defects of the race. Ideas of "mine" and "thine" are much less strong than with the Briton or American. It has been said of the Spaniard that he makes excellent laws, but ever considers that he personally has a right to break them. This sentiment becomes very evident in America: yet not only with the Spanish-American, for it is a marked characteristic of the United States, and of all American republics, where licence is often indulged in under the name of liberty.

The Mexican character must be summed up as that of a people in the making. The fact is stamped upon their physiognomies even. Let us turn over the pages of any book issued in Mexico and observe the portraits of public men and of their biographies, for it will generally be full of these, often pandering to their vanity. The features are strongly pronounced, and at times verge upon the grotesque—we mean it in no offensive spirit. A high intelligence runs riot, and an idealism untempered by sobriety and practice, with strong passions, and love of show. But they mark a people, not decadent, but evolving. The Mexicans are at the beginning, not the end, of their civilisation; the rise, not the fall, of their life. Here is the material of a vigorous and prolific race which may be destined to bulk largely—like the whole of Spanish-America—in the future *régime* of the civilisation of the white man.

A FAMOUS MINISTER OF FINANCE: SEÑOR LIMANTOUR.

A FAMOUS GENERAL AND MINISTER OF PUBLIC WORKS.

AN ARCHBISHOP.   A STATE GOVERNOR.
TYPES OF MEXICANS OF THE UPPER CLASS.

The "era of glorious progress"—to use the Mexican term—which the long dictatorship of the present famous President of Mexico inaugurated is a theme which occupies the Mexican mind and pen very largely. The European writer ungrudgingly records it, and the much-used adjective has much of truth for its constant use. General Porfirio Diaz has been wise and fortunate, and has been able to surround his administration with the talented men of his time—*una pléiade incontable de hombres conspicuos,* to quote from a Mexican description of his colleagues—"an innumerable pleiades of conspicuous men!" in their own grandiloquent phrases. As for the President, it might be supposed that the tendency to deify him by his contemporaries, and the constant pouring out of adulation and flattery upon him for the last twenty years, has made him proof against the workings of vanity. He well deserves this praise, both from his countrymen and from foreigners; but so long and varied a course of it must prove unpalatable, notwithstanding that the Spanish-American, as a rule, is capable of absorbing an infinite amount of praise. Porfirio Diaz has brought his country up from chaos, and for this fortunate work he has to thank his own staunch character and the fact that a time had arrived in the natural evolution of America when even the most turbulent States are called upon to perform their function and carry out their destiny. The man and the hour arrived together, and Diaz deserves to rank among the historic statesmen of the world.

The Mexicans, in their oratory and writings, are still congratulating themselves upon their overthrow of the power of the Church, and of the other ancient tyrannies which were a bar to their progress as a modern nation. But the tendency—though growing less as time goes on—is to overrate this. They pride themselves on being "modern," and congratulate themselves on every occasion upon having destroyed past traditions. But it is easy, in wiping away the evils of the past with too vigorous a hand, to destroy at the same time much that is of good report. Mexico possesses traditions, religious influences, historical and literary associations which are of great value, and possessed by no other American community upon that continent. These can never be replaced by the plumed hat of the General and all that it conveys, nor by the freethinker, nor by the factory whistle and overalled mechanic, nor, indeed, by the elements of a strenuous commercialism generally. As time goes on and civil life broadens and develops this attitude will be moderated—it is but a phase of the country's history, and indeed a healthy one, to cry for progress and the modern spirit.

Much of this cry for modern things, as well as some other of the characteristics of the Spanish-American, comes from the desire to be considered *highly civilised*. This feeling, whether in Mexico or South America, gives birth at times to a certain feverish spirit of construction, and is responsible for the existence of railways, but no roads; electric light in streets without sewers, and pretentious-looking stucco buildings where solid stone should have been employed. Buenos Ayres, Lima, Santiago, Mexico—all bear witness to this tendency, in more or less degree. And under the garish electric arc at night, or silhouetted against the new white stucco wall of some costly hygienic institution, or art gallery, or Governor's palace, glaring in the bright sun, stands the incongruous figure of the half-naked and sandalled Indian, ignorant and poverty-stricken! These, indeed, are elements of Spanish-American civilisation which the philosopher sees and ponders upon. In fact, the character of the Latin races seems sometimes to tend to run off into ultra-scientific methods and institutions before the every-day welfare of its citizens is secured. Elaborate meteorological observations, great schools of medicine with costly apparatus, and great penitentiaries are to be found as prominent features in all Spanish-American capitals, where they have been inaugurated with much fanfare of oratory regarding civilisation. In Mexico, Lima, Buenos Ayres, and other great centres of Spanish-American life, the *Penetenciaria* is always a showplace, or notable institution to which visitors' attention is drawn. This, however, seems to be rather a development of modern American civilisation all through, and whether in New York—and indeed Canada—or whether in Mexico, Peru, Chile, or Argentina, greater care seems to be expended upon the welfare of the criminal than on the ordinary poor citizen!

MEXICAN LIFE: THE CATHEDRAL AND THE PENITENTIARY, CITY OF PUEBLA.

As previously observed, Mexican society falls into lines of marked class distinction. The rich and the educated stand in sharp juxtaposition to the great bulk of poor and uneducated, and the high silk hat and frock-coat form a striking contrast to the half-naked and sandalled *peon* in the *plazas* and streets of the cities. Similarly does the *caballero*, the horseman on caparisoned steed, spurn the dust on country roads through which the humble cotton-clad Indian labourer slinks to his toil. The horse, in Mexico, is always an outward sign of social superiority, and no self-respecting Mexican would ever be seen on foot beyond the paved streets of his cities. The noble animal is an integral part of Mexican life, social or industrial, and the Mexicans are in some respects the most expert horsemen in the world, as elsewhere shown.

The upper-class Mexican is generally a large landowner. The great estates which form his *hacienda* lie in one or the other part of the country, whether upon the great tableland or in the tropical regions which surround it. He spends a certain period of the year upon his *hacienda*, returning to the capital or journeying to Europe as desire or necessity may dictate. Great plantations of cotton, or immense areas of sugar-cane, or *maguey*, or other products yield him the considerable income which he enjoys; and, as a rule, the fertile lands of the Republic are in the hands of this class, to the exclusion of the great bulk of the inhabitants. But the *haciendas* are important centres of industry, supporting the rural population in their vicinity.

The Mexican shares the characteristics of the Latin race in his love for politics, military and other titles and distinctions, and his predilection for holding some Government office. The law, the army, medicine are professions which appeal to him as affording distinction or degree, as well as giving outlet to the love of scientific pursuits, generally, however, theoretical rather than practical. On all sides one hears men addressed as "Doctor," whether it be of science, laws, medicine, or divinity. This condition is observed by the traveller in all Spanish-American republics, and it seems to the foreign observer that the practical and plodding class of workers and trade-makers is insufficiently represented, bearing in mind the large amount of scientific and theoretical leadership. This is in accordance with the dictates of caste, inherited from Spain. The upper class have always had Indians to wait upon them, and a Quixotic tendency to the despising of manual labour has naturally resulted, as among the leisured class of any other country. Any occupation that cannot be performed in the habiliments of the frock-coat and silk hat seems derogatory to the Spanish-American, and, filtering down through all the strata of society above the *peones* this sentiment has the effect of keeping the young men in the cities and robbing the country of a race of intelligent peasants of white descent. The Spanish-American youth of the poorer class prefers to pass the days behind a counter selling cashmeres and silks to bargaining *señoritas* rather than to take up work on the land, which urgently requires more distributed and intelligent cultivation.

The young Mexican of the upper class cares little for sport as understood by the Anglo-Saxon, and the strenuous games of the young Briton or American, or the hard work of British sport, are alien to his ease-loving nature. It is true that tennis and football and even polo are played to a limited extent by enthusiastic young men in the capital, who have followed the example of British or American residents, but it is not to be expected that these alien games could be grafted upon a different stock. Horsemanship is, of course, a natural pastime; but this has nothing in common with the pastime of the English hunting-fields, notwithstanding that a certain class of Mexicans are exceedingly famous as horsemen and have no superiors in the world in this art, in some respects.

As regards political distinction and career, the system obtaining in Spanish-American countries—like that of the United States—causes a change every few years of almost the whole official body, from President and Cabinet Ministers downwards. This has advantages and disadvantages. It certainly creates a large and generally capable governing class or clique. It is rare in the society of the capitals of these countries to find prominent men who, at one time or other, have not been Cabinet Ministers or held other important State office. This gives—to the foreigner at least—a somewhat farcical impression of the life of the community, but, at any rate, it may be conceded that the Republican method gives nearly all good citizens "a show," to use an Americanism, in the State or municipal life.

Whilst, up to recent years, almost all the administrative positions were filled by men with military titles, there is now a tendency to use the talent of men of civil professions in those departments of State corresponding thereto. Thus it is refreshing to observe that the Department of *Fomento*—Development or Promotion—one of the most important, has at its head and secondary positions men who are Engineers, not Generals. This Department is concerned with the railways, roads, mines, irrigation, and all matters of a similar nature, and its administration naturally calls for technical knowledge which the ubiquitous General does not often possess. The Minister of Foreign Affairs has been a lawyer (*licenciado*) as well as his seconds; others of the Cabinet Ministers are of the same professions, and the principal representatives of the country abroad, their ambassadors, are men whose simple titles of "Señor Don," and "Honourable" show their civil origin. So the picturesque and vigorous military element, invaluable in its place, is kept within its natural bounds, and as the pages of the book of Mexico are turned over the portraits of distinguished men with plumed hats and sword and uniform tend to become less and the civilian dress and the thoughtful brow of the educated civil statesman take their place. Among the ancient Mexicans, in pre-Hispanic days, commerce was a most honourable calling, as indeed were the handicrafts. But until recent years the titles of soldier and priest in Christian Mexico—as, indeed, it was in mediæval Europe—seemed to be those which alone called for respect.

The Mexicans are very careful to preserve the forms of their Republican system of government in the conduct of affairs of State, whether in principle or nomenclature. A decree is prefaced with "The Citizen President so decrees," is addressed to a "Citizen Secretary, Citizen Governor," or other, and terminates with the words "Independence and Liberty." Statues and streets, and institutions on every hand convey the recollections of liberty and reform. The *Calle de la Independencia*, that of the *Cinco de Mayo* (Fifth of May), the *Paseo de la Reforma*, and other kindred names are much in evidence, and the Anglo-Saxon observer is startled from his own prosaic world to one where the matters of civic machinery and romantic pretension people its everyday life. It is safe to say that the average Mexican knows more about the chief men of his *patria*, and its history and institutions, than does the average Briton or American of his country. The educated Mexican speaks correct and expressive Spanish, which language—the *Castellano*—is, of course, the language of the country. In addition, he invariably speaks French, for in his generation this has ever been considered the mark of a polite education. English he may speak in addition, but not so universally. When we ask the Mexican gentleman of the old school if he speaks English there will the slightest shrug of the shoulders or lifting of the eyebrows. "No, señor," he will reply, perhaps with a polite expression of regret; "but, on the other hand, I speak French." Nevertheless, he very often does speak English, and with fluency, acquired in England or the United States—preferably the former, he will add.

The Spanish of Mexico is very similar to that of Peru, and this says much for a language separated by such vast distances. The same good accent and facility of expression and gesture, the same native eloquence, grandiloquent similies, philosophical allusions and vivid descriptions, not only concerning things great and important, but things commonplace and everyday. The Mexican, however, partakes less of this character than the Peruvian. The pronunciation of the words, and especially of their termination, marks a great difference between the Mexican and Peruvian on the one hand and the Chilian on the other. The latter has developed a chopped and incomplete pronunciation, although it betrays the energetic and virile character of the Chileno in contrast to the more effeminate Peruvian.

Life in Mexican cities does not lack colour and interest, and the peoples to be encountered in the streets show very varying traits and occupations. Here is the carriage of a wealthy citizen, drawn by a splendid pair of imported English horses; here is a sweet-faced señorita, bending her steps towards her favourite temple, accompanied by some vigilant chaperon or domestic; here two Mexican gentlemen pass each other on the narrow curb, each insisting upon giving the other the inside—the place of honour—and ceremoniously raising their silk hats to each other in salutation. Along comes a bull-fighter now, with his distinctive hat, slouch, and shaven face, the redoubtable *torero*, accompanied by admiring *amigos*, ready to pay for all the *copas* their hero might, with lordly dignity, desire to partake of. In the middle of the stone-paved street the *peones*, or perhaps some Indians from the country, porters, *cargadores*, or other humble occupation, slink along—the footpath is not for them—with their pantaloons of cotton *manta* rolled up to their knees and their feet unshod or sandalled. The Mexican woman of the Indian class prefers to carry her shoes in her hand when she enters or leaves the city streets, putting them on only as a concession to civilisation and removing them when away. Some years ago it was necessary to pass a regulation to the effect that the Indians must wear trousers or other covering when in the city, as they continually asserted their aboriginal love of bodily freedom by appearing without them! The life and colour of Mexican towns is characteristic, and the Mexican journeying to Britain's cities finds life flat and colourless, without gleam of interest for him, its more solid basis of existence not easily falling into his comprehension.

THE FAMOUS MEXICAN "RURALES," OR RURAL MOUNTED POLICE.

It is the spectacular which more readily appeals to the Mexican. The bull-fight, with its accompaniments of showy dress, tense excitement, and elements of danger and bloodshed, is his favourite amusement. Military parades and political functions enter largely into the distractions of polite life, as indeed is the case throughout Spanish-America generally. Military titles are exceedingly numerous. Formerly it was rare that a President, a Cabinet Minister, the Governor of a State, or the official head of a department did not carry the distinction of general or colonel. The dormant military spirit, indeed—and in view of Mexico's history it could hardly be otherwise—permeates the whole body politic, and its influence and effects give place very slowly to civil ideas. The tramp of armed men and accoutred horses, the roll of drum and call of trumpet, appeal ever to this race of warlike instinct. The gleam of arms and sabre possesses for them an attraction which the ploughshare or the miner's drill can never impart. Their ancestors, on the one side, were the warlike Aztecs and other aboriginal races, and on the other the Conquistadores and martial men of Spain. A note of their stirring national anthem, with its warlike words and martial strain, and the soldier—and warrior—instinct arises:—

> "Mexicanos al grito de guerra
> El fierro apretad i el bridón!
> Y retumba sus entrañas la tierra
> Al sonoro rugir del cañón!"

Which might almost be translated in the fiery words of the—

> "Pibroch of Donnel Dhu; pibroch of Donnel,
> Wake thy wild voice anew; summon clan Connel.
> Come away! come away! hark to the summons,
> Come in your war array, gentles and commons!"

*   *   *   *   *

From such stern matters let us turn to a gentler theme—the woman of Mexico. The cultured upper-class are extremely exclusive as regards their women. Any sense of liberty or independence such as characterises the English or American girl is impossible with the Mexican. Between the sexes social intercourse before marriage is much restricted; the rigid etiquette and seclusion of years gone by—almost Moorish in its character—scarcely giving way to the more tolerant ideas which pervade society in general elsewhere. Nevertheless, there has been some improvement in this condition, partly due to the influence of the numerous foreigners who reside in the capital, and, no doubt, time will effect a change. But far be it from the philosophical observer to suggest that such conditions should be hastily swept away. The Mexican, and Spanish-American woman generally, retains qualities and attributes, due partly to her up-bringing, which in some respects gain rather than lose in comparison with the Anglo-Saxon woman.

The Mexican lady is generally of refined and distinguished manner and of a characteristically handsome type, with expressive eyes and a wealth of fine hair. As a girl she is of voluptuous form, remarkably attractive, and of romantic disposition. Her outlook on life is naturally somewhat restricted; its main culminating point is in love and marriage; and indeed the amorous passions in the Mexican race of both sexes are exceedingly strongly developed, and very largely determine their friendships or quarrels. There is a slumberous Southern fire in the Mexican girls' eyes and love. Her passion is consuming, and has not the sense of expediency of the cold Northern races.

This attractiveness of outward demeanour is accompanied often by sterling qualities which make for happy motherhood. But most women of Spanish-American countries sacrifice themselves to their children, nor endeavour to preserve their youth much beyond its allotted span. Also, lack of hygienic measures—as that of active exercise—and the too excessive use of paint and powder in the toilette seem to bring on an early middle age. But apart from this it is a natural condition of the race that it matures early—the Mexican girl is ripe for marriage long before her Anglo-Saxon sisters—and then pays the penalty of an earlier fading. When there is an admixture of the aboriginal strain—and in few families this is absent—a tendency to extreme stoutness exists as middle age approaches, especially among women of the leisure class, whose life calls for no active labour as among their poorer sisters. Sweet, soft, and melancholy, yet often vivacious and always *simpatica*—such is the impression of the Mexican girl which remains upon the mind of the foreigner who has known her. It is always evident to the foreign observer that a too exaggerated habit of seclusion and reserve between the sexes, such as prevails in Spanish-American countries, defeats its own ends to some extent. The men of these countries, whilst outwardly courteous and *correcto* towards their women, to an almost excessive degree, have not the real respect towards them which the less polite Anglo-Saxon entertains towards his feminine world. Nor does this too artificial barrier conduce to any rigid condition of morality. It rather tends to encourage clandestine courtship and amours.

But the Mexican girl's nature calls for admiration and notice. Behold the main street of the city during the fashionable shopping hours, lined with admiring young men, who make audible remarks as to the beauty of eyes, hair, or figure of the passing *señoritas*—remarks which would give grave offence in cold-blooded England, but which are heard with inward gratification by their recipients. These young men of fashion make it an event of the day to line up in this way, attired in fashionable garb, with an exaggerated height of collar and length of cuff! *Largartijos*—lizards—they are dubbed in the language of the country.

In the social life of Mexican cities religion plays an important part. Indeed, religion is the basis of politics—that is to say, the two political parties of the country are divided upon questions of religious control. Mexico, although the State divorced itself long ago from the Church, is, nevertheless, one of the firmest strongholds of Roman Catholicism in the New World. The handsome cathedral and numerous fine churches in the capital City of Mexico, as in the capitals of the various States, attest the fervour of the people's religion. The numerous Church feast-days and varying functions form the most important events of society. On the more special occasions, as during the *Semana Santa*, or Passion Week, almost frenzied multitudes—men as well as women—attend the churches, entrance to which, unless one has gone early, it is impossible to gain on account of the multitude. Among a large section of the Mexican people, however, religious observance has very greatly fallen into disuse, a result of matters which have been previously dealt with, and which include the influence of former French thought; for Mexicans have always made an intense study and example of French philosophers and methods. But in the main it is the natural reaction against centuries of clerical domination, which the evolving modern spirit will have none of. The Roman Catholic Church in Mexico brought about its own downfall. The following translation from a recently published Mexican book shows the spirit pervading the modern Mexico in this connection: "The prevailing religion is Roman Catholicism, but it may be said that its cult is confined to the weaker sex, as the majority of the men, although Catholic, do not practise any religion. Thus the State of Vera Cruz (for example) enjoys the fame of being Liberal. Marriage statistics show that in one year 2,500 civil marriages were consummated against 1,218 ecclesiastical." This is the State of Vera Cruz, of the "True Cross," where the Conquistadores tumbled down the Aztec idols from their *teocallis* and set up the image of the Virgin and Child!

SPANISH COLONIAL CHURCH ARCHITECTURE: A TYPICAL MEXICAN TEMPLE.

But the Church and her religion is the Spanish-American woman's special kingdom. The attendance at Mass upon the Sabbath is the most important of her engagements. Whether in the cool of the early morning, before the dewdrops have fallen from the flowers in the *plaza*, or whether at a later fashionable hour, she is to be seen, in charge of her chaperon, her fair face shaded by the romantic *mantilla* whose use time has failed to banish, devoutly directing her steps towards her favourite temple. Perhaps—confess it!—you have followed her, and one bright glance has rewarded you before she disappeared within the portal—

"Para que te miré, mujer divina;
  Para que contemplé tu faz hermosa?
  Y tu labio encendido, cual rosa
  Es mi delirio ..."

*   *   *   *   *

Otherwise, the distractions of the Mexican women are few. Yet our sweet damsel of the dark eyes and demure lips who daily enters her temple, applauds with her little gloved hands—with the approval and accompaniment of her mamma—the onslaught of the fierce bull at the bull-fight, and sees the torturing of the unfortunate horses as, their life-blood rushing forth, they expire in the arena before her. And the populace—ha! the populace of holiday *peones*—how frenziedly they shout! And the band plays a soft air, and the blue Mexican sky shimmers overhead. Love, blood, wine, dust—*O tempora! O mores!* This is Mexico; carrying into the twentieth century the romance of the Middle Ages, tinging her new civilisation still with the strong passions of the old, and refusing—whether unwisely, whether wisely, time shall show—to assimilate the doctrines of sheer commercialism whose votaries are hammering at her gates. But it is time now to review the cities and homes of this picturesque and developing people.

CHAPTER X

THE CITIES AND INSTITUTIONS OF MEXICO

Character of Mexican cities—Value of Mexican civilisation—Types of Mexican architecture—Mexican homes and buildings—The *Plaza*—Social relations of classes—The City of Mexico—Valley of Mexico—Latitude, elevation, and temperature—Buildings—Bird's-eye view—The lakes—Drainage works—Viga canal and floating gardens—General description—The cathedral—Art treasures—Religious orders—Chapultepec—Pasco de la Reforma—The President—Description of a bull-fight—Country homes and suburbs—Colleges, clubs, literary institutions—Churches and public buildings—Army and Navy—Cost of living—Police—Lighting and tramways—Canadian enterprise—British commercial relations—The American—United States influence—A general impression of Mexico.

Mexico is a land of numerous capital cities—far more numerous than those of any South American country. These cities are entirely distinct in type to the centres of population of Anglo-Saxon North America. Their structure, environment, atmosphere, are those of the Old World rather than the New—that is to say, if the cities of the United States and Canada are to be taken as American types.

Their character is that distinct Spanish-American one ever encountered in the countries which were the main centres of Spanish civilisation. Consequently there is much similarity between them. Standing in the Zocalo, or *plaza* of the City of Mexico, in front of the fine cathedral, we might imagine ourselves transported 2,500 miles, more or less, to the south-east, to the handsome city of Lima with its *plaza* and cathedral. But we may journey over the whole of Anglo-Saxon America, north of the Mexican border, and we shall find nothing similar.

The difference in character of the two nationalities of the Americas is plainly stamped upon their respective cities. The one is sealed with a hurried activity —the mark of the exigencies of commerce; the windows and doors of a business world, where men look out or emerge to the strife of money-making. Notwithstanding its wealth and solidity it bears a certain ephemeral stamp which the Mexican type does not convey. The atmosphere of this is one of serenity, of indifference to the feverish haste of money-getting, and its windows and doors give sight and footstep to less modern, less useful, perchance, but less evanescent a phase of civilisation. Let us theorise as we may, let us say what we will, about the progress of the world, but we continue to hope that the quiet civilisation of Spanish-America will preserve its character, for who can doubt that in the plan of nature there is some meaning in this preservation of a race which refuses to make the strife of commerce its main basis of progress.

History and tradition are stamped upon the façades of the stone-built cities of Mexico—religion and aristocracy have left their mark. They are cities of churches and convents, and of the abodes of the authoritative and the wealthy. They are far from being "republican" in aspect—that is, if the term is meant to convey the idea of democracy. The Governor's palace, the military *cuartel*, the ecclesiastical seat, form the centres from which the ordinary streets and life of the people radiate. The general structure and disposition of these cities is dignified and convenient. The dominant idea is the central *plaza*, upon whose four sides are the abodes of the authorities. First is the cathedral, whose façade takes up a whole side, or, if the place is not a capital, an extensive church—the *iglesia*—occupies the place of honour. Following this are the national or municipal palaces, where the public business is transacted, whilst on the opposite sides are clubs, shops, or other main centres of business or pleasure.

Generally, the upper storeys of the buildings in the *plaza*—except the ecclesiastical—overhang the footpaths, or, rather, are built over them, supported by the characteristic *portales*, or series of arches and pillars facing the roadway. This type of structure is prevalent in almost all the older Spanish-American cities. It is a feature of Mexican and Peruvian cities, and is encountered even in remote places such as Arequipa and Cuzco, the old Inca capital in the heart of the Andes, where it was introduced by the Spanish builders.

SPANISH-COLONIAL ARCHITECTURE: THE PORTALES OF CHOLULA.

A similar type of architecture, especially as regards the houses, characterises all Mexican cities and towns. The plan of town dwelling is that with interior *patio*, wide *saguan*, or entrance door, and windows covered with outside grilles, either of bars or of wrought-iron scrollwork. From this *patio*, which in the wealthier houses is paved with marble, the doorways of the lower apartments open. The houses are of two storeys, and access to the upper is gained by a broad staircase which terminates on a wide balcony, or, rather, gallery, above the *patio*. From this gallery the doors of the upper rooms open. A balustrade runs round the outer side of the gallery, and this is generally covered with flowering plants, ferns, and palms, in pots or tubs, which lend an air of coolness and luxury to the interior. Above, the *patio* is open to the sky, except that the overhanging roof of the house covers the gallery, from which it is supported by pillars. The whole arrangement is pleasing, and adapted to the climate, and the foreigner who has become accustomed to it finds that it possesses certain advantages which the houses of his own country do not enjoy.

On the other hand, this plan of building has grave drawbacks. The absence of a garden or grounds in front of, or surrounding the house, gives a restricted feeling. The main difference between an English and a Mexican house is that the Briton loves to cut off too-close intercourse with humanity by retiring his dwelling far from the road, whilst the Spanish-American builds his fronting immediately upon the street. In these houses, moreover, the rooms generally open one into the other, which is far from the Northerner's idea of privacy. This fact, indeed, is born of a race characteristic—the closer association between the members of families which obtains with the Latin race. The guest in these houses—somewhat to his embarrassment if he be an Englishman—sometimes finds a glass door, with no means of screening him from observation, the division between his apartment and that of some other —possibly a reception-room! Moreover, light and ventilation often seem quite secondary matters, for as a rule the rooms—in the case of the interior one—simply open on to the *patio* gallery above it if it be the second floor, with glass door and no windows. Consequently, if light or air are required, it is necessary to keep these open, and this is, of course, difficult at night. The Mexican thinks nothing of sleeping in a closed-up room all night, and shuts his doors and windows—where windows exist—and closes his shutters to the "dangers" of the outside air!

There are rarely fireplaces or stoves in Mexican houses. Of course, in the tropics these are not required, but in the cities of the uplands it is often bitterly cold. There is a popular belief that warming the air of a room by artificial heat in the rarefied air of the uplands induces pneumonia, but it is doubtful if this has any real foundation. And the Mexican prefers to shiver under cover of a *poncho*, rather than to sit in comfort and warmth, after the European or American fashion. On the other hand, the Englishman who has experienced the inveterate habit of overheating of the houses and offices of New York or other parts of the United States will prefer the Mexican method. Nothing is more trying to the Briton than the sudden change of temperature from the high-heated American office or house to the bitter cold of its winter streets, such conditions as prevail in the United States: or the overheating of American trains.

The architecture of Mexican cities is often of a solid and enduring type, especially the buildings of older construction; and many of these date from the time of the earlier viceroys. All public buildings and ecclesiastical edifices are of this nature. The modern buildings have, in some instances, followed out the same style, eminently suitable for the country, but others have adopted a bastard and incongruous so-called "modern" type, copied from similar structures in Europe or the United States, where pure utility of interior has been clothed with undignified exterior of commercial character, marking a certain spirit of transition in its inhabitants. This is partly due to the ruthless American industrial invasion, which, whilst it has valuable elements for the country, should not be allowed to stamp a shoddy modernism upon the more dignified antiquity of environment. This tendency, however, has not yet had time to show itself, except in a few instances in the capital. Nevertheless, some portions of the City of Mexico have already been spoilt by the speculative Anglo-American builder, who has generally called himself an architect in order to perpetrate appalling rows of cheap *adobe* houses or pretentious-looking villas, made of the slimmest material and faced with that sin-covering cloak of *tepetatl*, or plaster "staff." Even some of the principal streets of the capital have been disfigured with hideous pretentious business structures, for which the Anglo-American element, whether in fact or example, has been responsible. If the Mexicans are wise they will sternly refuse to adopt much of steel construction or of "staff" and corrugated iron covering imported from the north, but to limit their buildings to native materials of stone or brick and their elevation to two or, at most, three storeys. The skyscraper is at home in New York or Chicago; in Mexico (or in London) it is the abomination of desolation. In San Francisco the outraged earth endeavoured to shake them off a year or so ago in an earthquake! An attractive feature of Mexican houses is the flat roofs, or *azoteas*. These are often made accessible from the interior and adorned with plants and flowers, and even the heavy rain-storms of certain regions do not seem to influence this type of construction or demand the rapid watershed of the gabled roof. During the time of the conquest of the City of Mexico these *azoteas* formed veritable coigns of vantage for the Aztecs, who poured down a hail of darts and stones upon the besiegers.

The *plaza* of the Spanish-American city is its main centre. Thence the principal streets emerge, and there, upon its prettily planted and shady promenade foregather the people to listen to the *serenata*, or playing of the band on frequent occasions. The Mexicans are passionately fond of music, and a wise governmental sentiment has found that it is a useful part of government. Therefore it is decreed that the bands shall play, free of cost, to the multitude. In some cities the plaza-promenade has two paved footpaths adjoining each other—the inner for the *élite* and well-dressed class, the outer for the *peon* and Indian class. It would be manifestly impossible that the hordes of blanket-clothed, *pulque*-saturated, ill-smelling, and picturesque lower class could rub shoulders with the *gente decente* or upper class, nor do they desire to do so. They take their fill of the music quite indifferent to the presence of their superiors in the social grade, and the vendors of native sweetmeats, cooling drinks, and fruits ply their trade among them. On one side of the plaza, in the smaller towns, there are booths or tables where food is being cooked and displayed for the lower orders; and the savoury odour of *frijoles* and *tortillas*, or other matters of satisfaction to the *peon*, greet the nostrils of the promenader from time to time. The well-dressed *señoritas* and their male acquaintances, with ceaseless *charla*, or small-talk, promenade round and round the plaza, flirting, laughing, and enjoying life in a way that seems only possible to the Latin race. Indeed, the plaza is the principal meeting-place of the sexes.

As has been remarked, Mexico is a land of many capital cities. From the City of Mexico, northward along the plateau and southward, eastward, and westward, we may visit a score of handsome State capitals, a hundred towns, and an endless succession of remote villages and hamlets. Their environments embrace every change of scenery—from arid plains and rocky steeps to fertile valleys; and the larger communities share the quaint—if not always hygienic—disposition and atmosphere of their especial national character. At times, however, the smaller hamlets, or collection of primitive habitations of the plateau, have an inexpressibly dreary and squalid aspect, the backwardness and poverty of their people being well stamped thereon. Treeless, dusty, and *triste*, they strike a note of melancholy within us. The towns of the Pacific and Gulf slopes have generally some added charm afforded by the tropic vegetation surrounding them, and we shall often mark with surprise, after days of dusty and arduous journeying, that we have suddenly entered a handsomely built town, sequestered far from beaten routes of travel, yet bearing a stamp of permanence and solidity and the air of an independent entity.

A PUBLIC GARDEN IN TROPICAL MEXICO: VIEW AT COLIMA.

The first city of importance in the country is, of course, the Federal capital of the Republic, with its population of 369,000 inhabitants.

Standing towards the southern extremity of the great plateau of Anahuac, reposing in a beautiful valley full of natural resources, and rich with historic lore, is the City of Mexico. Of singular and varied interest is this capital of the prosperous North American Republic whose name it bears, for its geographical situation and historical associations are such as assign it a leading place among the great centres of Spanish-American civilisation.

In many respects the capital of Mexico may be considered the queen city of Latin America. Buenos Ayres is much larger and of greater importance as a centre of population, but it has not Mexico's history and tradition. The commerce of Santiago and Valparaiso are potent factors in the life of the Pacific coast, but the Chilean capital and seaport are but modern creations in comparison with the old city of the land of Anahuac. Only Lima, the beautiful and interesting capital of her sister nation—Peru—is comparable with Mexico as a centre of historical tradition and Spanish-American culture. Of course, the City of Mexico with its large population is much larger than Lima, with less than 150,000.

Indeed, there are many points of similarity between Mexico and Peru, such as have been discussed elsewhere, and which are the common knowledge of the student, but the City of Mexico possesses a special interest in that it was actually the seat of a prehistoric American civilisation—that of the Aztecs—whilst its position between the great oceans which bathe the American coasts, give it a value for the future of untold possibilities.

The Valley of Mexico, wherein the capital is situated, is a broad elevated plain, or basin, surrounded by hills, which culminate far away to the south-east in the snow-clad summits of Popocatepetl and Ixtaccihuatl—the extinct volcanoes of the Sierra Madre. The combined conditions of its latitude and elevation above sea-level—19° 26 N., 99° 7 W., and 7,410 feet—have dowered it with an agreeable and salubrious climate, with an annual range of temperature from 60° F. to 75° F. The mornings are cool and bracing, often bitterly cold indeed; whilst the midday sun is often hot, and the Mexican stays within the cool of his thick-walled house, for it is the hour of *siesta*. Excessive extremes of heat and cold are not encountered, although at night the Mexican gladly dons his velvet-lined cape, and the foreigner his overcoat, whilst the poor *peon* shrouds himself in his *serape*.

The city is one of handsome buildings, wide streets, and fine avenues. Its architecture bears the stamp of its Spanish origin—the typical and picturesque façades of the houses, the grille-covered windows, the balconies looking on to the streets, and other characteristic features well known to the traveller in Spanish-America. The great plaza, ever the pulse and centre of these communities, is known here as the Zocalo; and this ample square is that same one around which the Aztec city—the famous Tenochtitlan—was built, upon whose foundations the Mexican capital arose.

The plan of the city is more or less the geometrically regular one of main and cross-streets running at right angles to each other, and the principal of these are lined with shops, whose windows display luxurious articles of jewellery, clothing, and other effects such as betoken the taste and purchasing power of a wealthy upper class. It is a city of domes and towers, which rise above the surrounding roofs, and convey that aspect of charm and refinement unknown to the purely business cities of Anglo North America. The strong part which the Church has played is shown by the numerous and handsome churches in every quarter of the city. There are more than one hundred and twenty churches and other edifices which were built and formerly occupied for ecclesiastical purposes. The cathedral is the dominating structure, and its two great towers, nearly 200 feet high, are conspicuous from any point of view.

Let us behold this pleasing city from afar before examining more in detail the institutions and habitations of its people. The environs of the capital form a good setting to its beauty. Taking our stand on the range of hills which bound the Valley of Mexico, our eyes rest upon the cultivated fields and gardens of the smaller towns which dot the plain and lead up to the central mass. Green meadows, running streams, great plantation of *maguey*, giving their characteristic semi-tropical aspect to the landscape, surround *haciendas* and villages embowered in luxuriant foliage, all lying beneath the azure vault of the Mexican sky. The gleam of domes and towers, softened in the glamour of the distance, catches our eyes; and the reposeful atmosphere and mediæval tints seem to belie the strife of its past, or even the incidents of its modern industrial life. There is the Castle of Chapultepec surrounded by trees, the beautiful and venerable *ahuahuetes*, or cypresses, surmounting its hill—the Aztec "Hill of the Grasshoppers" where Montezuma's palace was, and where stands the fine structure reared by the viceroys, now the official residence of the Presidents of Mexico of to-day. And there lies Guadalupe gleaming in the sun, with its famous shrine of miraculous visions and cures—the Lourdes of Mexico. There lie Tacubaya, San Angel, and Tlalpam, luxurious and aristocratic suburban homes of Mexico's wealthy citizens, surrounded by their exuberant vegetation on fertile hillsides mid soft and soothing colour and balmy atmosphere. From the pine-clad hills whereon we stand, which form the rim of this singular valley, the whole panorama is open to the view, of lakes and flat plain, the latter crossed by the dusty roads cut by centuries of traffic through the white *adobe* soil, giving access to the surrounding villages and the serried lines of the *maguey* plantations, or the chess-board chequers of dark green *alfalfa*, lighter barley, and yellow *maiz*. And from plain and dusty road, and vivid *hacienda* and city domes and whitened walls, our gaze rises to the clear-cut, snowy crest of "The Sleeping Woman," Ixtaccihuatl, in her gleaming porcelain sheen, where she hoards the treasures of the snow, reminding us of the peaks of the great South American Cordillera, to whose system she and her consort Popocatepetl are but a more recent addition. Like legendary sentinels of a vanished past, they seem to overwatch the valley.

The Valley of Mexico is a flat plain, in the lowest portion of which the City of Mexico is situated, two or three miles from Lake Texcoco. The plain consists of lands barren and lands cultivated, marshes and swamps, all intersected by numerous streams falling into the lakes, as well as irrigation and drainage canals, whilst on the rising ground which appears in places the volcanic understructure is laid bare, often in the form of great lava sheets. The group of lakes have been elsewhere described in these pages. Lake Texcoco, whose shores are now distant from the city, is a dreary waste of brackish water with scarcely any fish-life, inhabited by water-fowl at certain seasons. During the period of overflow its rising waters cover many added square miles of ground, but in the dry season the water recedes, leaving saline-covered marshes of desolate aspect. Lakes Chalco and Xochimilco, however, are very different in their regimen and aspect. They are of fresh water, and stand at an elevation some 10 feet higher than Texcoco, into which they discharge. Fertile meadows surround these, and Xochimilco is now, as it was at the time of the Conquest, a "Field of Flowers," which is the meaning of its native nomenclature, not unworthy of the designation of an "earthly paradise," which the modern Mexicans bestow upon it.

THE VALLEY OF MEXICO: THE GREAT DRAINAGE CANAL.

The position of the City of Mexico near Lake Texcoco, which receives the waters of all the other lakes of the system, has ever rendered it liable to inundation, and to a saturated and unhealthy subsoil, conditions which, were it not for the healthy atmosphere of the bracing uplands whereon the valley is situated, would undoubtedly make for a high death-rate. The drainage and control of the waters of the valley have formed matters of thought for Mexico's successive Governments for more than four centuries. Work to this end was begun under Montezuma in 1449, nearly three-quarters of a century before the Conquest. During the colonial *régime* further works were undertaken, in 1553, to replace those destroyed by Cortes, followed by other works in 1604 and 1708. But only after the Republican *régime* was established was the work carried to completion, upon a plan brought forward by a Mexican engineer. These works, which were mainly carried out during the closing years of last century by English firms of engineers and contractors,[28] consist of a canal and tunnel. The canal is thirty miles long, flowing from the city and bearing its sewage and storm-waters, and taking the overflow from Lake Texcoco: and discharging thence into a tunnel, perforating the rim of the valley, about six and a half miles long. This in turn empties into a discharge conduit and a ravine, and the waters, after having served for purposes of irrigation and for actuating a hydro-electric station, fall into an affluent of the Panuco river and so into the Gulf of Mexico. This work, which is the climax of the attempts of four hundred years or more, reflects much credit upon its constructors and the Government of Diaz, which financed it at a total cost of sixteen million Mexican dollars.

28 S. Pearson & Sons, Ltd., London, and Read, Campbell & Co.

An Aztec hydraulic work of the Valley of Mexico is the Viga Canal, which leads from the Indian quarter of the city, crossing swamps, plantations, and waste lands to Xochimilco, the "Field of Flowers." Along this canal ply daily primitive canoes and punts laden with vegetables, flowers, and other produce for the native market. The floating gardens, or *chinampas*, far-famed of Mexico, are encountered upon this canal. But, alas! the "floating gardens" do not float, nor is it possible to prove that they ever did, in plain, prosaic fact. They consist of areas of spongy soil intersected by numerous irrigation ditches, where the traveller may observe the Indian owners industrially watering them and tending their profuse array of flowers and vegetables. New "floating gardens" are sometimes made by the method of driving stakes into the shallow bottom of the lake, winding rushes about them and filling in with the fertile mud.

The city itself is surrounded on all sides, except that leading to Chapultepec, by miles of squalid streets, where dwell the poor and outcast of the community—and their name is legion. Yet these surroundings, if squalid, are less painful than the frightful East End dens of London, or the appalling Bowery and east side of New York. American cities, whether North or South, have produced nothing in their boasted march towards "liberty," which is an alleviation for the proletariat, above the cities of Europe. These mean yet picturesque streets give place as we enter to those inhabited by the better class, whose dwellings generally exist side by side and interspersed with the shops and commercial establishments, after the general fashion of Spanish-American cities. This is indeed a notable feature of their regimen. Here is the old home of a former viceroy or of a modern grandee, cheek by jowl with a little bread or liquor shop; its handsome doorway, worthy of study, but a few paces away from the humble entrance of the *tienda* aforesaid. The names of some of Mexico's streets and squares are reminiscent of the past or of fanciful story and legend and heroic incident. Here is the *puente de* Alvarado, formerly the Teolticalli, or Toltec canal; here the street of the *Indio triste*, or that of the *Niño perdido*; the "sad Indian" and the "lost child" respectively. Redolent of the Mexico of the viceroys, of political intrigue, of love and *liasons*, of the cloak and the dagger, are some of the old streets, balconies, and portals of Mexico. Here the Spanish cavalier, with sword and muffling cape, stalked through the gloom to some intrigue of love or villainy, and here passed cassocked priest and barefooted friars, long years ago. Here sparkling eyes looked forth from some twilight lattice what time from the street below arose the soft notes of a serenading guitar. As to the sparkling eyes and the serenading lover and the balconies, these are not gone; they are imperishable in Mexico. Here is a description of Mexico of years ago—the Mexico of the viceroys—which I will translate freely from the description of a Mexican writer of to-day, and which in some respects might almost describe the city at the present time: "Hail, mediæval city, redolent of sentimental recollections and romantic impressions such as well might be the creation of fantastic romance! Clustered with monasteries and convents, turreted dwellings and sombre monuments, bathed in an atmosphere of orisons and melancholy, threaded by foul and ill-paved alleys, made for crime, intrigue, and mystery; where buried in the profundity of night love and wickedness both stalked forth; strange temples and niches lit by twinkling lamps before the images of saints; recollections of diabolical Inquisitorial rites—a romantic and fantastic shroud, dissipated now, torn into shreds by the iron hand of destiny, and banished or transfigured by the torch of progress!"

THE CATHEDRAL OF THE CITY OF MEXICO.

As has been said, the construction of the houses of Mexico was of solid type, with walls such as might serve for fortresses rather than dwellings, and when from necessity, some old building is demolished it can only be performed by the aid of dynamite. So builded the Spaniards, and their work will outlast the more ephemeral structures of to-day. Indeed, at the beginning of the colonial period and throughout the sixteenth century, the buildings actually were constructed both as dwellings and fortresses. At the end of that century a greater refinement of architectural art appeared—as a natural outcome of corresponding conditions in Spain—in the colonies. The great cathedral of Mexico was constructed, due to a mandate of Philip II. It was dedicated in 1667, but not concluded until the beginning of the nineteenth century, and into its façade enter the Doric, Ionic, and Corinthian orders. It is an exceedingly handsome building, both interiorily and exteriorily, and it stands upon the spot where the great Aztec *teocalli* stood—the shrine of the abominable war-god of the early Mexicans. The edifice stands upon the soft subsoil of which the city's foundation is composed, softness which has caused the subsidence of other buildings; but the cathedral, although it has suffered somewhat from earthquake shocks, stands firm and solid as ever. Valuable art treasures exist within, among the pictures being a Murillo, and possibly a

Velasquez. So numerous are these old pictures that they overlap each other upon the walls. The cathedral is nearly 400 feet long, and its interior rises upon twenty splendid Doric columns for 180 feet, whilst the apices of the great towers are 204 feet above the pavement. But this splendid temple—as is often the case with the cathedrals of Spanish-American capitals—is not the fashionable or aristocratic resort of Mexico's religious people. Nevertheless, its aisles are generally thronged, and the highborn and expensively attired lady and the poor *peon* woman, with her modest *rebosa*, or shawl, may be seen side by side kneeling upon its knee-worn floor, whilst before the images in the seven chapels of its aisles there are never wanting supplicating figures, nor the numerous little written supplications pinned upon their altar rails.

It would be endless to describe the other numerous ecclesiastical buildings and temples of the City of Mexico. Their number and beauty are indicative of the strength and rooted persistence of religion and monastic orders in New Spain. Among the principal of these Orders and the dates at which their corresponding habitations were erected, were those of the Franciscans, 1524; Dominicans, 1526; Augustinians, 1533; Jesuits, 1572; Carmelites, 1585; and various others, with numerous convents.

The principal commercial and fashionable street of Mexico City is that of Plateros, somewhat narrow and congested, but full of high-class shops. Thence it continues along Bucareli[29] and the broad Avenida de Juarez, which in turn is continued by the famous Paseo de la Reforma, a splendid drive and promenade of several miles in length, which terminates at the Castle of Chapultepec. This great road is planted throughout its length with trees and adorned with a profusion—almost too great—of statues, and along both sides are private houses of modern construction. These are less picturesque, but more comfortable, than the old Spanish-built dwellings before described, although at times somewhat bizarre in their façades, with a certain *nouveau riche* air, consequent upon the transition period of Mexican life of recent years. The beautiful monument and statue of Guatemoc is planted in this avenue, and is worthily deemed a successful embodiment of Aztec art sculptured by modern chisels. Upon Sunday morning—the fashionable time of *serenata* or promenade concert—the wealth and beauty of the capital foregather in carriages and upon foot and listen to the strains of the band. Here we may, from the seats of our victoria, observe the Mexican upper class at our—and their—ease. Hats off! A private carriage comes driving swiftly by; its coachman attired after the English fashion, and the whole equipage of similar character. In it is a well-dressed gentleman well past the middle age, with dark complexion and characteristic features. It is the citizen-President, the redoubtable General Diaz, and the universal salutations are evidence of his popularity. The air is balmy and the warmth of the sun pleasant. But at any moment these conditions may change, and a ruthless dust-storm, swept by the wind from the dry *adobe* plains surrounding the city, descend upon us, the fine dust covering our clothes and bidding us direct our coachman to turn his horses' heads towards our hotel. This, however, is not frequent, but when it does occur it brings a certain sense of disillusion akin to that felt by the British holiday-maker when he has gone down to an English seaside place to enjoy the balmy air and finds a bitter east wind blowing!

29 Named after the viceroy who caused its construction.

But the bull-fight—ha! the bull-fight—takes place this—Sunday—afternoon, for this is the Mexican Sunday sport: a kind of licence, possibly, after the numerous *misas* of the early morning! We have purchased our seat in the *sombra* of the great bull-ring, and the *corrida* is about to begin. Let us glance round the assembly of many thousands of persons. The seats of the great amphitheatre are divided into two classes—the *sol* and the *sombra*, "sun" and "shade." That is to say, that the seats in the shady portion—for the structure is open to the sky—are of one class, and command a high price of, say, ten *pesos* each, whilst the sun-beat portion is of an inferior class, and price, say, one *peso*. It is a sea of faces we gaze upon, the *élite* of the city in the *sombra*, and the lower classes, the *peones* and others, in the *sol*.

The arena is empty, but suddenly a bugle-call sounds from the judges' platform, and the *picadores*, men on horseback, with their legs protected by armour and bearing sharp-pointed lances in their hands, enter and ride around the arena, bowing to the judges and assembled multitude, who receive them with plaudits. Again a bugle-call, and the sliding doors leading from the *corral* are opened, and a bull, bounding forward therefrom, stops short a moment and eyes the assembled multitude and the men on horseback with wrathful yet inquiring eye. A moment only. Sniffing the air and lashing his tail, the noble bovine rushes forward and engages the *picadores*; the little pennants of the national colours, which, attached to a barbed point, have been jabbed into his back by an unseen hand as he passed the barrier, fluttering in the wind created by his rush. Furiously he charges the *picadores*. If they are clever they goad him to madness with their lances, keeping him at bay; if he is resolute down go horse and man—both results tickling the popular fancy immensely—and those frightful horns are buried deep in the bowels of the unfortunate steed, which, maddened with agony and fright, leaps up and tears around the arena, trampling perhaps upon his own entrails which have gushed forth from the gaping wound! At times the wound is hastily sewn up, and the unfortunate horse, with a man behind him with a heavy whip, another tugging at the bridle, and the *picador* on his back with his enormous spurs, forces the trembling brute to face the savage bull again, whilst the audience once more roars out its applause. As many as ten horses are killed or ruined at times by a single bull, who returns again and again to plunge his horns into the prostrate carcase ere it is dragged away. This is sport!

BULL-FIGHT IN THE CITY OF MEXICO, SHOWING THE SPECTATORS OF THE "SOL," THE PICADORES, AND THE ENTERING BULL.

But perhaps the bull himself is faint-hearted! Then, indeed, the noble Spanish blood of the audience is aroused to fever pitch. "*Otro toro! Otro toro*"—"Another bull! bring another bull!"—rises from a thousand throats. Otherwise the other acts of the performance take their course, and the *banderilleros*, bull-fighters armed with short gaudily decorated spears with barbed points, come on. Some "pretty" play now ensues, the *banderilleros* constantly facing the bull at arm's length with the object of gracefully sticking the spears or *banderillas* in the neck of the animal, where, if successful, they hang dangling as, smarting with the pain, the bull tears round the arena, to the accompaniment of the delighted roar of the crowd. This scene is repeated again and again, until perhaps several pairs of *banderillas* are depending from the shoulders of the maddened animal. The *capeadores* have not been idle, and the bull, repeatedly charging them and meeting only the empty flapping of the *capas*—the scarlet cloaks which the bull-fighters charged with this office wield—works himself into a paroxysm of rage, which must be seen to be understood. Oftentimes the *capeadores* are severely injured; sometimes killed in the act by a terrific stroke of the bull's horns.

But hark! once more a bugle-call, strong and sonorous, from the judges' box; the well-known notes which call the *espada* to his task; the last act in the drama—for drama it is. The *espada* is the most famous bull-fighter of all. His salary is a princely one; his reputation extends over two continents, from Old Madrid to Old Mexico. He is the great star in all that richly-dressed galaxy of *toreros*—for their gorgeous silver and gold spangled attire baffles description—and all his *compañeros* are but lesser lights, paling before his name and powers. And now the band, which has hitherto sent forth joyous music, plays a sad and mournful air. The *espada* takes the sword from an attendant and examines and curves it with critical and expert eye. Then, taking off his gold and silver-embroidered cocked-hat, he bows low towards the judges and to the fair ladies of the *sombra*; and in fitting phrase "dedicates" the stroke he is about to perform to them. Or otherwise, with his hand upon his heart, he turns towards the occupants of the *sol*, and again bowing low dedicates the coming stroke and the doomed bull thus: "*Al Querido Pueblo!*"—"To the beloved people"! A hush falls upon the great assembly: a pin might be heard to drop: the bull, who during these preliminaries—somewhat fatigued but full of life and anger—has been standing in the arena with his attention diverted by the *capeadores*, is now left to face his doom at the hands of the expert *espada*. Bull and man slowly approach, eyeing each other as those whose quarrel is to the death, whilst the notes of the music sound low and mournful. Within arm's length the *espada* extends his shining blade. He glances along it; the bull leaps forward to charge; there is a swift thrust; the blade goes home in that fatal spot which only the expert knows; and tottering, swaying, and falling, the noble bull leans over and falls prone to the dust. He raises his head with a last effort; the *espada* rushes forward, places his foot upon the prostrate neck, and, exerting a mighty strength, draws forth the scarlet, dripping blade, and a crimson stream of life-blood spurts forth from the wound, whilst the animal, making "the sign of the cross" with its forefoot upon the sand, lowers his noble crest—dead!

Then are the bounds of pandemonium let loose. How the audience of the *sol* shrieks and cheers! Hats, sticks, cloaks, belts, even money, are thrown into the arena like hail, and nothing is too good for the successful *espada* and the idol of the moment. Even the dignified *sombra* shouts itself hoarse, and at times showers bank-notes and jewellery down, and perhaps—let it be whispered low, for it is not unknown!—a billet-doux or *papelito* for the brave *torero* from some newly-created female admirer. Grave gentlemen in frock-coats and ladies in elegant attire, on the one hand, discuss the points of the entertainment, whilst the red *serapes* of the *peones* and *pelados* and their great *sombreros* rush animatedly to and fro. The band plays, the crowd pours into the street, and the long shadows fall from the blue Mexican sky across the dust of their departure, whilst a team of horses drag forth the quivering flesh of the vanquished bull to the *corral*, and the Sabbath Day draws to its close.

The Mexican upper and middle class share the general Spanish-American characteristic of preference for life in their cities. Expeditions into the country are matters to be avoided if possible. The gilded youth of the capital and members of polite society generally, do not like to leave the conveniences of good pavements, restaurants, fashionable bars and clubs and the like, and to venture into the hot sun or cold winds of the country regions. It is true, however, that there is a certain exodus to their *haciendas* of the upper-class families in the season corresponding thereto; but the love of the country for its own sake, or for sport, exercise, or exploration, as understood by Englishmen, is unknown. There are no country houses, as in Great Britain, where wealthy people reside because they prefer it; for the Mexican prefers to live in the main streets of his cities, the great doorway of his *patio* and his barred windows opening and looking immediately on to the streets.

On the other hand, the wealthy inhabitant of the capital often lives in the quaint and beautiful towns adjacent thereto, and reached by rail or electric car with a few miles' journey. Such places are Tacubaya, San Angel, Tlalpam, and others, and here spacious and picturesque stone houses—some of considerable age—surrounded by luxuriant gardens where oranges, pomegranates, and other semi-tropical *flora* lend shade and beauty, attest the wealth and taste of their inhabitants. Serene and old-world is the atmosphere surrounding these "palaces"—for some are worthy of this designation—and with their environment of summer sky and glorious landscape they form real oases of that romantic and luxurious character which the foreigner in his fancy has attributed to Mexico, but which he fails to encounter in the newer quarters of the city.

To treat at much length of the numerous institutions and buildings of the capital would be to fill a volume. The parks, monuments, museums, art gallery, public library, theatres, hygienic establishments, hospitals, prisons, new drainage-system, pure water-supply, national palaces and public buildings, colleges, schools, clubs: mining, engineering, medical science, and art institutions: all mark the character of the people as lovers of progress, art, and science, with strongly developed literary and artistic perceptions and idealistic aims, which they are striving to apply to the good of their people, as far as circumstances render it possible. All the machinery of State affairs and municipal and social life are excellently ordered theoretically, and in time may be expected to work out in general practice to a fuller extent.

Education is provided for by compulsory primary instruction throughout the Republic, and by preparatory and professional schools and colleges in the capital, all of which are free. The principal of these latter in the capital are the Preparatory College, or High School, providing a general curriculum; the College of Jurisprudence, devoted to law and sociology; the Medical College, to medicine and kindred subjects; the School of Engineering, whether civil, mining, electrical, or all other branches of that profession, which is looked upon as a very important one; School of Agriculture; School of Commerce; School of Fine Arts; Conservatory of Music; Schools of Arts and Trades, for boys and girls respectively; Normal Colleges, for men and women respectively. All these educational institutions are supported by the Federal Government in the capital, by which it is seen that the Mexican nation is holding forth good opportunity to its citizens for acquiring knowledge. Notwithstanding these facilities the education of the lower classes proceeds but slowly, and at present less than 13 per cent. of the entire population can read and write. It is to be recollected, however, that the great bulk of the population consist of the *peones* and the Indians, and the conditions of the life of these render the acquisition of education by them often impossible. Knowledge cannot else but slowly unfold for the indigenous peoples of Spanish-America, weighed down as they are by conditions of race, caste, and inherited and imposed social burdens.

MEXICAN STREET SCENE: A PULQUE SHOP WITH ARTISTICALLY-PAINTED EXTERIOR.

Prominent among the literary, scientific, and art institutions of Mexico City are the Geographical Society, the oldest of all, founded in 1833; the Geological Society; the Association of Engineers and Architects; Society of Natural History; the five Academies of Medicine, Jurisprudence, Physical and Natural Science, Spanish Language, Social Science, respectively; also the Antonio Alzate Scientific Society and the Pedro Escobedo Medical Society. Of museums and galleries are the Academy of San Carlos, with fine specimens of European and Mexican art, among the former of which are works by Velasquez, Murillo, Ribera, and others attributed to Rubens, Leonardo da Vinci, Van Dyck, &c. The National Museum, which was founded in 1865, is an important and interesting institution, in which are preserved the famous archæological and ethnological objects and collections illustrative of prehistoric Mexico. It was founded in 1865, and attracts Mexican and foreign visitors to the annual number of nearly a quarter of a million. The famous prehistoric Calendar Stone is preserved here.[30] There are various other museums devoted to special subjects. Of libraries, the *Biblioteca Nacional* ranks first—a handsome building with 365,000 volumes for public use. The building is a massive stone structure, and was originally built for a church. A garden surrounds it, and upon the stone pillars of the enclosure are busts of Mexicans and Aztecs famous in history, as Ixtlilxochitl, Tezozomoc, Nezahualcoyotl, the king-poet; Clavijero, the historian, and others. Other libraries are maintained by various museums and professions.

30 Also the Aztec sacrificial stone.

There are some sixty or more Catholic churches in the city, and numerous other buildings formerly of ecclesiastical purpose. Most of these were built during the colonial *régime,* the Spanish Renaissance being the prevailing style. Several Protestant places of worship exist—religious observance being absolutely free—and these include Episcopalians, Presbyterians, Methodists, Baptists, and others. The religious census, made in 1900, of the whole of the Republic gave thirteen and a half million persons declaring themselves as Catholics, about 52,000 Protestants, 1,500 Mormons, 2,000 Buddhists, and about 19,000 who made no statement of religious faith.

There are some twelve hospitals, asylums, and kindred establishments for the afflicted, in the capital or Federal districts, as public charities, and eight of a private nature, including the benevolent societies and hospitals of the various foreign colonies, as the Americans, Spanish, and others. Among the semi-charitable or benevolent institutions must be mentioned the famous Monte de Piedad, or National Pawnshop, which, as its name implies, carries on the business of such for the benefit of poor people, who thus avoid the usurious rates of interest of private pawnbrokers. This worthy institution was founded in 1775, by Terreros, Count of Regla, of mining fame, and during a single month of 1907 the establishment and its branches loaned money to the people against articles to the amount of nearly half a million *pesos*. Of penal establishments the Penitentiary, opened in 1900, at a cost of about two and a half million *pesos*, ranks first. It has a strict scientific *régime* for its inmates, with more than seven hundred cells for convicts and others.

Some of the public buildings are good types of structure of the colonial period. Among these is the Palacio Nacional, spacious and massive, but monotonous and plain in its outward appearance. Here the Government business is transacted, and this edifice occupies a whole side of the Zocalo, or Plaza de Armas, with a long arcade of the characteristic *portales*, or arches, facing the square, above the footpath. It is of historic interest, having sheltered nearly all Mexican rulers from Montezuma onwards, Cortes, the viceroys, Iturbide, Maximilian, and all the Presidents in succession. The Palacio Municipal is a somewhat similar structure also facing the plaza, and not far away is the handsome building known as Mineria—the School of Mines—which was founded by royal edict in 1813. This building, unfortunately, has subsided somewhat into the soft subsoil. Within its spacious hall an enormous meteorite confronts the view, brought there from a distant part of the country, entire. The Geological Institute is another public building of kindred nature. The famous Castle of Chapultepec, embowered in its cypresses, and surrounded by its handsome park, is at a distance of two miles away along the Paseo de la Reforma, before described, and serves both as a summer residence for the President and as a military academy. Around it is a public park. Here it was that the heroic incident of the American War took place, of the young Mexican military cadets and the national standard, which has been touched upon in the historical chapter. A monument is erected here to their memory. A new post-office was opened in the capital, in 1907, at a cost of three million *pesos*, to cope with the growing postal business of the Republic. Among the numerous public squares and gardens of the city is the Alameda, dating from the time of Spanish rule. Six theatres of good class and other minor ones attest the play-going inclinations of the Mexicans, and a grand opera-house is in course of construction out of the national exchequer, which is designed to bear comparison with that of Paris. The Governments of Mexico, like those of Spanish-America generally, consider it a natural part of their function to support popular amusements of a refined nature. The foreigner might feel called on to remark that this laudable motive might well be brought to bear upon bull-fights, lotteries, and other institutions of a kindred nature! The chief evil of the bull-fight is that it keeps alive the love of the sight of bloodshed, which is naturally too strong in the Mexican *peon* without artificial stimulation, and its brutalising tendency must go far to offset the good effects of education and musical entertainment. As for the lotteries, they constitute a bad moral; the petty gambling and principle of hoping to obtain something for nothing is evil, and they are banned by all truly civilised nations.

The chief club and sport centre of the wealthy Mexicans is the Jockey Club, in a handsome old building in the plaza of Guardiola, and it is considered a mark of distinction by the foreigner to be invited as visiting member to this institution. The British and the American Colonies each have comfortable club-houses, the Spanish their casino, and the French and Germans their respective centres.

The Army of Mexico consists of some 28,000 officers and men, efficient and disciplined, on a footing far superior to the dilapidated soldiery that the traveller generally observes in, and ascribes to, Spanish-America. The rank and file have that remarkable power of performing long marches and heavy work on short rations, which characterises the Spanish-American native soldier in times of stress. Their officers receive an excellent training, and the military schools are considered to take high rank as such. Every citizen, by law, is obliged to serve in the army, but this is not necessarily carried out, and needless to say the upper class, except as officers, do not figure therein. A picturesque and remarkably efficient body of men are the *rurales*, exceedingly expert horsemen, who range the country, and whose work of the last few decades has entirely wiped out the prevalent highway-robbery of earlier years. Mexico's Navy is small: she does not require a large one, and it consists at present of two training ships, five gunboats, and two transports.

MEXICAN ARTILLERY: A WAYSIDE ENCAMPMENT.

The cost of living in the capital, like all other cities, varies much according to style, but in general it may be considered high. Even native produce is not cheap necessarily, whilst imported goods are very expensive. Correspondingly high is the rent of houses or flats. The houses of Mexico City are very generally constructed and let as *viviendas*, or flats, usually of about six rooms to each floor, a time-honoured arrangement among all classes. Such a flat, according to its position, costs from £5 to £15 per month; and a private house, such as in England would rent at, say, £200 per annum, or, say, £300 in the United States, brings £50 per month in Mexico City, whilst the rents in the suburbs, and those of business establishments are scarcely less. Such property is always expected to yield 12 to 15 per cent. per annum upon the investment. The values of landed property or real estate in the city have risen in an unprecedented manner of late years, from a few cents per square yard a few years ago to 30s. or 50s. per square yard at present, and they are still rising. The cost of building is also exceedingly high. These conditions refer, of course, to the capital. Elsewhere values are often exceedingly low.

The capital and the Federal District, which is that containing the city and its suburban towns, are administered by *Ayuntamientos*, or Municipal Councils, with Boards of Health and Department of Public Works. The city is policed by mounted and unmounted *gendarmes*, a total of some 2,300, and travellers may bear witness to the vigilance and courtesy of these officials. Whilst the ordinary *gendarmes* are recruited from the Indian class largely, they are efficient. The British traveller finds them as obliging as London police, in their more humble sphere, and the American is startled at the possibilities of official courtesy after the rude and aggressive policemen of the United States. The water-supply of the city belongs to the Federal authorities, and is being augmented from the springs of Xochimilco, as the present amount *per capita* of 137 litres is not sufficient. The new works will ensure a *per capita* supply of 400 litres, for a population of 550,000 inhabitants. The lighting of the city and suburbs is by electricity, and is efficiently performed, giving the capital the reputation of being an excellently illumined community. A Canadian Company, the Mexican Light and Power Company, holds the contract for this work. The drainage and sewerage of the capital form a fine modern sanitation system, which has recently been completed at a cost of nearly six million *pesos*; and these works, in connection with the great drainage canal and tunnel already described, form one of the most perfect systems in the world, and a point of interest to visitors.

The system of electric tramways embodies more than 100 miles of line, and gives an efficient urban service as well as furnishing communication with the suburbs and residential towns, as Tacubaya, San Angel, Tlalpam, Guadalupe, and others. There are still some 40 miles of mule-car in operation, such as a few years ago existed over the whole system. The mules were kept going at a gallop over these lines by the incessant thwacking and shouts of the drivers, and the modern system, if less picturesque, is more humane and speedier. The Mexicans, both upper and lower class, are inveterate travellers—many of the latter simply journey on the cars for amusement—and, picturesque and ill-smelling, they crowd the third-class coaches on every journey. In the year 1907 a total of nearly 65 million passengers were carried. The enterprise is in the hands of Canadians—The Mexico Tramways Company, in connection with the Mexico Electric Tramways, Limited, a British corporation. The great plaza, the Zocalo, presents an animated scene with the numerous starting and stopping cars on their incessant journey; and the figures of the saints upon the cathedral façade gaze stonily down upon the electric flashes from the trolley line, whilst the native *peon* and Indian on the cars has not yet ceased wondering what power it is "that makes them go"!

Life in the City of Mexico for the foreigner contains much of varied interest and colour, although he or she will have to support with philosophy much that is incident upon its peculiar character. The hotels often leave a good deal to be desired, yet they are sufficient for the transient visitor, and the more permanent resident prefers to take up his abode in a hired house. The former palace of Iturbide, a building of handsome architectural form, with a *patio* of noteworthy style, forms one of the principal hotels. It has been shown that the Republic contains a considerable foreign population, and in addition there is a constantly floating one, brought about largely by American tourists from the United States. The Americans and Spaniards are by far the most numerous among the foreign element, and Great Britain is represented mainly by the fine works of public utility constructed by British contractors, and by other railway and banking interests. British commercial enterprise in Mexico has almost entirely fallen away of recent years, and has been supplanted by American and German activity. Various reasons are assigned to this loss of a once paramount commercial pre-eminence; possibly the real one lies in the diverting of British enterprise to various parts of the British Empire, and also to a slackening of activity from the great centres of British industry as regards foreign lands, which seems to be apparent of recent years. Capital does not venture forth so easily as it did some decades ago, from the shores of Albion, due to a variety of causes.

A noticeable feature of Mexican business life in the capital is what may be termed the Anglo-Saxon—or rather Anglo-American—invasion, for of Britons there are but few in comparison with the ubiquitous American from the United States; and smart, capable-looking men from New York, or more generally from Chicago, or Kansas City, or St. Louis, or other great commercial centres of the middle west, have set up numerous offices and enterprises. They have brought a good deal of wealth into the country, in the form of capital invested in mines and railways, and Mexico has welcomed her *primos*, or cousins from the North, both for their gold and for their spirit of enterprise. The class of American business-man who goes to Mexico has much improved of late years; and these *hijos del Tio Samuel,* "sons of Uncle Sam," as the Mexicans sometimes jocularly dub them, are more representative of their country than the doubtful element of a few years since. The junction of these two tides of humanity which roll together but never mingle—the Americans and the Mexicans—affords much matter for interesting observation. The American influence on Mexican civilisation is partly good, partly bad, but it cannot yet be considered more than a drop in the ocean of change in the deep-seated Spanish individuality of the Mexican people.

To sum up a mental impression of Mexico City, there rise before us the old and the new on the threshold of change; the antique, the quaint, and the refined, pressed close by the modern, the commercial, and the cheap: the hand of a haughty Castilian hidalgo-spirit held forth to the "cute" and business Yankee. But there is a great breach yet between the Chicago "drummer," or the American land-shark; and the Mexican gentleman. Here is a rich and developing soil, with—perhaps—some benefit for the masses: a new civilisation in the making; a new people being fashioned from an old; a plutocratic bulk trailing off into a mass of white and red-clothed poor *peones* and swarthy Indians. Beautiful women, *serenatas*, bull-fights, courtesy, azure sky—all have inscribed upon the traveller's mind a pleasing and semi-romantic impression, a *conjunto,* whose interest and attraction, with perchance a regretful note, time does not easily dispel.

CHAPTER XI

MEXICAN LIFE AND TRAVEL

Travel and description—Mexican cities—Guadalajara—Lake Chapala—Falls of Juanacatlan—The Pacific slope—Colima—Puebla—Cities of the Great Plateau—Guanajuato—Chihuahua—The Apaches—The *peones*—Comparison with Americans—*Peon* labour system—Mode of living—Houses of the *peon* class—Diet—*Tortillas* and *frijoles*—Chilli—*Pulque*—Habits of the *peon* class—Their religion—The wayside crosses and their tragedies—Ruthless political executions—The fallen cross—Similarity to Bible scenes—*Peon* superstitions—The ignis fatuus, or *relacion*—Caves and buried treasure—Prehistoric Mexican religion—The Teocallis—Comparison with modern religious systems—Philosophical considerations.

The City of Mexico, typical as it is of Mexican people and their life, by no means embodies or monopolises the whole interest of the country, and the mere tourist who, having paid a flying visit thereto, thinks thereby to gain much idea of the nation as a whole, will naturally fall short in his observations. We must depart thence, and visit the other handsome and interesting centres of Mexico's life and population, and sojourn for a season among her people, and observe something of the "short and simple annals" of her labouring classes. During the several years which it fell to my lot to pass in this interesting land the various phases of Spanish-American life as portrayed in Mexico were often brought vividly before me, and indeed it is only after arduous journeyings in a land of this nature that pictures of its life and topography can be truly portrayed.

CITY OF GUADALAJARA: INTERIOR OF THE CATHEDRAL.

The general type of Mexican cities has been set forth in the former chapter: their distinctive Spanish-American character and atmosphere. The city next in importance to the capital is Guadalajara, in the State of Jalisco. This is a really handsome community, with fine public buildings; and it forms a centre of Mexican civilisation and education of which its inhabitants are proud: not without sufficient reason. The people of Guadalajara love to term their city the "The Queen of the West," for the city lies upon the Pacific watershed, although the Western Sierra Madre intervenes between her and the great ocean. The population of Guadalajara numbers rather more than 101,000, and the city is famed for its public monuments and institutions, religious and secular. The elevation above sea-level of 5,175 feet insures an equable climate, tending to a spring-like warmth, yet of an exhilarating character, due to the breezes which sweep over the broad valley in which it is situated. The region around the city is one of varied topographical interest. To the southeast is the great Lake Chapala, eighty miles long—a sheet of water of marked scenic beauty—and from its broad bosom the Santiago river flows upon its two-hundred-mile journey to the Pacific, near Tepic, of Toltec fame, but first forming the well-known falls of Juanacatlan. Surrounding this region are great plains of wheat-growing capacities, and indeed this State has been termed the "Granary of Mexico." The railway carries us westwardly to Ameca, a picturesque town, and thence the saddle is our means of conveyance. Far down towards the Pacific coast, and southwardly, one of my journeys took me, over vast stretches of plains and among timber-clad hills: timber-clad, as the devouring wood-burning locomotive has not yet reached so far, and the stump-studded lands as along the railway are not encountered. Further on are the abrupt precipices of the Pacific slope, and above them rises the high volcano of Colima with its everlasting crest of smoke, breaking in leaden spirals against the sky by day, and illuminating the night scenery of *haciendas* and palm groves with its fitful flames. Colima is the only active Mexican volcano at present.

In quite a different direction is the city of Puebla, one of the foremost of the State capitals, lying within a short distance by rail from the City of Mexico. This city has acquired a considerable commercial and industrial importance of recent years, largely due to the local cotton-manufacturing industries and general flourishing agricultural resources. The city is not, however, spoilt by the manufacturing element as regards its character and appearance, and the cleanliness of its streets and general beauty and severity, in their various fields, of its church and domestic architecture charm the traveller, and elicit admiration from those who had expected a less advanced community. The cathedral is one of those handsome colonial structures for which Mexico is famous. The elevation of the city is slightly over 7,000 feet above sea-level, with a corresponding excellence of climatic conditions, whilst the general environment and azure tropic sky form a whole which remains pleasingly upon the memory. A busy population of more than 93,000 people is supported in the city, mainly by the natural products and manufactures of its environment. Overlooked by the picturesque hills where the struggle for independence was raged in the historic years of last century, and sentinelled to the north-west by the two volcanic peaks of snow-crowned altitude, Popocatepetl and Ixtaccihuatl, the city of Puebla is of much interest.

To the north, and of a somewhat different character as regards their environment and population, are the cities along the Great Plateau, especially those upon the mineral belt, although they bear the inseparable stamp of the Spanish-American people and their life. Some of these cities sprang to being upon the very flanks of the mountains which give them their source of life—silver—centuries ago. Among these great towns of the plateau, especially those whose wealth and population have accrued from or depend upon the business of delving into the earth for minerals, is Guanajuato, picturesquely situated among the foothills of a mountain range known as the Sierra of Santa Rosa. Its elevation above sea-level is 6,850 feet, and the dry, clear atmosphere, bright hues of buildings and churches, sloping hills with houses and gardens perforce terraced thereon, with the brilliant sunlight overhead, form a characteristic Mexican centre of industry. The houses of Guanajuato are built of a species of freestone, which as a fine-grained tufa caps the Sierra in places here, and is known as *cantera*. It is easily worked and hardens on weathering, and its use gives a well-constructed appearance to the streets. I have noted the same aspect in other Spanish-American countries, notably the Peruvian city of Arequipa. According to the calculation of Humboldt, the great *veta madre*, or "mother lode," of Guanajuato, had yielded, up to his time, silver to the value of fifty-eight million pounds sterling; and, indeed, it is to be recollected that, a century ago, Guanajuato was a larger city than New York!

Of Zacatecas, Durango, San Luis Potosi, Aguascalientes, and others of the numerous important cities and towns, linked together by the great trunk lines of railway along the vast reaches of the *mesa central*, we cannot speak save by name. Each has its peculiar circumstance and interest, and the different States of which they form the political and industrial centres are described in the chapter devoted thereto. We will, however, take a momentary flight to the fine city of Chihuahua, far to the north, situated among its great plains and mineral-bearing mountain ranges. Among these vast deserts, now slowly yielding to reclamation by the hand of civilised man, scorched by a merciless sun by day and bitterly cold by night, which form this part of Mexico, the savage Apaches formerly roamed—the abominable Apaches: the cruellest and most treacherous race the world has ever known. Well might these savages have been hunted to the death by the invaders of the white race, both here and on the great American deserts north of the Rio Grande, and well might their scalpings and torturings form the theme for those adventurous novels which made our flesh creep as we perused them in boyhood's days! Now the degenerate descendants of these once formidable Redskins seek a living in desultory cultivation of the soil, although bands of them and of other tribes still cause trouble to soldiery of the Mexican Republic at times. But the capital city of Chihuahua is an example of man rising superior to savagery and Nature, and this splendid centre of modern life and industry is far removed from the condition of its natural surroundings. It stands at an elevation of nearly 5,000 feet above the level of the sea. The climate is a healthy one, eminently suitable for the white race and its activities; and the population of 30,000 inhabitants forms the centre of a great growing region whose natural resources are manifold. Upon the river Conchos, and upon the Casas Grandes, affluents of the Rio Grande or Bravo, are some of the ruins which are amongst the oldest and most interesting of Mexico, from an archæological point of view.

We have said that the Mexicans are an hospitable people, and this is eminently true of the upper class. As to the *peones*, they are, in the more remote districts, by no means of an untractable or surly character, although the lowest in the scale, and some of the Indian tribes, are excessively stupid and suspicious. The Mexicans of better class divide these people into *gente de razon*, or "rational" people, and *gente intratable*, or people with whom it is almost impossible to treat or to comprehend. These people vary much throughout the country, but as a rule they are unaggressive and harmless. Whilst thieving is generally ascribed as a strong vice of the Mexican lower class, this must not be rashly applied. The *peon*, or Indian, may take articles of small value which are left about, but he does not commit crime in order to rob; and the extraordinary outrages constantly perpetrated in the "Wild West" of the United States, in the shootings, "holding-up" of passenger trains, wrecking of express cars by dynamite, bank robbery, and the like exploits of the Anglo-American desperado, to steal, are unknown to the temperament of the Spanish-American. The latter are creatures of impulse, and lack the "nerve" for a well-planned murderous exploit of the above nature. Nor are they capable of the lynching, burnings of negroes, and race riots which characterise those parts of the United States which bound Mexico on the north, and once formed part of her territory. If, however, their crimes are smaller, so is their power of initiative, sustained effort, and the working for to-morrow characteristic of the Anglo-Saxon and Anglo-American peoples. Yet the police are much in evidence in Mexican travel. A *gendarme* with sabre and revolver accompanies every car on the trains which cross the great plateau. Indeed, in former years robbery with violence was the chief "incident" of travel in Mexico. Footpads and armed *bandidos* infested every highway and mountain road twenty years ago, and travel was impossible except with an armed escort. But this was before the work of President Diaz and his *rurales*. The conditions are now very different, and the traveller may journey almost anywhere, except in a few districts, without danger of molestation, with ordinary precautions such as the characteristic conditions of the country call for. In those places where the *peones* are distrustful of the white foreigners it is generally due to the influence of these, who have ingrained their own bad habits and vices upon them. A gentleman, if he holds the demeanour covered by the designation, ever carries respect in Mexico.

Incidents of life and travel in remote regions, among the petty authorities and the *hacendados*, *rancheros*, and landowners generally, are full of colour and interest for the traveller. Our belongings are securely packed upon a couple of well-appointed mules; we are astride passable Mexican horses, seated on comfortable saddles, with our servant and the *arriero* in attendance, and we have left the last of the city streets; with our face to the open country the true charm of travel comes upon us—the touch of Nature, solitude, and the far horizon which nothing else can ever supply. Thus accoutred we shall hold real converse with Nature, and with the typical people of the land over which we pass.

Let us therefore turn our attention to the picturesque world of the great bulk of the Mexican population, the class which earns its daily bread by the sweat of its brow. These are the *peones*, and to their work is due the cultivation of the ground, the working of the mines, and all the manual labour without which the industries of the country would be non-existent. The *peon* is not necessarily a forced labourer. Nevertheless, the conditions of his life are such that he is not a free agent as the working men of other countries are. His payment is largely received in goods which he is obliged to purchase in the general store of the *hacienda*, belonging to the proprietor, or by some one licensed thereby. This is a species of "truck" system. High prices and short weight—in accordance with the business principles underlying such systems—generally accompany these dealings. Moreover, as the *peon* has often been granted supplies in advance, against future wages, he is generally in debt to the store, a condition which, purposely, is not discouraged. The law does not support the system, but as the whole area of land surrounding the *hacienda* belongs thereto, the proprietor may or may not—generally the latter—permit the establishment of any independent shop in the vicinity. Indeed, such temerity on the part of any would-be merchant would soon call down punishment—if such it may be termed—from the myrmidons of the landowner, to whom the hunting of "contraband" vendors of goods or liquor is fair game.

A TOBACCO-PRODUCING HACIENDA: STATE OF VERA CRUZ.

The house of the *peon*—the single-roomed adobe-built habitation, or the wattle-built *jacal* in which he dwells, belongs to the estate owner; and if the dweller, through laziness or other similar cause, fails to put in an appearance in the fields, he is soon forced to vacate it, and, supposing him to be free from debt, to leave the *hacienda*. He toils all day in the fields, drawing a scanty wage, and retires at night to this primitive abode, which he shares with his female consort and her progeny.

Yet it is not to be supposed that under this autocratic and patriarchal rule—for the *régime* in some respects has an atmosphere of the pastoral scenes of the Old Testament—the *peones* are oppressed or unhappy. Men who know no other state are contented with their lot, and the poor Mexican creates matters of pastime and enjoyment in his simple life. Bull-fights, horse-racing, cock-fighting, together with dancing and the consumption of liquor—the latter his serious and principal vice—furnish him with distraction, whilst religious feast-days make up the sum.

This description applies mainly to the agricultural labourer. The miner stands somewhat apart as a class, pursuing his more arduous, yet possibly more independent, labour under the ground, and living in the clustered *adobe* huts upon the bare hillside in the vicinity of the mine-mouth. With his pick, bar, and dynamite he jovially enters his subterranean passage, where, generally working under some system of contract, his energies are spurred by the hope of profit depending upon his own efforts—ever a stimulus which the mere day-worker lacks.

The system of contract work also obtains in some cases with the agricultural labourer, especially in the cultivation of sugar-cane, which is an important Mexican industry. Fields, with water for irrigation, are allotted to the responsible worker—Mexico is a country whose rainfall generally is insufficient for cultivation without irrigation—and this he cultivates, the *hacienda* lending seed and implements, and taking as payment a stated portion of the crop.

So, if the people generally are poor, they are not discontented. Their wants are exceedingly simple and easily supplied. Furniture and other household chattels are not acquired nor required by the poorer class of *peon*. If he has no bedstead, the earthen floor serves the purpose, and here he and his family sleep, rolled together in their *ponchos* or blankets for warmth, with an utter disregard for ventilation, damp, or kindred matters. Indeed, if need be, the hardy *peon* will sleep out upon the open plain without feeling any particular discomfort.

The interior *ménage* of a Mexican hut is naturally primitive. The fireplace is often outside, and consists of unshaped stones, between which charcoal or firewood is ignited, and upon these the earthen pot, or *olla*, is balanced, containing whatever comestible the moment may have afforded, and whose contents we will proceed to investigate. If the fireplace is inside, there is often no chimney, and the habitation is smoky and dark, with only a hole in the roof for ventilation. *En passant*, it may be said that some of the methods of the poorer Mexican *peones* are not much in advance of those of our common ancestor—primeval man!

To observe now the contents of the *olla*. First it should be noted that earthenware vessels fulfil nearly all the purposes of the *peones'* culinary requirements. In these seemingly fragile articles the women bake, stew, boil, and fry in a fashion which would astonish the English or American housewife, accustomed to the use of iron utensils. The diet of the *peon* is largely vegetarian, and indeed he is a living example of the working force contained in cereals and leguminous plants. Meat is a scarce and expensive luxury which he is rarely able to obtain.

MEXICAN PEON LIFE: TYPICAL VILLAGE MARKET-PLACE.

Most important of all in this primitive menu is the *tortilla*; and, indeed, this simple article of food is worthy of being blazoned upon the country's escutcheon! for it may be said to be the basis of all labour here. The *tortilla* is simply an unsweetened pancake of *maiz* flour, patted out thin in the hands and baked, and its preparation is the principal occupation of the women of the *peones* during the time their men are toiling in the fields. Let us watch a Mexican woman of the working class making her *tortillas*, probably sitting on the threshold of her habitation for purposes of light and neighbourly gossip. She has brought forth a grinding-stone or flat mortar known as a *metate*, for the purpose of grinding the *maiz*—an article shaped out of a block of a special kind of volcanic stone, called *recinta*, an implement inherited from Aztec times. The *maiz* has been boiled with a little lime, and is somewhat softened, and she places handfuls of the grain upon the *metate*, adding water, and shortly reduces it to a stiff paste under the grinding of the upper stone. The *tortilla* is then patted out into the form of a thin pancake and baked in an earthenware dish, or *casuela*. If it is to be our fortune to partake of this preparation—and if we have been travelling in a remote part of the country it may be so—it is advisable not to inquire too closely into the cleanliness of the operation, for the Mexican *peon* and his woman do not consider morning ablutions at all a necessary part of their toilette! The supply of *tortillas* being finished, they are sufficient for the day's requirements, and take the place of bread, and, indeed, of plates, knives and forks, for the *peones* scoop up their food or put it upon these handy pancakes for depositing it in their mouths, and munch them with their *frijoles* with the utmost gusto. To re-heat the *tortillas* they are placed for a few moments upon the glowing embers of the fire, and with a roll of *tortillas* in his pocket the *peon* will undertake a day's work, or toilsome march, and ask little else. The *tortilla*, and, indeed, the consumption of *maiz* in this form, seems to be peculiar to Mexico. In Peru, Chile, or other Spanish-American countries it is unknown.

Mention has been made of *frijoles*. There is more contained in that word—which we should translate as haricot beans, a small white variety—than might be supposed. Next to the *tortilla* it is the staple article of diet of a good many millions of Mexico's inhabitants. The preparation of the *frijoles* is simple. They are boiled in an earthen pot until they are cooked, and then fried in lard or other fat. They acquire a rich brown colour, and are appetising and wholesome. Even in the homes of the upper class *frijoles* are—or were—served as one of the courses, although there is a certain tendency to despise this as a national or *Indian* dish—a little weakness of advancing civilisation! But beans cooked in the Mexican way might well be adapted in English households, whether for reasons of novelty or economy. In the United States they are used in the form of "Boston baked pork and beans," but are considered a delicacy rather than an article of ordinary diet.

The next important item on the Mexican *peones'* bill of fare is *Chile*. This is the chilli; the pepper-pods of that name, a species of capsicum; the guinea-pepper. The pods are eaten either green, which is their unripe condition, or ripe or sun-dried, when they acquire a scarlet colour. In the first state they are only slightly piquant and are consumed largely, cooked with cheese or pork, which latter favourite dish is known as *Chile con carne*. When red they are exceedingly piquant, but are largely consumed with the *frijoles* and *tortillas*. They might certainly form a useful article of diet in England or the United States, where they are practically unknown, except in the form of chilli pepper.

Potatoes come next in the diet of the *peones*. The Mexican potato, however, seems often to be small and of inferior quality, and probably the soil and climate are not favourable to its production. Camotes and sweet potatoes, however, are excellent.

The national beverage of the Mexican is the well-known *pulque,* a fermented and intoxicating drink made from the *maguey*, and elsewhere described. Coffee is much esteemed by the *peones,* and purchased when circumstances will allow, and tea also, although in lesser degree. Milk and butter are scarce, and rarely used by the *peones*, but cheese made from goats' milk is a favourite article of diet. Meat is often used—when obtainable—dried, in strips, generally of beef. Mutton, or *carne de borrego* is consumed to some extent, and goats' flesh more frequently. The Mexican *peon* is not necessarily particular as to the quality of this meat. If a cow or bullock perishes upon the plain from drought or accident, the villagers soon get wind of the fact and the carcase is cut up and appropriated in short order. Indeed, the flesh of horses is not despised at times! And, as may be supposed, there are no troublesome municipal restrictions or health officers in such places to interpose authority against the practice, and the struggle for life, especially upon the great plateau, is keen.

Of course, as we rise in the social scale a large variety of foods are consumed, of excellent quality and unstinted quantity, such as we have described in speaking of the upper class. Even here, however, a Mexican "Mrs. Beeton" would have to describe a number of novel and appetising dishes of national character, and peculiar to the country.

The *peon*, like his superior the educated and wealthy Mexican, is excessively fond of tobacco. His cigarette is his great solace and enjoyment. No manufactured and papered article is the *peones'* cigarette. The dried husk of the *maiz* is taken and cut into pieces of the required size. Into this he sprinkles a small portion of strong tobacco and rolling it into a thin roll in a certain dexterous way, smokes it without necessity of gumming or fastening the edge. These cigarettes have a distinctive and agreeable taste and aroma, and the foreigner who has grown accustomed to them will certainly find nothing superior in the machine-made cigarettes of the United States or Great Britain—especially the former. The upper-class Mexican does not use these cigarettes of *hoja de maiz*, or *maiz* husk, but unceasingly smokes either the imported Havannas, or the Mexican paper-covered varieties, which are generally excellent.

The *peon* does not generally use matches to light his cigarette. He produces an *eslabon*, or small steel link, which he strikes upon his piece of flint, deftly dropping a spark upon his rag tinder, and so creates the means of ignition. Matches cost money—why spend unnecessarily? Or, seated at the camp-fire, he takes a glowing wood ember for the purpose, and indeed the traveller finds that this method of lighting a husk cigarette imparts a peculiar flavour or sense of satisfaction, unknown before. The *peon* who accompanied me on my expeditions picked up the cartridge cases, especially the brass ones, which I had ejected from the rifle, or *carabina*, after firing at bird or animal, and preserved them carefully. What for? "It forms an excellent tinder-box," he replied, asking permission to retain it.

The Mexican *peon*, like the *Cholo* of Peru, has become deeply imbued with the Roman Catholic religion, as expounded by the priests of Spanish-America. His was a nature to which the realistic ceremony and outward show of this system strongly appealed, and the superstition which in Spanish-America is an inseparable adjunct of this religion among the poorer class—and indeed to a certain extent among the upper—is at times scarcely distinguishable therefrom. To speak first of the religion. This manifests itself in their excessive reverence displayed towards the priests, the adoration of saints, and the naming of objects and places after these, and in the devout method of expression employed even in their ordinary tasks. Shrines and crosses are found everywhere—upon inaccessible hill-tops and in the depths of mines. As we ride along the dusty road our eyes rest suddenly upon a cross set by the way-side, apparently without any explanation of its presence at that spot. We turn to our *mozo*, or servant, who himself is only a more or less intelligent *peon*, and ask him the reason. "Señor," he will make reply, "may God preserve you: a highwayman—*un bandido*—was overtaken and shot here some years ago," or some kindred explanation wherein death has befallen some one by the wayside, whether by accident or punishment. There is much that is attractive and good about this religious sentiment—far be it from the philosophical observer to scoff thereat.

Yet the frequent occurrences of these crosses along the mountain-roads are terribly indicative of past disorders, and of private and political revenge, and even murder. Inquiry reveals that highway robbery and assassination, private feuds, love, drunken quarrels, and—frequent as any—*pronunciamientos* and revolutions are responsible for the deeds of bloodshed upon the spots where the emblem of Christian love and brotherhood is raised up. A certain lonely hill, which it was my fortune to pass on one occasion, was marked by three decaying crosses set among the stones and thorns at its base. I inquired the reason of their presence there from my servant, a faithful old *peon* who was a native of the vicinity. "Ah, señor," he replied, crossing himself devoutly as we drew rein and gazed upon the melancholy spot, "three *caballeros* died here—*pasado por las armas*[31]—twenty years ago." "For what reason?" I inquired. "That no one has ever known," he answered. "They were roused from their sleep in yonder town"—pointing to the white cluster of buildings and trees on the far-off horizon which we had that morning left—"taken by a file of soldiers under arrest, with orders—it was said—to conduct them to the capital." "Well?" I said as he paused; and the old fellow looked round as if fearful that rocks and cactuses had ears and might report his utterances to some *jefe politico*, and continued, "A volley was heard, and the officers afterwards reported that the prisoners had *attempted to escape* and had been shot down." Drawing closer to me he added, "But, señor, it was not true. My brother happened to be on this very hill and saw it, and the prisoners had been stood up in a line and shot."

31 That is to say, shot.

I did not feel called upon to doubt the old fellow's words. Probably the three *caballeros* had been implicated in some political plot, and the Federal Government had—as was common in Mexico a few years ago—disposed of them by this swift and ruthless method. The pretext of "endeavouring to escape" was often a convenient one to hide the summary execution both of political suspects and criminals in the turbulent days of Mexico's recent history, and indeed has not altogether disappeared yet! *Pasado por las armas* was a common penalty, and is a somewhat poetic nomenclature for that form of execution which the soldier prefers.

Absorbed in such reflections, I rode on for some distance through the rocky defiles and over the alternating plains—absolutely sterile and verdureless—which some parts of the great *mesa central* present. On the summit of a small eminence I beheld yet another cross—a large wooden structure, which, however, had fallen from its base of loose rocks and lay upon the ground. Old

José, my servant, was some distance behind assisting the mule-driver with my baggage with a refractory mule, and there was no one to say why the cross had been erected. The dusk was rapidly falling and we had yet some leagues to my objective-point. But there was something pathetic about the lone, fallen cross, and I felt loath to pass and leave it there, prone. Dismounting, I looped the long bridle over a projecting rock, and, ascending the eminence, took hold of the fallen cross, exerting my strength to raise it. It was large and heavy, and the footing on the slippery rock made it difficult, but at length I managed to lift it up and put it in position, piling heavy stones round its base to keep it there. Engaged in this self-imposed task, I did not observe that my horse—a spirited animal I had bought some months before—had freed its bridle from the rock below, and when I looked round it was just breaking into a gentle trot away across the desert! At this juncture old José rode up with the mule-driver and took in the situation, and I directed the latter individual to tie up his pack-mule and pursue my horse at all speed. "This cross," said José, in response to my questions, "was placed here when I was a boy," and he recounted how it had been erected in memory of an old Spaniard, a rich landowner of that region, who had been murdered there by the lover of his wife; she a beautiful young Mexican woman. The details of the history are too long to record here, but according to the legend current among the people, which José recounted, the spirit of the penitent wife visited the cross at evening, and hung a phantom wreath of white flowers upon it. "But," added the old *peon*, whose diction and ideas, notwithstanding his superstition, were superior to his kind generally, "the cross has never fallen before, and when from afar I saw the señor lifting it up I was astonished. But it is a blessed act, and no evil can now befall the señor!"

Inquiring what he meant by this, I learned that, in the opinion of the natives of some regions, the raising up of a fallen cross secures immunity from danger for him who has performed it for a season afterwards! This belief of old José's seemed put to the test, in his view, for half an hour afterwards, on crossing a steep-sided ravine, my horse slipped and fell, and carried me down the almost vertical cliff face for 50 feet or more. The sand and stones poured down in an avalanche, but I kept my horse's head up, and we landed on the sandy bottom below, unscratched, in a normal position! "The señor has been saved because of the cross!" José and the *arriero* both averred, after congratulating me upon the almost miraculous escape from injury.

But the cross set up in Mexico means many things, and is always in evidence among the lower orders. Here is a little path winding away among the rocks, pressed flat by the bare feet of generations of Indian women. Let us follow it. It leads to a feeble spring of clear water, which flows from the bare hillside into a scooped-out rock basin, and close beside it is a rude wooden cross, adorned with fading flowers. Perhaps we have met on the path a damsel with peasant dress and bare brown feet, who passes us with downcast eyes, bearing upon her shoulder a huge earthenware *olla* of water of quaint form— a figure such as in the land and time of Jacob and Rachel might have graced the sterile landscape. The cross has been placed there as a mark of gratitude for the existence of this frail water supply. Indeed, in these Spanish-American countries—as Mexico, Peru, and others—the conditions and atmosphere of everyday life often remind us of the scenes and colour of the Bible narratives. The absence of the conditions of modern life—railways, factories, the scramble for commercial wealth—induce this. The quaint and primitive methods of travel, the long distances, the sterile landscape, and the simple dress and pastoral life of the people, all contribute to this environment. Amid the haze of some long, shimmering road as we ride along a figure approaches. We do not *see* him; we "behold him while he is yet afar off," and if he happens to be a native friend he does not greet us with a handshake, but "falls upon our neck." Here in these wilds what typical places there are where the traveller might "fall among thieves" in some rocky defile or on the desert's edge! Here men are close to nature. They are unconsciously tinged and imbued with its picturesque and chequered incident, as was the great singer of Israel. Nature is ever present in Mexico, and man's struggle with her is his daily task. The wilderness is ever before his eyes, and circumstances often compel him to fast there in the wilderness, whose broad, arid bosom does but accentuate the valleys which intersect it, flowing veritably with milk and honey, and which we ofttimes behold from some Pisgah's mountain of the rocky Sierra. The "patriarchal" condition of life, moreover, as regards family life, "handmaidens" and natural sons, are reminiscent of Biblical story. Nature will not admit too rigid regulations against increase of population in Mexico: Hagar and Ishmael dwell in every hamlet!

Just as the religion of the Mexican *peon* causes him to people his daily surroundings with the presence of the saints, so does his superstitious mind assign supernatural causes to things not easily explained, and bid him see evil spirits and hobgoblins in strange or unfrequented places. Naturally, much of this superstition has come down with the traditions of his Aztec forbears, whose polytheistic religion set up many imaginary gods and spirits. The devil and his attendant hobgoblins are active people in this people's minds. But—happy tribute to the strength of Christianity!—the sign of the cross is potent to banish imaginary fiends on all ordinary occasions.

But the *peon* loves not to journey alone at night, nor to enter dark caves and grottoes where the bones and mummies of dead men are found. Peculiar superstition attaches to the vicinity of buried treasure. Enter into conversation with your *mozo*, or other of the *peones*, in their hours of relaxation, and they will impart strange stories of apparitions drawn from their own or some acquaintance's experience, and—for they are given to romancing—partly from their imagination. As to buried treasure, it is supposed that this is always guarded by a spirit, sometimes good, sometimes evil, and generally that some evil will befall those who meddle with it. In the immediate vicinity of concealed treasure at night, upon the plain, the *peones* say that a mysterious light is seen hovering over the spot, especially when damp and misty. This light they term a *relacion*; and although they dare not approach it, it serves as a guide to mark the place, which they proceed to dig over when daylight comes—although in some cases they dare not do so, fearing that an evil spirit will draw them in—in the hope of enriching themselves with treasure trove. The same light is said by the Mexican miners to "burn" over the place where a lode of rich metallic ore exists undiscovered, or even within the workings of a mine, sometimes, when a body of rich ore has escaped attention.

The truth or falsity of these stories of the *peones* I must leave to the inclination of the reader. On one occasion I observed a phenomenon of this nature, however. It was a damp, misty night, and I was sitting in my tent after a long day's examination of the hills. "Señor," suddenly exclaimed one of my men, entering the tent, "there is a *relacion* burning on the plain by the point of the hill!" I started up, willing to observe whatever might be visible, or have the satisfaction of showing them what *tontos* they were. They conducted me round the spur of the hill close at hand. The sky was dark and frowning, and an eerie feeling took possession—at least of the two *peones*!

"There!" they exclaimed, and following the direction indicated I observed a pale fluctuating flame or light a few hundred feet distant. I began to advance towards it, but the fearful *peones* strove to detain me. "No, señor," they urged; "it is a spirit; do not approach." But disregarding this admonition, I began to walk towards the spot, telling them to follow, which, however, they would not do. In unknown situations in wild countries a revolver gives a certain sense of security, and drawing mine I approached the mysterious light, which went and came intermittently. I knew it must be an *ignis fatuus*. As I reached the place it disappeared; my feet suddenly sank in marshy ground, and a heavy mist-cloud enveloped the place, so that I could see absolutely nothing. I confess I felt a species of "gooseflesh" creeping over me. But my feet were sinking deeper in the bog, and more by good luck than anything else I floundered out and regained the rock, and, directed by the shouts of the *peones*, made my way through the dense mist to the tent. I heard some time afterwards that excavations had been made at the spot in the hope of finding treasure, but could not learn the result.

Ancient caves in different parts of Mexico often contain the skulls and bones of former inhabitants, whether prehistoric or of later times, sometimes containing finely fashioned flint implements. The natives, as a rule, fear to go into these places. "Do not enter, señor," they will say, as, with Anglo-Saxon lack of superstition, you determine to explore them; "some evil befalls those who meddle with the remains of the dead." And if they are prevailed upon to assist they cross themselves devoutly before descending or entering. Weird tales they unfold afterwards of men who have gone into such places and found their exit barred by some evil spirit, they themselves having been encountered dead and cold upon the cavern floor when discovered by their relatives, who had searched for the missing one! According to the *peones*, the scenes of murder or wickedness which may have taken place in such situations are enacted again to the terrified vision of the unhappy witness who had the temerity to venture into these places possessed of the devil, for the King of Darkness is an ever-present and active element of the poor Mexican's superstitious world.

As to buried treasure, it is a favourite subject of the *peon* for conversation. Quantities of silver money and other articles are frequently found concealed throughout the country, where they were often placed for safety in the turbulent times of former history. At the time of the dispossession of the clergy it is probable that a good deal of concealment of this nature was made, whether in lonely places in the hills or plains, or in the floors and walls of convents and houses.

It was with considerable difficulty that I persuaded my *peones* on one occasion to assist me in the examination of a cave which was said to contain the remains of the dead. The cave had a corkscrew-like opening from the surface of the hill, a barren limestone hog-back in the State of Durango. It descended spirally for some 30 feet or more, as I found when my men lowered me down with a rope, at my command. When my feet touched bottom I lighted the candle, which had been put out in the descent, and looked around. The place was of small extent—little more than a pit—and it seemed to be a natural cavity, with nothing remarkable about it. But I turned my attention to the floor, which felt curiously soft and greasy to the touch. It was strewn with pieces of human bones and skulls! The gruesome place weighed rather upon me, I confess, silent and stifling as it was, but having come to explore I proceeded to excavate lightly in the yielding material of the floor with a light pick. The singular nature of this material aroused my attention, and well it might, for I afterwards learned that there was a legend to the effect that the pit had been the scene of a massacre, and that numbers of persons alive and dead, had been thrown into it, and the soft material was the decayed human remains! When this had taken place no one knew, but it must have been at a very remote or prehistoric period, for during my digging in the floor I unearthed a flint spearhead, beautifully chipped and fashioned, lying by a skull it had cloven. The spearhead, or blade, is some 6 inches in length and 4 inches in width, about a quarter of an inch thick, and I still preserve it.

So, as we have seen, religion and superstition are much combined in the mind of the Mexicans, the result of both ancient and modern creeds. As to the antique beliefs and cult, there is much that appeals to the philosopher in the religious structures and history of the prehistoric, semi-civilised peoples of Mexico, or indeed of Spanish-America, whether North or South. The pyramids and temples, which the Toltecs and the Aztecs and the Incas built, have something grand and broad underlying their main idea, the idea of being able to get *on* their temples rather than *in* them. There is ever a source of inspiration in being upon the point of an eminence, to commune with Providence, rather than being immured within some gloomy walls, with toppling spires overhead. The spirit ever tries to get *out*, to ascend, and is exalted in accordance with its altitude. Did not Moses at Sinai bring forth the enduring Decalogue from the summit of a great natural pyramid, rather than from the gloomy interior of a temple? The exceedingly numerous pyramids throughout ancient Mexico seem to attest some exalted idea of a natural religion, which found outlet and habitation in the great Teocallis.

Man, semi-civilised or modern, ever strives to commune with a God, an unseen Being. Is it not nobler and more inspiring to gaze towards the setting sun with solitude around us? An environment of Nature, the nearest approach to the "unknown God" which exists, subtly attracts us as the handiwork of a power unknown. Well may the altar lights and emblems, and the oppressive enclosure of temples, be more and more rejected by the thinking mind, as the dark ages of religion leave us and true reverential knowledge unfolds. We might almost be tempted to say that the cathedrals of Mexico are not a philosophical exchange for its Teocallis, nor that the stake and axe of the Inquisition were much advance upon the sacrificial stone of the Aztec wargod! The frenzied priest who cut open the breast of the human sacrificial victim with an obsidian knife, and tore out the palpitating heart to cast it before his fanciful gods, does not present a picture of such refined cruelty as that of civilised European man, the Inquisitors in long black cloaks, calmly sitting by whilst their victims were slowly roasted to death at the stake because they would not change their faith, or for other equally reasonless cause. There is, and ever will be, something peculiarly sinister and abominable about the recollection of the Inquisition and its operations, under the sky of the New World. And to the philosophical observer, who pins his thoughts to no mere creed of whatever designation, the fact seems palpable that the sinister authority which did those things is only slumbering, and did not civilisation and antagonism restrain it those scenes would be repeated. The germs of an Inquisition exist in almost every religious organisation, but the old original one would burn its victims again if it could!

As to the Teocallis, perhaps their form was suggested by the natural pyramidal hills of the mountain landscape, whereon men must have stood to watch the sunset and feel nearer heaven, even in those savage lands. Even to-day this hill-ascending influence is not banished among the primitive class of the Mexican people. Every hill in the neighbourhood of a hamlet is surmounted by a cross, up to which culminating point processions constantly ascend. Indeed, at times the devout—or fanatic—Indian and *peon* ascends these rocky steeps upon his knees, leaving blood-spots to mark his way!

Processions of fanatic Indians were formerly common; they journeyed over great distances upon their knees towards some popular shrine, and although the law now prohibits these, they are surreptitiously carried out at times, and I have witnessed them myself. Onwards and upwards towards the "Unknown God" these poor people grope their way—

"Upon the great world's altar stairs."

Can we say much more of the most civilised among us?

Much of beauty and interest there is in a study of both the old and new religions of this land; much of the romance of the former we may feel, as, standing on the pyramid whence the rays of the orb of day were flashed back from the golden breastplate of Tonatiah in days of yore, we mark the sun-god of the Aztecs sink in the Occident.

CHAPTER XII

MEXICAN LIFE AND TRAVEL (*continued*)

Anthropogeographical conditions—The Great Plateau—The tropical belt—Primitive villages—Incidents of travel on the plateau—Lack of water—Hydrographic conditions—Venomous vermin—Travel by roads and *diligencias*—A journey with a priest—Courtesy of the *peon* class—The curse of alcohol—The dress of the working classes—The women of the *peon* class—Dexterity of the natives—The bull-fights—A narrow escape—Mexican horse equipment—The *vaquero* and the lasso—Native sports—A challenge to a duel—Foreigners in Mexico—Unexplored Guerrero—Sporting conditions—Camp life—A day's hunting.

The picturesque incidents of life and travel in Mexico vary much according to the particular part of the country we may be sojourning in or passing through. Civilisation has advanced more upon the great plateau, threaded by numerous railway systems, than in the less accessible regions of the Pacific and Atlantic slopes. Mexican national life has not developed much upon the littoral. A harbourless and riverless country, aboriginal civilisation made little use of its coasts, and the same natural conditions have existed until to-day, although now, at great cost, harbours are being created and transverse railway lines being built.

THE PACIFIC COAST ZONE: COCOA-NUT PALMS AT COLIMA.

Yet upon the great plateau, which, indeed, embodies a large part of Mexico, life is harder—at any rate for the labouring classes—than in the tropical regions bordering upon the Pacific and Atlantic slopes, and of that equally or more tropical region to the south of the Sierra Madres. Scantily clad, the *peon* suffers from the brusque change from torrid day to bitterly cold night which the climate of the great tableland produces. The ground is generally sterile by nature—as elsewhere described—and all produce is grown under irrigation. In many parts of the region water is scarce, or is employed for the irrigation of highly remunerative crops, such as cotton, leaving a minimum for the growing of food products. In this arid region natural pasture is scarce, with a consequent dearth of cattle and their produce, whilst cereals, fruits, and vegetables are far from plentiful. Consequently the *peon* has but a small choice of comestibles.

In the more tropical belt, however, the vegetation is profuse, and fruits, cereals, and any product of the vegetable world grows almost spontaneously, or with a minimum of care. Bananas, oranges, sweet potatoes, sugar-cane, and a variety of eatables—all easily acquired—increase his range of food products, even if they do not augment his working powers.

Not all the *peon* inhabitants of Mexico are necessarily attached to the large estates. Upon the great tableland the traveller, as he pursues his sun-beat and dusty road, will constantly come upon small hamlets and even single dwellings, set near the base of some hill or in the broken ground of a ravine, or *arroyo*, where perchance a feeble stream or spring provides the inhabitants with the means of satisfying their thirst. Failing that a dammed-up pond may form the only supply of water.

These places are generally of the most primitive and miserable character. Often, were it not for the sterile nature of the land and the lack of water they would not be in the possession of the people at all, but would long ago have been taken by the nearest *hacienda*. Indeed, possibly they may be upon the territory claimed by such, but of too insignificant a nature to be disturbed. Let us survey briefly these poor dwellers on Nature's waste places. We have ridden for hours under the sun and wind; our faces are scorched and our lips are cracked. "Is there no *sombra* where we can eat our lunch and take a *siesta*?" I ask of my servant, who is acting in the double capacity of *mozo* and guide. He shakes his head doubtfully. "Quien sabe, señor," he replies, but recollects a *publecito*, a little farther on, where we may obtain shade. We ride on. Oh for a drink from some crystal stream! The water in the bottle is lukewarm; it is not a bottle, but a gourd, such as in Mexico are fashioned from the wild *calabazas* for this purpose, stoppered with maize-cob freed from the grain, and it preserves the water fairly fresh.

The vociferous barking of a legion of dogs announces our approach, for however poor the inhabitants of these places may be the bands of mongrel curs which they keep seem to find means of living. We approach the huts, our horses kicking and snorting at the attacks of the dogs. A few of the houses are built of the usual *adobe* bricks; the major portion—there may be a dozen or so—are simply *jacales*, as the Mexican wattle-hut is termed. Dirt, rags, and evil odours surround the place, for primitive man is a filthy being, and defiles the environs of his habitation for a considerable area around him. My visions of the crystal stream vanish. Close at hand is a foul pond of waters collected from the last rainstorm, wherein a lean-backed hog wallows, and we learn that this is the villagers' water supply! Naked children of both sexes run about under our horses' legs, and supplicate me for a *centavito*. A horse, or at least the framework of a horse—for the animal is attenuated beyond description—stands tethered under the shade of a rude roof of boughs and whinnies feebly to our sturdy mounts.

"There is no water, señor," the old crone, who has emerged from one of the huts, replies. "God has sent us no rain for many days, but if the señor would like some *pulque*—" I close with the suggestion and instruct the *mozo* to try it, to see if, in his experienced judgment, it is good. This he does, nothing loath, and pronounces it fresh. *Pulque* is a refreshing and not unwholesome drink. It is not a spirit, although in quantities it is intoxicating. Its manufacture is unknown outside Mexico, and in Peru the *chicha*, or *maiz* beer of the natives, takes its place.

I quaff a gourd of the liquid; custom has rendered it not unpleasant to the palate, and its singular odour I disregard. And in the cool shade of the interior of the most respectable of the *adobe* huts we rest awhile until the sun's fiery disc has descended somewhat from the zenith. Then I distribute some small largesse to the woman and her numerous progeny, for am I not an *inglés*, of that famous race whose pockets are ever lined with silver and who are known even throughout these remote regions?

How do these people live? The only vegetation at hand is some gaunt *nopales* or prickly pear cactus, forming a protective hedge around the settlement, and a few other specimens, all armed with spines and prickles after the fashion of Nature's handiwork in arid regions. Truly, these outcasts must gather "grapes of thorns and figs of thistles" if they reap anything here! But probably at the head of the *arroyo* there is a little tilled patch of *maiz* and *alfalfa*, such as supply the inevitable *tortilla* for the denizens of the place, and fodder—and thereby some small revenue, as in our own case—for the beasts of passing travellers.

But this region is not always dry. At certain seasons heavy rainstorms occur, and a veritable deluge descends upon the cracked ground and fills the dry river-beds and *arroyos* with a turgid flood. In some situations, as, for example, on the river Nazas, a wave of water comes down, covering 10 or 15 feet deep and 500 feet wide in an irresistible flood what a few moments before was a parched and sandy bottom. In the great gullies of the plains similar conditions occur, and woebetide the unfortunate horseman or foot passenger who may be journeying along them at the moment! These sudden freshets are a remarkable feature of the hydrography of the great plateau, and have been more fully described in another chapter.

Such a storm we shall have encountered in our expeditions. The rain comes down in torrents, and the lightning flashes and the thunder reverberates among the rocks and canyons; for we have approached a mountain spur, perhaps, in our examination of its mineral resources.

The *peon* in such situations, if there be no shelter at hand, not infrequently, when alone or only with his companions, takes off his clothing and places it in some sheltered rock-crevice, where it keeps dry, until the storm has passed, he himself remaining nude and unconcerned amid the downpour. A mouthful of *mezcal*, or fiery native spirit, will ward off a chill.

At night we have sought the hospitality of the owner of some *adobe* hut. He has done his best for me, but sleeping on the floor is ever trying, and the pack-mule with my baggage and camp-bed has tarried on the road. A rainstorm in this region has the effect of bringing out the noxious vermin from the soil, where they have lain during the heat. Among the most uncomfortable of these are the *alacran*, or scorpion, and the centipede, both of which reptiles are found freely upon the walls and roofs of the *adobe* dwellings. For my peace of mind we have carefully examined the interior, with a candle, before turning in, and the *mozo*, with a piece of firewood, has smashed the offending centipedes, of which there were a number. Both the scorpion and centipede have a venomous sting, the former sometimes fatal.

As to the *peones*, they display small concern at the presence of these vermin. "God willing we shall not be stung," they say, and, rolling themselves in their *ponchos* on the bare floor in a corner of the habitation, they are soon asleep. But sleep does not visit me so easily. An uncomfortable impression remains, which has not been lessened by the casual remark of the owner of the hut regarding the habits of the scorpions. "Very knowing creatures, señor," he says, as he obsequiously helps to arrange my couch in the middle of the floor—a position chosen by myself—"they have a habit of dropping from the roof on to a person sleeping beneath"!

Mexico, unlike other Cordilleran countries, lends itself to travel in certain directions by means of roads and vehicles. The *diligencias* which give communication from remote places to the wayside stations of the railways, where the nature of the topography admits of roads for wheeled vehicles, are canvas-topped carriages drawn by half a dozen mules. Over the dusty plains of the tableland and through the rugged scenery of hill-passes these somewhat crazy vehicles perform their journeys, starting often before sunrise and arriving after sunset in order to accomplish their toilsome trajectory. Jolting over the ruts and *arroyos* of the scarcely-tended "roads"—if by courtesy they may be termed such—and baked by the sun blazing upon the carriage-hood, the traveller would often prefer to exchange his uncomfortable seat for that of the saddle. Often a more agreeable method is by alternating these methods.

LIFE AND TRAVEL IN MEXICO: MULES, PEON, AND CACTUS.

I journeyed, on one occasion, with a *padre*, or village priest; not, however, in a public *diligencia*, but in a vehicle of similar nature which I had chartered to convey me to a distant point. As I was starting some Mexican friends of a neighbouring *hacienda* approached the vehicle, accompanied by a stout *padre*. "Would I do them and the *padre* the great favour of taking the latter in my coach, which would save the worthy representative of the Church a long, hot ride?" they asked. "Of course I would; nothing would afford me greater pleasure," I replied, although in strict truth this was an expression of courtesy rather than of actual fact, for the *padre* looked very heavy, and I had desired to journey rapidly without a change of mules. The reverend gentleman was of a type commonly met with in Spanish-America, of little education and predominant native physiognomy, but jovial withal. A basket containing good and liberal provisions to sustain the *padre* upon his arduous journey was put into the coach by his friends, and simultaneously put at my service, as a matter of course. From the covering of the basket protruded the tops of various bottles of wine and beer, which my travelling companion eyed with satisfaction, and indeed before we started he insisted upon opening one—of cognac—and giving us a *copa* all round. This habit of drinking brandy in the early morning is a common one in Latin America—it is said to ward off malaria!—but is not an acceptable one to the temperate Briton.

Well, the coach started. The *peon* who held the mules' heads—a necessary precaution—let go, and the half-broken animals bounded forward along the rough and dusty road, in a way which rendered both the *padre* and myself quite speechless for a space. However, they soon settled down into their rapid jog-trot, and I found my companion quite loquacious. His mission had been to marry a number of *peones* at the *hacienda*, who, at such places, where the visits of a representative of the Church are apt to be few and delayed, have to wait for the Church's blessing for some time, and then receive it in batches. This delay, however, does not necessarily cause a postponement of their matrimonial relations in other respects—as, indeed, the reverend father informed me! Other interesting matters and views of men (and women) and their customs the *padre* unfolded as we went along, drawn from his professional experience, and recounted, perhaps, with more freedom to a foreigner who understood his language, and doubtless rendered of more facile delivery by the frequent investigations of the contents of the bottles which he made as the day wore on.

As evening approached my coach halted at a small village at the foot of a range of hills which intersected the desert, in order that the mules might water. The inhabitants of the place, eager for the least distraction, approached; and, learning that a *padre* was within the vehicle, the women and girls crowded round to receive the good man's benediction and kiss his hand, which he graciously extended from the carriage window. But the throng was considerable, and our stay short, and it seemed that many of them would not be able to kiss the brown hand of the priest. And now I absolve myself from having done it on purpose! My own hand lay upon the sill of the window upon my side of the coach, and suddenly I felt the pressure of a pair of lips upon it! Looking out, I saw that some of the girls and women had come round to that side of the vehicle, and, doubtless, supposing that I was also a padre, had begun to kiss my hand. A certain feeling of pity or delicacy caused me to refrain from removing it—let them be happy in thinking they were also the recipient of some attention; and so I left it there. No one peered into the gloom of the vehicle's interior, or the supposed *padre* would have been discovered as a clean-shaven young Englishman, dressed, not in priestly black and cassock, but in riding garments! And when the vehicle started I did not consider it necessary to inform my companion of the *rôle* I had unwittingly played.

But the day's adventures were not over. In crossing the dry bed of an *arroyo* a wheel gave way and the coach overturned, fortunately for me on the side of the *padre*! Had it been otherwise the weight of the good priest might have caused me much inconvenience; but as it was I fell *upon* him. It was in no irreverent spirit that I afterwards cogitated that, at least on one occasion of my life, the Romish Church had interposed between me and injury! And as the priest was not hurt, I could afford to impart this view to him.

The poor *peon* class is there much under the influence of the priest, especially the women, and, indeed, among the upper classes the confessional and other priestly operations are attended with as much rigidity as in past centuries, although the male sex has very greatly emancipated itself therefrom, and receives any allusions to the priest with a shrug of the shoulders, or, at times, with coldness or open hostility towards that worthy. The Church has fallen into disrepute in Mexico, and it is impossible that it should ever regain its former preeminence. The humble *peones* arouse the foreigner's pity. Poor people! they are bound by centuries of class-distinction and priestly craft transplanted from an old-world monarchy. These people are generally affectionate and respectful; they will undergo hardship and toil to serve us if we have by justice and tolerance won their respect and sympathy; and with a faithfulness that is almost canine. Their feasts, ceremonies, griefs, are quaint and full of colour and the human touch. Their simple state of life and humble dress take nothing from their native courtesy. Behold yon sandalled and *manta-* (cheap calico) clad worker. He will never think of addressing us without taking off his grimy and battered hat, nor will he speak to his acquaintance or fellow worker save as "Don"—Don Tomás, Don Juan, or whatever it may be. His first salutation in the morning is always to ask how we have slept. Indeed this is a common form of salutation with all classes in Mexico, "*Como ha pasado usted la noche?*" And it is but an indication of that importance which they attach to sleep. None would think to disturb our *siesta*, no matter who might be waiting to see us, and nothing short of actual danger to us would cause us to be awakened before the usual hour, or aroused after we had retired.

The great enemy of the *peon* and Indian class is alcohol. Whether it be the mild intoxicant *pulque* of the plateau—for the beverage will not keep in the *tierra caliente*—or whether the fiery *aguadiente*, or cane-rum, or the potent *mezcal*, also made from *maguey*, the habit of drinking to excess is the ruination of the working class. Wherever it may be, whether under the shade of a tree in the noonday sun, or riding an attenuated horse across the plains, or at the dwelling of some *compadre* or other acquaintance, there is a bottle protruding from pocket or saddle-bags, and the odour of spirits in the air. The remedy lies largely in prohibition, but, alas! the country's legislators are generally great landowners, and part of their revenue comes from the growing of the *maguey*, or of the sugar-cane, and in the making and sale of *pulque* and *aguadiente*.

The dress of the *peon* is picturesque, and to the foreign observer ever strikes a note of almost operatic strain. As the sun sets the *peon* dons his *poncho*, or *serape*, as the red blanket which is his invariable outer garment is termed. In the cool air of the morning or evening he speaks but little, covering his mouth with a corner of the *serape*, for he has a constant and, as far as the foreigner can observe, unfounded fear of pneumonia. The crowning point of his dress is the great conical, broad-brimmed hat, which is the main and peculiar characteristic of the inhabitants of this land; a national and remarkable headgear which is met with nowhere else. There is ever a brigand-like local colour about the Mexican *peon*, and indeed of some of the upper classes in their national dress. The *peon*, or the *vaquero*,[32] as he stalks muffled through the streets or *plaza*, or lurks within his habitation with a corner of the *serape* thrown over his shoulder and a knife stuck in his belt, is a subject which might have stepped from the boards of a theatre! Although he is respectful in his demeanour, and often devout in his language, the open greeting and confident demeanour of the Anglo-Saxon is absent. Who can blame him? The oppression of centuries weighs upon him; he has been doomed to ignorance and poverty ever since his Iberian conquerors set foot upon the soil which was his, and the descendants of this same conquering race do little but perpetuate his melancholy state. In the years since the Republic was established he has been constantly dragged from his peaceful labours to serve this or that revolutionary malcontent, and so made to destroy rather than create industry. And to-day he is the subject of such unequal wealth and class distinction whose change it seems impossible to hope for. Yet there is some progress.

32 Cowboy.

As to the women of the *peones*, their dress is generally sombre-hued and modest. No scarlet blanket covers them, but a blue *reboso*, or shawl, which is generally placed over the head in lieu of a hat. The women of the poorer classes accept, with what to the foreigner seems almost a pathetic resignation, the style of dress which custom has dictated to their class. There is no aping of the rich in their attire. Whether it be the fine lace *mantilla* or the Parisian hat which the far-distant-from-her señorita wears, as in temple or *plaza* she takes her dainty way, or the pretty frock or delicate shoes, the poor woman of the *peon*, or the *mujer* of the petty shopkeeper, casts no envious glance—but no, that would not be true! She casts them, but she will not strive to imitate. Is there not some virtue in such non-emulation, or is it but the spirit of a deadened race? Yet this rather sombre and unattractive apparel is found more among the *peon* class; the Indian girl in some parts of Mexico—as at Tehuantepec—wears a handsome native costume, derived from Aztec days, at holiday time.

NATIVE WOMEN OF TEHUANTEPEC: ORDINARY DRESS AND CHURCH-GOING COSTUMES.

The *reboso*, or shawl, is a useful article of clothing of the women of this class. We shall meet her trudging along dusty roads or over steep mountain trails, sad-faced and patient, with her baby slung behind her in a *reboso* tied round her waist; or possibly she has utilised it to collect some scanty *leña*, or firewood, from among the dry scrub of the *arroyo*, just as her man uses his *serape* as a universal hold-all on occasions for potatoes, maize, or other articles which he has purchased at the village market.

The complexion of the Mexican *peon* class is generally exceedingly dark, approaching coffee-colour, although they have, of course, no strain of African blood in their composition. But the types of faces vary much for different parts of the country—due to the numerous distinct races. Some purely aboriginal faces are almost clear-cut and attractive, especially among the women. The *peon* women, too, are often soft and pretty, and attract, and are attracted, by the foreigner. Near the lines of the railroads the progeny of Mexican women—Anglo-Saxon in type—are often seen!

The Mexicans, *peones* and Indians, have a remarkable aptitude—like those other peoples of aboriginal blood in America, as Peru—for making things by hand which require care and patience. The exquisite figures with delicately carved features and dress, pottery, woven material, as mats and pouches, straw (and Panama) hats, and so forth, are such in delicacy and texture as it is improbable could be made by the workmen of Europe.

Indeed, the elements of care and patience are much developed among these semi-civilised peoples. A Mexican *peon* will not miss his way on the plains or in the mountains—the least indication will serve his recollection of the route, and, indeed, it is not necessary to enlarge upon the aborigine's natural science of woodcraft. Moreover, the *peon* will carry any delicate object—a theodolite or barometer, or other scientific instrument, for example—with such care over the roughest and most precipitous places that it will never be injured, and where in similar situations, the clumsy European or American would inevitably bring it to disaster.

The Mexicans are dexterous in pottery-making, and they fashion great *ollas* to a wonderfully symmetrical form without other appliance than that of a small wooden paddle or beater, with which the red earth-mortar is shaped and patted into form. This method, indeed, dates from Aztec time, when there was no potter's wheel. They are sun-dried first and then baked. The makers of these, or the vendors, carry numbers of them about bound up in crates, a huge load on their backs; and as they are much in demand, the women rush out of their houses eager to purchase, as the *olla*-carriers enter the villages. These huge pots are mainly used for carrying water from the spring, and with a *reboso* or shawl as a pad upon their shoulder or their head, the women walk gracefully along with their heavy burden of the necessary water-supply, at morning or evening.

The *peon* is ever ready to exchange work for play, or indeed to shelve the former altogether at times, and the numerous feast-days—the *dias de fiesta*—which are the despair of the foreign employer of labour in Mexico, fall in well with this disposition. The spectacle of the bull-fight appeals greatly to him, ever the national sport. Even in the small villages and *haciendas*, remote from the capitals, bull-fighting is the favourite sport, and local *toreros* from among the middle-class young men of the place enter the arena to display their valour. A bull-ring is easily made in the *plaza*, or a *corral* or courtyard, and young bulls, sometimes with their horns blunted to render the pastime less dangerous, are harried about the improvised arena in the usual style, the *picadores*, *bandilleros* and *capeadores* all taking up their office in approved style. The sport tries the mettle of these *aficionados*, as the amateur bull-fighters are termed, and many, considering discretion the better part of valour, promptly retreat and hurriedly climb the barrier as the angry bovine makes his entrance to the ring. As a rule, however, the young Spanish-Mexicans show a bold front to the animal. Is this not the sacred and national sport of the land of their forefathers? Does not the *sangre española* run in their veins? None so low as to turn before a bull, or if he does the howls of the *peon* spectators who line the walls will make him blush for shame.

In such a scene I found myself on one occasion. A remote *hacienda*, and bull-fight, of *aficionado* nature, inaugurated in honour of some occasion of birthday or other anniversary of the proprietor, whose guest I was. Some lively bulls were performing in the arena, and more than one ambitious amateur bull-fighter had retired the worse for his temerity. "Señor," said one of the guests turning to me, "doubtless you would like to try your hand!" The idea met with instant approval by the others present, and the word went round that the *inglés* was to enter the ring. I confess the invitation did not appeal to me. The bull at that moment occupying the arena had already drawn blood from one of his tormentors, who was outside repairing his injuries, and the animal stood in the centre of the space, lashing his tail and throwing earth over his shoulder after the manner of his kind, what time he wrathfully eyed the audience. My host—he was a Spaniard, a large landowner—possibly seeing some disinclination reflected on my face, interposed: "There is no shame in refusing," he said. "It is not to be expected that an Englishman knows anything about this sport." But the ladies of the party looked, I thought, disappointed, and the *peones* around the walls were already shouting my name, and calling upon me to "*entrar*"! This would never do. "Señores," I said in the most grandiloquent Spanish I could muster, "you are much mistaken if you think an Englishman is any more afraid of a bull than a Mexican or a Spaniard"; and, taking a proffered pair of *banderillas*, I descended from the platform and entered the arena.

The cheers and yells which arose from the *peon* audience were deafening, and then an ominous calm. The bull advanced towards me and—I must confess it—loomed large as a locomotive! But perhaps fortune favours the brave, and whether from often having seen it done or whether from good luck alone, I placed the decorated *banderillas* successfully in the animal's neck, and instantly leaped aside with instinctive agility, having felt the breath from his nostrils upon my face, whilst the animal, smarting with the pain from the barbed points, bounded some paces away, and the audience cheered itself hoarse and gave repealed *vivas* for the *inglés*. Now was the moment to retire in "peace with honour," but desirous of showing how little I cared for the animal—a sentiment I did not really feel—I turned my back to the bull, and ostentatiously unrolled a Havana cigar from its lead-foil covering, and calmly cutting off the end, I proceeded to light it. The bull saw it. With a bound he was upon me, and as I turned to leap aside his horns passed clean under my waistcoat and shirt, and ripped them open to the flesh. Hurled aside by the impact, I lost my balance and staggered wildly, but faced the brute again, whilst deafening yells—whether of delight at possible disaster or encouragement to go on, I could not tell—arose from the spectators who thronged the barriers. But up came the *capeadores*, and diverting the animal's attention as was their office, I retired, not without dignity, and received the congratulations of my friends, and a Spanish sash from the presiding "queen" of the entertainment. But I took no credit for it myself; rather I felt that I had done wrong and barely escaped punishment, in countenancing and taking part in what every Englishman must consider an uncivilising form of sport.

Horsemanship and its accompanying callings play a prominent part in rural life in Mexico. The *hacendado*, or estate owner, or *ranchero*, mounts his horse directly after early morning coffee, in order to make the round of his plantations. The *vaquero*, or cowboy of Mexico, is possibly the most expert horseman in the world, and the method of training the horse to the lightest touch of the rein, and the comfortable yet swift *paso*, or rapid march to which the animal is trained, are such as the foreign observer notes with interest. Indeed, is he wise he adopts this *paso* himself, instead of the English trot.

A distinctive riding dress is used by the Mexican horseman—the *charro* costume, which is a remarkable and even gorgeous habiliment, both as regards man and horse. The short coat and tightly-fitting trousers are made of soft deerskin, tanned to a rich burnt-sienna hue. Down the edges of the coat and upon its lappels a border of luxuriant gold or silver lace is worked, and round the buttonhole similar profuse ornament is planted, and upon the cuffs. A stripe of intricately patterned gold lace runs down the seams of the trousers, which latter, tight-fitting at the top, are adjusted very closely at the calf of the leg. For riding in rough country a further leg-covering is worn; a kind of loose trousers put over the others and buckled round the waist, called *chaparreras*, made and ornamented with similar material. The crowning glory of the whole is the huge Mexican hat. This is made of thick beaver-looking felt, with a soft silky surface. Its form is well known with a very high tapering dome-like crown and very broad brim. This great headgear is also profusely ornamented with gold or silver lace, worn principally by the *rancheros*, and the owner's initials are generally worked upon the front of the crown in large gold letters. The hat is of considerable weight. To return to the lower members again, the feet are armed with a pair of spurs of appalling size and weight, the "wheel" portion being several inches in diameter, and the whole weighing several pounds each. These are often of steel inlaid with gold or silver, and are buckled upon the foot with an elaborate strap and embossed medallion. These spurs do not lacerate the horse, as their points are blunt. The effect of the whole dress is almost dazzling, but the big hat set over the tight trousers and short coat gives a somewhat top-heavy appearance.

The trappings of the horse are not unworthy of the gorgeous habiliments of the *jinete*, or horseman. The Mexican *montura*, or saddle, is of beautifully tanned leather of a high colour, and profusely-embroidered with silver patterns and ornamentations, and the whole is exceedingly heavy. It is, however, remarkably comfortable, and "the horse carries the weight," the Mexican will inform you if you criticise its bulk in comparison with an English saddle. For work in the country no experienced traveller would ever think of using the English form of saddle. In Mexico or South American countries it is altogether unsuitable, both for horse and rider, giving a maximum of fatigue and minimum of comfort. Also the heavy Mexican bit and single rein are better for travel in these regions, as ever used by the natives. This bit is not necessarily cruel, and in fact the Mexican horses are so remarkably trained as to their mouths, that the faintest touch of a single finger on the bridle is sufficient for instant obedience. As to the huge spurs they are not necessarily cruel, indeed they are less so than the sharp English kind, which draw blood easily where the native instrument does not abrade the skin.

The remarkable and dexterous management of the lasso, or *riata*, by the rural Mexican is such as fills the beholder with admiration and surprise that so skilful a combination of hemp and horseflesh, managed by a man's hand, could exist. Behold the *vaquero*, with his *riata* whirling aloft as at full gallop he pursues a fleeing bull! Closing upon it a few yards away the lasso swings its unerring coils through the air, the noose descends upon horns or hoofs at the will of the *vaquero*, and it is quite common to lasso the two hind legs of the animal whilst he is in full gallop. And now the horse plays his intelligent part. The noose has fallen with the accuracy desired; the *vaquero* winds his end rapidly around the horn of the saddle; the horse gives a half-turn in the quickness of thought, in obedience to his own knowledge and a touch of the bridle, so presenting his flank and a long base to the direction of the strain; the rope tightens tense and smoking with the pull; horse and rider stand unmoved, but the great bulk of the arrested bovine falls prone to the ground. It is an art, a wonderful dexterity we have witnessed, acquired from birth. I ambitiously tried it once, but failed to turn the horse quickly enough, and was pulled over to the ground. Of sports on horseback the

Mexicans indulge in several. Mark our friend the *ranchero,* in his holiday dress, upon a *dia de fiesta*. He is going to show us the "raya." His man marks a spot on the flat ground; the horseman retires with his steed to a short distance, put spurs to the animal, comes thundering along towards us at full gallop, and as he reaches the mark on the soil he suddenly draws rein, and the obedient horse putting his legs rigidly together, slides forward on his hoofs with his own momentum, scoring out a mark about his own length on the ground, and stops dead without moving a muscle. This mark is the "raya." Another diversion is that where gaily-be-ribboned chickens—alive—are provided by the *novias,* or sweethearts of the young men: and these, mounted on their steeds, ride fast and furious to capture the bird from the one who holds it. The unfortunate chicken is generally torn to pieces, and sometimes in jealous anger and rivalry other blood is shed than that of the innocent bird!

The *riata* at times serves the Mexican as a lethal weapon. Perhaps a quarrel between two hot-blooded *vaqueros* has taken place. One draws his revolver—if his circumstances permit him the possession of so expensive a weapon, and they are generally carried—whilst the other lays hand to his *riata*. It might be supposed that the man with the revolver would triumph, but woebetide him if he fails to bring down his enemy—both are darting about on their agile horses—before the chambers are exhausted, for the other, whirling the rope aloft, lassoes him, and putting spurs to his own beast, drags the unfortunate man from his horse and gallops away across the plain, dragging him mercilessly to death among the rocks and thorns. For the Mexican when aroused to anger—and his fiercest passions are generally the outcome of love affairs or of drink—is mercilessly cruel and revengeful, and thinks little of shedding the blood of a fellow-creature in the heat of a personal encounter. Among the lower class the knife, or *puñal,* is a ready weapon, and a stab, whether in the dark or in the daylight, is a common way of terminating a personal question. This is the shadow of the Aztec war-god thus thrown across the ages! Again it may be said of the Mexicans—love blood, wine, dust!

Among the upper class Mexicans such matters are, of course, unknown, but the challenge and the duel is still a custom of the country, as it is throughout Spanish-America generally. It fell to my lot in one Spanish-American country to receive a challenge. The gentleman who thought himself aggrieved formally sent two friends to wait upon me, requesting that I would name my seconds and select weapons. There was something operatic about the matter to my mind, although they appeared to be in earnest, and I could not help reminding my two visitors of the proposal of a famous American humourist regarding a choice of weapons in such a case—"brick-bats at half-a-mile, or gatling-guns," or something of that nature. However, they would not be turned from their purpose even when I seriously asked if they really desired the shedding of gore. I gravely replied that Englishmen did not enter into such affairs and that I considered it uncivilised; and absolutely refused to have anything to do with them. This they pretended to attribute to cowardice, and said that in such a case I should be exposed to affront or attack in the street, to which I made reply that I expected to be able to take care of myself and to punish any one who should dare to attempt such a course. I easily gathered that an elaborate duel was in their minds, a show or scene, such the Latin races love and the Anglo-Saxon abhors, and I accused them of this. At length, in order to get rid of them I made the following proposal: "If your friend is really desirous that his blood or mine shall be shed, let him meet me alone—I want no seconds, nor friends nor any other fanfare. I go out every morning on horseback along a certain mountain road. To-morrow I will go alone—let your friend meet me, also alone, and there, without more witnesses than Heaven, we can settle all accounts." This grandiloquent-sounding exhortation had the advantage of coming straight from the heart; it was what I had resolved to do, and moreover my side was the just one. The two seconds departed without much comment, and on the following morning I mounted my horse and went out alone, along the described road. But in the front holster of the saddle there was a long-barrelled Colts revolver, and the Winchester carbine I had occasionally brought down a deer with was strapped in its usual place alongside the saddle. Yet upon all that expanse of road not a soul did I meet, neither that day nor on the several following ones during which I remained in the vicinity.

But such matters are comparatively rare, and the Spanish-American is generally a warm and courteous friend, with a considerable regard for Englishmen, and ever ready to show his hospitality, and those general qualities which are ever esteemed of the *caballero*.

The *riata*, which appliance or weapon has been described, is ever the accompaniment of the Mexican horseman, and part of his equipment. No rider would ever go forth without, for its multiplicity of uses in woodcraft and travel is remarkable. It is one of the main accoutrements of the *rurales*, the fine body of county police which were called into being by President Diaz. At the time of the war with the French of Maximilian the *riata* was sometimes employed by the Mexican soldiers with deadly effect in foraging or scouting parties. Two Mexicans, each with the end of a *riata* wound round the horn of his saddle, would charge suddenly from ambush upon some unsuspecting *Franceses*, tearing them from their horses with the taut rope. "The Mexicans have a terrible and barbarous weapon—the *riata*!"—was recorded by the French soldiery at that time.

As to foreigners in Mexico at the present time, those most in evidence are the Spaniards and the Americans of the United States. Spaniards are continually arriving, and they generally settle down and make good and useful citizens, and often amass much wealth. They are not, however, of the upper or cultivated class from Spain, and their manners and language are far inferior to those of the cultured Mexicans. The Spaniard of a certain class is possibly the worst-spoken man to be met with. His speech teems with indecent words and profane oaths, and whilst he does not mean to use these except as a mere habit, it marks him out from other races, even from the American with his own peculiar and constant "god-dam" and other characteristic terms, both profane and indecent. The most noticeable and objectionable American habit, however, which is shared by the Mexican and South American to the full, is that of continually expectorating. The Anglo-American never leaves it off, whilst, as to the Spanish-American, it is necessary to put up notices in the churches in some places requesting people "not to spit in the house of God!" There is a considerable population of Americans in Mexico, and some of these are of doubtful class and antecedents. But it would be unjust to pretend that only the Americans have furnished a doubtful element for Mexico's floating population. The shores of Albion have furnished a good many examples in the form of "unspeakable" Scotchmen, Englishmen, and Irishmen, at times. Yet the British name has, as a rule, been well established throughout Mexico and Spanish-America, and the American from the United States has often enjoyed the benefit of a reputation he had not earned, for, to the native mind, the distinction between the two English-speaking races is not always apparent at first sight, although it is upon closer acquaintance.

Whilst there is a growing sense of respect and esteem between the Mexicans and the Americans, the former have never quite forgotten that the latter despoiled them of an empire—from their point of view—by the Texan war, half a century ago or more, and only recently have the Mexicans come to believe that the big republic to the north no longer cherishes desires of further annexation of territory. The Americans, for their part, have given up dubbing the Mexicans as "greasers," and have acknowledged the pleasing and refined civilisation of their southern neighbours. The North American, or *Americano*, is often known in Mexico as the "Yankee"—not used in an offensive sense, but as a convenient designation. This is varied by the still less distinguished term of "gringo," and indeed, both these terms are employed, not only in Mexico, but thousands of miles below, in South America—Ecuador, Peru, Chile. The latter is not necessarily an opprobrious term, and it is applied to all Anglo-Saxons, British or American, and, indeed, in South America, to all Europeans of a fair complexion. Its derivation has been expounded by various writers as having come from the words of a song sung by some British or American sailors upon landing at a Mexican port, but the etymology seems doubtful. That of "Yankee" is more assured—the corruption of "English," or "Anglais," or "Ingles," employed by the Indians of North America towards the early settlers.

Conditions of life and travel in Mexico vary greatly according to the region we may be called upon to traverse. On the great plateau such as I have described, the hand of civilisation prevails, even if its evidences are at times far apart. In the tropical lowlands, whether of the Gulf or of the Pacific side of the country, we may be much more seriously thrown upon our own resources, whether for food, transport, or habitation. In the State of Guerrero there are yet large tracts of land absolutely unexplored, and the numerous tribes of Indians inhabiting certain of the tropical regions are under scarcely more than the semblance of control. Yet it cannot be said that they are ferocious or dangerous. Some of them, indeed, are cowardly, and will not even venture far from their villages for fear of wild beasts, whilst others form the most active and fearless guides, varying characteristics which show the wide range of peoples embodied in the country, as set forth in a previous chapter. Whilst Mexico cannot be called a "sportsman's paradise," there is in certain regions a great profusion of game, from turkeys to crocodiles. The *guajalote*, or Mexican wild turkey, with its great red beard and shimmering blue-black plumage, is a conspicuous inhabitant of Tamaulipas and other wild regions, and its low flight and plump body render it comparatively easy of securing, whilst it forms an excellent addition to the bill of fare. Huge wild cats abound in the broken country, and *osos*, or Mexican bears. Of sport, adventure, and romantic travel we may take our fill among these semi-tropical valleys, rivers, and mountains. Of noxious insects, malaria, wild beasts; of flooded streams and parched deserts; of sand-storms, snow-storms, and rain-storms; of precipitous mountains, tracts, and dangerous bogs; of gloomy forest and appalling crags; of delay, danger, and hardship, we shall have all that adventurous spirits may seek, and count the time well lost. Of pleasure in nature and solitude we shall have much, and of the study of primitive and civilised man, and of coquettish maidens and Indian maids, we shall carry away enduring recollections.

We are in camp. The exigencies of our travel have bid us take up our abode in that hastily-constructed *jacal*, or hut built of branches and plastered outside with mud, such as the *peon* knows cunningly how to contrive. Indeed, in such habitations a large part of Mexico's fifteen million inhabitants dwell. I inspect the well-ventilated walls, for numerous open chinks are left. "The wind will come in," I say. "Yes, señor," José, my *peon*-constructor, replies with unconscious wit, "it will not only come in but it will go out"—and he proceeds to remedy the defect.

Our residence in this spot may be for some weeks whilst at our leisure we examine mines, hydrographic conditions, flora, or other matters of scientific or commercial interest which our self-chosen exile demands. The simple habitation is pitched when possible, of course, near to a water supply, a clear running stream, or lake, and if the latter we can take a morning plunge. This excites the surprise of our *mozo*, or servant, and the other men in our employ.

"No, señor," they hasten to urge us, "it is dangerous to bathe the body." This objection to the use of cold water in this way does not arise from a dislike of cleanliness necessarily. The traveller in Western America soon finds that care must be exercised in bathing in the open, for the effect of the sun and the water is to bring on malaria sometimes, which is more easily acquired than cured.

On the edge of our lake great white herons stand in the cool of the early morning, and the wild ducks swimming lazily on its surface invite a shot. If it is winter and we are upon the high regions of the great plateau, the lake may freeze at its edges, imprisoning the unfortunate birds in the ice. The heat of the midday sun at these high elevations is succeeded at night by the bitter cold of the rarefied air, and the white drill suit we have worn must be supplemented by heavier garments.

The sun sets in gorgeous splendour over the plain and upon the grey-blue hills, and the short tropic twilight gives place to darkness, save perchance as the silvery moon of Mexico may cast its peaceful beams over the desolate landscape. Cigarettes and coffee are finished. No sound breaks the silence; our men's tales are all told as they crouch round the campfire. We have sought our couch and turned in, bidding the *peones* look to the horses, which, tethered near at hand, champ their oats or maize contentedly, giving from time to time that half-human sign with which the equine expresses his contentment and comfortable weariness. All is still. Sleep falls upon us.... Hark! what is that? A long mournful howl comes from the plain and winds through the canyon, and is repeated in chorus. "What is it, José?" I call to my *mozo* and the other men. "Coyotes, Señor," he replies, "they are crying to heaven for rain." Of course, I had forgotten for a moment that they have this habit, and the sound seemed almost unearthly.

To return to the game. We are going a-hunting to-day. The great barren plains and sterile rocky ribs which intersect them, the stony foothills and the dry *arroyos* do not seem to offer much prospect of sport. But our friend the Mexican *hacendado*, who has ridden up from his *hacienda* for the purpose of inviting us, assures us to the contrary. And, indeed, his words are soon justified. He and his men have led us far away towards the head of the canyon, and the dry stream-bed is fringed with *mesquite* and cactus which might offer shelter to quarry of some nature. A dozen dark forms start suddenly from the shadow of the bank upon whose verge we stand. Bang! bang! bang! In the twinkling of an eye we had dismounted, flung our horses' reins to the attendant *mozos*, and pointed our Winchesters. Several of the dark forms lie upon the sand below, inert; the others, already squealing far enough off, scrambling away. What are they? "*Javelines*, Señor," the *mozos* make reply. They are peccaries. A good bag indeed and excellent eating, as their ribs, roasted over a fire at the bottom of the *arroyo*, attest. Later on we look round for our host, but he is away after a plump *venado*—deer— which, passing near at hand, proves too strong for the sportsman's instinct. But the night falls ere he returns. "Never mind," is his greeting, "although we have to sleep here we may eat good venison," and across the horse of his *mozo* lies the drooping body of the deer, its eyes glazed in death, and the blood still dripping from the bullet wound which laid it low.

And so our *hacendado* friend, who owns the land we are upon for leagues away, and knows it well, leads us to a cave snugly hidden in the rocky wall, with a floor of purest quartz sand, and a limpid rivulet flowing thereby. The saddle bags are brought in; they are full of bread and tinned meats and native fruits, brandy and wine from his own vineyards. We are his honoured guest, and he plies us with all this fare, not forgetting the venison roasting outside. And filled and comforted with good food we discourse far into the night of weird things tinged with our friend's strange superstition and curious lore. Outside the coyotes howl, far away on the plain, and the mournful cry of the *tecolote*, or Mexican night owl, faintly reaches my ears, as, wrapped in my blankets with a saddle for a pillow, I fall asleep upon the cavern floor.

CHAPTER XIII

MINERAL WEALTH. ROMANCE AND ACTUALITY.

Forced labour in the mines—Silver and bloodshed—History of discovery—Guanajuato—the *veta Madre*—Spanish methods—Durango—Zacatecas—Pachuca—The *patio* process—Quicksilver from Peru—Cornish miners' graves—Aztec mining—Spanish advent—Old mining methods—Romance of mining—The Cerro de Mercado—Guanajuato and Hidalgo—Real del Monte—Religion and mining—Silver and churches—Subterranean altars—Mining and the nobility—Spanish mining school—Modern conditions—The mineral-bearing zone—Distribution of minerals geographically—Silver—The *patio* process—Gold-mining and production—El Oro and other districts—Copper—Other minerals—General mineral production—Mining claims and laws.

"Grant me, oh! rock-ribbed matrix, here to know
 Thy minerall'd sanctuary;
 To none but me the sesame disclose,
 Un-oped since chaos fled!"

There is much of interest and something of pathos and romance attending the old mines of Spanish-American countries—Mexico, Peru, and others. They are so interwoven with the history of these countries, so redolent of the past, and of the hope, despair, piety, greed of the old taskmasters who worked them, and of the generations of toiling Indian workers who spent their lives in wresting treasure from the bowels of the earth. Religion, superstition, cruelty have marked their exploitation in past ages, and as we explore their grim abandoned corridors, and pass half fearfully their yawning pits, our imagination might conjure up some phantoms of those who toiled amid these old scenes of man's sweat and avarice.

The cruelty innate in the Spanish race has been shown in their mining methods, and the native population of Mexico, and in a larger scale of Peru, suffered severely at their hands. Guanajuato, one of the most famous and richest of the mining centres of Mexico—in past times as to-day—bears in its archives the stories of oppression which marked the methods of the Spaniards, and may be taken as a concrete example. It was a system of slavery under which these mines were worked—an atrocious system of forced labour which took no heed of Indian life, save as it might most cheaply extract a given quantity of gold or silver ore from the pits and adits beneath the ground. Thousands of *peones* were impressed into this forced labour; armed soldiers were stationed at the entrances of these labyrinths to see that each wretched serf deposited his sack of rock, under the load of which he had toiled up fathoms of notched pole, or ladder, from the infernal regions below, panting, sweating, expiring, and presently driven down again by the brutal taskmasters, jealous lest he might enjoy too much of the light of day and so sacrifice some moments in the delving amid the rocks which furnished the wealth. In 1619, a law was promulgated in Guanajuato—it remains upon the archives to this day—prohibiting the branding of slaves upon the face!

But these inhuman methods brought about their own punishment. The great Valenciana mine, opened in 1760, which for fifty years was worked at a sacrifice of human life by these methods, producing more than 300 million dollars, became at last the scene of a terrible vengeance, for the serfs rose in rebellion and massacred every white man upon the place. Indeed, the brutalities practised by the Spanish mine-owners largely influenced the revolution and secession from the mother country.

For more than three centuries there flowed from the mines of Mexico and Peru, millions and millions of silver and gold, which went to fill the needy coffers of Spain, to enrich a distant and callous or careless monarch, and to prop up a moribund nation. The appalling system of the *mitad* and the *encomenderos*, by which silver and gold were extracted with indecent haste, form such pages as can never be erased from the history of metallurgy in the New World.

Yet there is another light in which to regard the picture of Mexican mining, and remembering that mining operations, whether in the sixteenth or the twentieth century, whether in Spanish-America or elsewhere, ever embody conditions of usury and oppression, we may turn to this more pleasing aspect. For unless under grave oppression, the native miner, be it on the plateau of Anahuac, or in the Andine Cordillera, has been a zealous worker. His picturesque surroundings, simple mode of life, and easy-going disposition, together with the pervading sentimental attributes which his religion lent, and the sunny skies under which he toiled, took from mining much of the material brutality and grey atmosphere which enshroud it in Anglo-Saxon communities.

Mining was a source of enrichment which appealed strongly to the Spanish nature, and it must not be forgotten that to the efforts of the men of Spain the science of mining owes much. And, indeed, these remote waste places of the earth owe the civilisation they possess to the early work of these *Conquistadores*. The Anglo-Saxon world prides itself on the great discoveries and exploitations which have marked epochs in its gold- and silver-getting history, Australia, California, Nevada, Africa; but we shall not forget that Mexico and Peru were yielding up stores of gold and silver centuries before Captain Cook sailed, or before those historic nuggets were found by accident in Sutter's mill-stream, in the Californian Sierra region. Scarcely six years after the Conquest the silver of Mexico was being eagerly sought, and easily found, with that remarkable *olfato* possessed by the Spaniards. Shakespeare was at work, and Drake was voyaging under the Elizabethan ægis at the time when the great silver mines of the Mexican Sierra Madre were giving up their rich ores to treatment.

At Guanajuato, one of the most famous of the silver mining centres, prospecting was begun in 1525, only a few years after the Conquest, and the mining regions still further away to the north, as those of the famous Zacatecas and San Luis Potosi, had already been discovered. History relates that the silver deposits of Guanajuato were discovered as a result of a camp-fire, made by some muleteers, who found refined silver among the ashes, melted from the rock beneath! Shortly after the middle of the sixteenth century the great *Veta Madre*, or "mother lode," of Guanajuato was pierced, with an ore-body 100 feet wide. This place, which to-day boasts a population of fifty thousand souls, had begun to grow and was granted a charter as a *Villa Real* at the beginning of the seventeenth century. This before the sailing of the *Mayflower*! So, as we look back upon those strenuous times of Mexican mining, we shall see much of good arising from the metallurgical conquest. We have a vision of fair cities, established within mountain fastnesses, within fertile plains, long centuries before the advent of the locomotive, cities whose wealth came from the fabulous riches of the great silver mines, whose ore was quarried from its lodes and deposits, cities where fine cathedrals arose, built from the taxes levied upon the product of these mines, by which fortunate national trait some good at least was perpetuated for the inhabitants and toilers who produced it. Does the mining director and shareholder of to-day loosen his greedy and capacious pocket for such works? We might ask the toiling nigger—Kaffir, or Chinese, and his Jewish employer in the mines of Africa. The Spaniards did not suck out the wealth of Mexico's soil only to enrich a decadent monarch and his coffers, thousands of miles away, for which we have reproached them. Some of the wealth their enterprise produced formed beautiful cities and made the desert blossom where, before, savage tribes of Indians roamed; and stimulated great thoughts and actions in men whose historic names remain upon the country's history.

It was a laborious journey from Spain to Mexico in those days, and mining was marked by difficulties due to the remoteness of the region from means of communication, and also from the hostile Indian tribes, who resented the advent of the white man into their territory. An example of the tenacity and courage of the invaders against these odds is shown in the founding of the fine city of Durango, 350 years ago. At that time this region was the home of savage tribes of Indians, who continually made raids upon the Spaniards. A marvellously rich mine, the Avino, worked as a huge open quarry, which exists to-day, was deeded by its owner to those white inhabitants there who would consent to build their houses together for mutual protection. Thus the beginning of the city of Durango was made.

Another famous mining centre in those early days, just as it is at present, was Zacatecas, and its name alone conveys the idea of silver and gold. In 1546 it was, that a lieutenant of Cortes, traversing the country, arrived there, observed its promise of mineral wealth, and formed a settlement. So rapidly did the place become renowned that, forty years afterwards, a Royal Charter was given to the city, and a coat of arms, with the title, "Noble and Loyal." The curious archives of the Alvarado Mines—they were worked by Fernando Cortes—which were kept, and which show the care in these matters exercised by the Spaniards, still exist; as is the case, indeed, with the records of many of the great mining centres of Mexico and Peru. Here it is shown that an enormous output of silver was made, the total from 1548 to 1867 amounting to nearly eight hundred million dollars.

The great lodes of the famous mining centre of Pachuca, which at the present day are the most productive, were discovered by the companions of Cortes soon after the Conquest. But knowledge of the great wealth in silver there was held by the Aztecs, who, in fact, showed the main veins to the Spaniards. It was here that Bartolomé de Medina discovered the famous method of treating silver ores by amalgamation with quicksilver, known as the *patio* process, in 1557. An improvement on his invention came from Peru, in 1783, which was the use of mules instead of men in treading out the crushed ore. From far-away Peru other matters had come, as the quicksilver from the great Huancavelica mines, the mercury necessary for the process. And the beautiful Peruvian pepper trees, which were brought to ornament the *plaza* of Pachuca by one of the last of the Viceroys from Lima, form another reminiscence of the sister land of the Incas, in Mexico. There is at Pachuca a link with the world of Anglo-Saxon mining—the cemetery where to-day lie the bones of clever Cornish miners, who, in the time of the British revival of Mexican mining, taught the native their more useful methods. There lie these hardy sons of Cornwall, "each in his narrow cell," within the foreign soil whereon he had laboured.

What is the earliest time at which man began to dig for minerals in Mexico? It is not possible to determine this, as it is involved in the obscure history of the races of prehispanic days. But it has been affirmed that the method of recovering gold by amalgamation with quicksilver must have been known to the Maya civilisation which preceded the Aztec times. This is adduced from the discovery of a vessel containing quicksilver, during the excavations, in 1897, of the celebrated ruins of Palenque, in Chiapas. The native miners of Mexico have always won gold from the rocks, it is stated, by the method of crushing ore and treating it with quicksilver in amalgamation, and it is considered that the method has not been derived from the white man, but was handed down from the Mayas. Be this as it may, the early Mexicans carried on regular mining operations, extracting metals and metallic ores from the rocks by means of pits and galleries, and these, in some cases, furnished the Spaniards, after the Conquest, with the first indication of the existence of mineral-bearing veins. Gold was taken, however, among these prehistoric people, mainly from the stream-beds, or *placer* deposits, where it had been concentrated by nature. Gold was used more as a decorative or useful material than as a medium of currency, among the Aztecs, as among the Incas of Peru. However, in Mexico, transparent quills full of gold-dust were used as money. Gold ornaments figured largely in the military pomp and domestic decoration. The wonderful representations of animals and plants which they fashioned, and the remarkable presents of gold and silver which Montezuma made to Cortes, among them two great circular plates "as large as the wheel of a carriage," attest the relative abundance of the precious metal which the early Mexican possessed. How similar were these objects to those which figured in the dramatic scenes enacted in the Andes of Peru nearly three thousand miles away, a few years later, the student will recollect. Cortes told Montezuma that the Spaniards "suffered from a disease, which only gold could cure," and the Aztec monarch sent supplies of the yellow metal to alleviate this!

In addition to the mining and reduction of the ores of the three noble metals, gold, silver, and mercury, which these people understood and practised, were similar operations regarding lead, copper, and tin. Of the two latter they formed an alloy, and made tools of the bronze. Small T-shaped pieces of tin, moreover, were used as a medium of exchange or currency. As to iron, it appears to be the case that they were unacquainted with its use, notwithstanding that the ore of the metal is exceedingly plentiful. Nevertheless, it is stated that iron was mined and wrought into use at Tula, the Toltec centre, in the State of Jalisco, long before the advent of Cortes and the Spaniards.

Regarding the subject of the mining and metallurgy of the Aztecs and their predecessors in prehispanic days, it must be recollected that historical knowledge about it is exceedingly meagre, and the details of their operations in this field of industry are buried in much obscurity.

The Spanish advent wrought a marked change in the history of mining in the country. The Spaniards began to work mines as early as 1526, and continued their exploitation until 1810, the time of the War of Independence, at which period the value of the yearly output was 27,000,000 dollars. There was a general expulsion of the Spaniards in 1829. It was, however, in 1700 that the most marked period of Spanish mining began. The production of gold and silver from 1522 to 1879, according to the most reliable authorities, is given approximately as 3,725,000,000 dollars, of which gold formed 4 to 8 per cent. Indeed, the staple product of Mexico has ever been silver, in those remote times as it is to-day, and it has been calculated that possibly one-third of the existing quantity of silver in the world has come from the lodes of the Sierra Madre of Mexico.

The early Spaniards, whilst they did not despise the indication left or given by the Aztecs in the discovery of rich mines, struck out for themselves and found the great lodes which yielded fabulous fortunes in silver to their fortunate owners. These adventurous spirits spread over the whole of the country bordering upon the Sierra Madres, stimulated by the rich finds of silver mines successively made in one region or another. They have left old workings in almost every region where minerals exist, and they extracted great *bonanzas* with their crude, old-fashioned appliances. Ancient corkscrew-like workings, analogous more to the burrowings of animals than the excavations of man, honeycomb the crests of lodes and veins in every part of the country. After yielding fortunes to their workers these mines were abandoned, not because they were worked out, but for lack of appliances for drainage and hoisting, and in this condition, flooded or caved-in, remain innumerable of their old treasure-chambers to this day.

But not all the Spaniards' workings were of this nature. Magnificent tunnels were run by them into the bowels of hills, tunnels whose enormous dimensions excite the wonder of the mining engineer of to-day. In some instances these *socavones*, or great adits, are of such a size that a mounted horseman can enter with ease, or a locomotive might easily traverse them. Indeed, the engineer of to-day hesitates to attack the mountain sides with such bold adits as the Spaniard, with inferior materials, drove into them. Similar tunnels were driven by the Spaniards in some of the famous mines of Peru.[33]

33 See my book, "The Andes and the Amazon."

Ancient ore-reduction works, *arrastres*, canals, ditches, excavations, tunnels, pits, ruined buildings, and in some cases falling church walls, all of this bygone age, are encountered throughout the country, scattered far and wide. Those who lived and moved and had their being therein lie mingled with the dust these centuries past, and kind nature has often covered up the evidences of their handiwork with flower and foliage.

There was a steady flow of the two precious metals to the City of Mexico from the innumerable mines of the regions which produced them. To attempt to describe these mines, even those renowned for their richness, would fill a chapter alone. Fantastic displays of wealth are recorded by the owners of some of the great silver-producing mines—the bridal chambers of a palace, lined by the father of a bride with silver bars; the footpath from the *plaza* to the church paved with great silver ingots, for the bridal party.

A famous hill of iron—standing on the plains of Durango, stands out also from the historical vista of metallurgical discovery of those early days. In 1552 Vasquez de Mercado, a Spaniard of wealth and family in Mexico, living in Guadalajara, heard from the Indians that a great mountain of pure silver existed on the boundless plateau far to the north. Arming an expedition he set forth with this vain illusion actuating him, and travelled on day after day expecting that every sunrise would gleam upon the burnished slopes of this silver mountain. Battles were fought with the savage Indians who inhabited the plains, but vanquishing these the deluded party pushed on. At last, on the horizon, the hill rose; they approached it: it was iron! Sleeping sore-hearted at its base that night, Mercado and his companions were attacked by Indians, various soldiers killed, and he himself wounded. Returning homeward towards Guadalajara, the unfortunate leader succumbed to his wounds, fatigue, and the ridicule of his companions, and he perished. But the great Cerro de Mercado, the hill of iron, still remains one of the wonders of Mexico.

The long years of the struggle for throwing off the dominions of Spain wrought a great change in Mexican mining, and even when independence was accomplished, the warring revolutionary factions of a country divided against itself destroyed all sense of security, alienated the labour, and so mining fell into disuse, and the mines into ruins. The history of the great Guanajuato silver mines is typical of the effect political conditions exercised upon this industry. The great output of silver from the Valenciana mine—300 million dollars during the last half of the eighteenth century—fell, after the first decade of the nineteenth, to insignificant proportions. The city was attacked in 1810, when in the zenith of her production, by the revolutionary army of the Republicans under Hidalgo, the famous instigator of independence. Sanguinary struggles took place in the city, which fell, and with it the mining industry. Work was stopped; the waters flooded the shafts and galleries, general lawlessness took the place of order, and bands of armed robbers helped themselves at will to the silver, and made forced loans upon the community. Indeed, at the great mining centres throughout the country, Mexican mine buildings resemble fortifications rather than the structures of a peaceable industry; those which were constructed during those turbulent times. Battlemented walls and loopholes give some of these places the appearance of the stronghold of robber barons of the Middle Ages, and remind the traveller, under the peaceful *régime* of to-day, how rapid has been the country's progress.

The troubled times of Iturbide followed, and mining operations practically ceased. The Indians at this period became unruly in some districts, due to the withdrawal of the Spanish soldiers who protected the mining communities; and in Sonora, one of the busiest of the mining states, a great uprising of the savage Apaches in 1825 caused the abandoning of towns and industries and the inauguration of a long period of ruin and bloodshed. In 1824 something of a revival had begun, by the operations of English capitalists in the great silver-producing centres of Real del Monte, at Pachuca, as already mentioned, and at Guanajuato. The history of this period at Real del Monte is a remarkable one, not yet forgotten, and the lavish outlay of funds made by the London company in Mexico and the extraordinary speculation upon the shares in London are still pointed to as an example of mining operations as conducted at that period. After spending twenty million dollars and extracting sixteen millions from its mines, the company was wound up in 1848. It was succeeded by a Mexican company, which operated to the present time, when sale has been made to American capitalists. The turbulent times of Maximilian and the struggles later for the Presidency of the Republic among its ambitious and unscrupulous military element in later years told against peaceful industry. Soldiers and bandits vied with each other in extortions and robberies, and the fortifications which it was necessary to construct around the mine buildings attest the state of lawlessness of that period.

Even towards the close of last century life and property were insecure, and men went armed in daylight in the streets of Pachuca even in 1890. At Guanajuato the English company which had acquired the great Valenciana and La Luz mines worked them successfully for years, but often under difficulties due to the raids of revolutionists—as in 1832. But a disastrous period followed, and during the last decade of the nineteenth century the end came. The regeneration of these historic groups of mines which is now taking place is due to American enterprise—the British *régime* is over. The Aztec, the Spaniard, the Mexican, the Briton, and the American—each have had their day in taking this treasure of the white metal from the mother lodes of Anahuac. Whatever their operations, good or evil, they have in succession done service to the world—putting into circulation added means of currency and commerce.

The extent into which religious matters and emblems entered into mining in these early days in the New World was remarkable. In many cases the entrances to the mines were through elaborate stone doorways, with pillar, capital, and pediment, carved figures of saints, and surmounted by a cross. Such are often encountered in Mexico and Peru, and they seem rather the portals to a temple than the entrance to a mine. There was some virtue in work which lavished its sentiment and artistic skill upon the surroundings of a purely industrial enterprise. Churches and chapels, in many instances, surmount the hills whose bowels are pierced by shaft and gallery, and upon the walls of these hang strange pictures, depicting, in some places, incidents of mining life and accidents, placed there perchance by some devout one who had escaped from danger. In some cases these churches were built by fortunate men who had become fabulously rich by the discovery of some great *bonanza*, and in token of their gratitude to their patron saint who had guided them to so fortunate a destiny they raised the temple which bore his name.

The fine cathedral of Chihuahua, which cost more than half a million dollars, was built from a tax levied upon every pound of silver from the rich Santa Eulalia mine—discovered in 1704—of that region; and in the State of Guerrero, at Taxco, a splendid church was built which cost, it is stated, one and a half million dollars to construct, yielded by the famous mine there. A huge gallery, or tunnel, which was begun by Cortes, forms part of the extensive workings. Another example embodying this strange medley of silver and piety is that of the celebrated shrine, or church, of Guadalupe, near the capital, whose sacred vessels, altar rails, candelabra, and other accessories of a like nature, are formed of silver contributed by the pilgrims who, since the time of the vision which made the place famous, journeyed thither. The weight of the silver contained in these articles is calculated at fifty tons. In the plateau-city of Durango stands a fine cathedral, and this was built from the taxes imposed upon the great Avino mine, and stands as a lasting monument to the great natural wealth of silver which gave it being and which for 350 years has enriched the inhabitants of that favoured spot. In some of the rich mines it is recorded that the miners were permitted to carry out each day a large piece of rich ore, which they presented as an offering to the priest, who devoted the total to the building of a temple. At Catorce a splendid church was so constructed, at a cost of nearly two million dollars.

The great Valenciana mine at Guanajuato, of which mention has been made as the scene of ruthless oppression practised upon the natives by the Spaniards, which terminated in bloody vengeance, left a monument to the fabulous wealth extracted from it. This was built by a miner, one Obregon, who, the chronicles of the city state, became the "richest man in the world." With that almost fanatic and inexhaustible credence and energy which has often characterised the Spanish miner, he drove his adit year after year into the bowels of the great "mother lode"; penniless, ruined at last, without credit, and earning by his losses and persistence the name of *el tonto*—"the fool." But—almost as if his patron saint had resolved to teach his detractors a lesson—the reward came. The richest *bonanza* that the "mother lode" ever yielded he struck. From the results of this great treasure—a mere fraction of it—he caused the fine Valenciana church to be raised, whose handsome façade still draws the traveller's attention and marks the romantic episode of mining lore which gave it birth. The building of the temple was begun in 1765; its cost was a million dollars.

Ancient and, in many cases, ruined churches, especially in some of the northern states, lie scattered throughout the regions where great mining communities dwelt—now dead and gone. But religion—or the barbaric custodian of religion, the Inquisition—claimed her victims among the workers of mines. At the beginning of the seventeenth century it was that a rich mine—the Monoloa, in the State of Jalisco—was being worked by one Treviño and his partner, who, having been denounced to the Holy Office by jealous neighbours, they were accused of invoking the aid of the devil in their work. The unfortunate mine-owner was brought to the capital in consequence in 1649 and burned alive!

The Mexican miner, like his brothers of Peru or Chile, not content with the churches and shrines above ground which his religion afforded, often formed chapels and set up images in the subterranean caverns to whose habitation his daily toil condemned him. Shrines and crosses are frequently encountered in the galleries and chambers of Mexican mines now, as ever. Often, candles are kept burning before them throughout the eternal night, which they illuminate, and in some cases the devout among the miners go through these underground labyrinths in their daily toil in the dark, saving their candles to light the shrine! As they pass this bright spot their accustomed hand comes up to make the sign of the cross, and wearied knees humble themselves in a genuflexion. In one of the mines at Guanajuato there is an elaborate underground shrine where as many as two hundred candles burn at times, shedding a radiance which contrasts weirdly with the gloomy depths of worked-out caverns which surround it.

Such vast wealth as was extracted from some of these mines brought not only material riches, but royal honours and State positions to their owners. Titles of nobility were given by the Spanish sovereigns to fortunate mine-owners, some of whom had afforded loans or rendered other services, and they received the high reward of being admitted into the ranks of the Spanish aristocracy. Thus the builder of the great church of Valenciana at Guanajuato, which has been described in this chapter, from plain Antonio Obregon became Count of Valenciana. And, again, another miner of that city, Sardañeta, who drew millions from the famous Rayas mine, from the *bonanza* which his persistent adit upon the "mother lode" laid bare, received the title of Marquis of Rayas. Still another—marquis and viscount—this wonderful city and its silver mountains afforded in Francisco Mathias, the owner and worker of mines upon this mighty ore deposit. To some of these men, as related, there have remained monuments in the great churches they built. The Marquis of Sardañeta raised up the massive and enduring structures which form the buildings of the Rayas mine at Guanajuato, whose striking architectural features of flying buttresses, massive walls, and sculptured portals arrest the traveller's attention. No sheds of props and corrugated roofs are there; but arches, pillars, and walls of solid stone, cut and carved, defying the centuries—and above their portal is the sculptured image of Michael the archangel.

Pachuca, the wonderful silver-producing city not far from the capital of Mexico, produced a Mexican noble. This was Pedro Romero de Terreros, who, in 1739, having discovered a great *bonanza*, enriched himself by this characteristic stroke of fortune. He rendered some service to the King—presenting a battleship to the Imperial Navy—and was created a count—Conde de Regla.

It is not to be supposed that the Spanish Government did not recognise, in its demands for bullion from its colony of Mexico, any necessity for scientific advancement in mining. A petition sent to Carlos III. in 1744 by various prominent persons, and originated by one of the foremost miners of the country, secured the Royal assent to the creation of a "Mining Tribunal," and towards the close of the century this was established, with a school where the sons of poor miners received gratuitous education in mining, without distinction of caste or colour. Indeed, the sons of Indian chiefs of the Philippines were brought over and instructed here, and returned later to stimulate gold mining in their native land. A special tax on miners was then imposed for the purpose of raising an adequate building, and this was completed in 1813, and it has been considered one of the best architectural features of the capital. It contained a special chapel, where services were held for the students up to the time of the Reform, after which it was turned into a library.

Important as mining has been in the past history of Mexico, it is, and must remain, the most important of the industries of the country—in the sense of wealth produced. This does not mean, of course, that it is the most beneficial to the interests of the country and its inhabitants at large, for agriculture is that by which the bulk of the native Mexicans earn their means of subsistence.

The mineral-bearing zone of the country is a very extensive one, and includes all that portion of the Republic traversed by the Sierra Madres and their offshoots. From the State of Sonora in the north, the boundary with the United States, to that of Chiapas in the south—bordering upon the neighbouring Republic of Guatemala—minerals are found. The region in which the most important mining districts exist, and in which the historic mines of Mexico lie, forms a great zone 1,600 miles long—between the States of Sonora in the north to Oaxaca in the south—and 250 miles wide. These more famous and largely-worked mines are chiefly upon the western slope of the Eastern Sierra, and their elevations above sea-level range from 3,000 feet to 9,000 feet, and more. The minerals which are found throughout this great region include almost all those known to commerce, and, more or less in relative order of their importance, are as follows:—

Silver, copper, gold, lead, quicksilver, iron, coal, zinc, salt, antimony, petroleum, sulphur, tin, bismuth, platinum; and others more rarely, as nickel, cobalt, &c. Onyx, marble, opals, emeralds, sapphires, topazes, rubies, are found, and other precious stones, whilst diamonds are said to exist in certain localities. Agates, cornelians, obsidian, are also among the products of this nature.

The following table shows the principal distribution of minerals in the various states:—

STATE.	MINERALS.													
	Silver.	Gold.	Copper.	Lead.	Tin.	Mercury.	Iron.	Coal.	Petroleum.	Zinc.	Antimony.	Sulphur.	Bismuth.	Salt.
Aguascalientes	"		"		"									
Campeche	"		"					"	"					
Chiapas	"	"	"	"			"	"						

State	1	2	3	4	5	6	7	8	9	10	11	12	13
Chihuahua	"	"	"	"			"			"			
Coahuila	"	"	"	"						"			
Colima	"	"	"										
Durango	"	"			"		"		"		"		
Guanajuato	"		"		"							"	
Guerrero	"	"	"			"	"						
Hidalgo	"			"			"						
Jalisco	"	"	"			"	"	"					
Lower California	"	"	"								"		"
Mexico	"	"									"		
Michoacan	"	"	"				"	"			"		
Nuevo Leon	"			"					"				
Oaxaca	"	"		"			"	"					
Puebla	"		"	"			"	"					
Querétaro	"	"	"	"	"	"				"			
San Luis Potosi	"	"				"	"				"		
Sinaloa	"	"								"			
Sonora	"	"	"	"	"		"	"					
Tabasco								"					
Tamaulipas	"		"	"									
Tepic	"	"	"	"			"	"					"
Vera Cruz	"	"					"	"	"	"			
Zacatecas	"	"	"		"	"				"			

The geological formation of the country does not bear special relation to the deposits of metalliferous minerals, which are distributed in many parts of the great zone. In general terms it may be said that the abundance of the ores rather than their richness characterises the mines of Mexico and is the source of their wealth. Those which have most steadily produced bullion generally consisted of a main lode containing enormous quantities of low-grade ore of about 60 ounces per ton; and typical of these are the mines of Guanajuato, Pachuca, Querétaro, Zacatecas, and others. The ores, however, are not always low-grade, for great *bonanzas* of exceedingly rich ore were encountered, making rapid fortunes for their discoverers.

Silver.—The main lodes in those places enumerated have ranged up to hundreds of feet in width, and form the most potent silver-ore deposits upon the globe. Their extensions in length and depth bear out their importance as metal-producing sources. Thus the Mellado vein, of Guanajuato, measures, in places, more than 300 feet in width; with workings ten miles in length, and extending to a present depth of nearly 2,000 feet. The *Veta Madre,* or "mother lode," ranges from 30 feet to 165 feet in width; whilst others of the famous lodes reach 50 to 100 feet. As to the ore-values, Humboldt, who visited Guanajuato in the height of its production, at the beginning of the nineteenth century, assigned as his calculation a value equal to about 80 ounces of silver per ton *for the whole lode*. For portions of the ore-bodies, and for many of the great *bonanzas,* much higher values have obtained, silver up to 7,000 ounces per ton having been encountered; whilst ores of 1,100 ounces have been frequently exported to Great Britain.

The almost fabulous wealth obtained from the silver mines has been shown in the foregoing pages, and these mines are far from being exhausted at the present day. The importance of the Pachuca mines is shown by the statement that they produce six million ounces of silver and 30,000 ounces of gold yearly. Of the population of the city, of forty thousand souls, seven thousand are employed underground.

All of the Mexican states are silver bearing, although those which contain the famous mines are the most important, as:—Sonora, Chihuahua, Sinaloa, Zacatecas, San Luis Potosi, Guanajuato, Querétaro, Hidalgo (Pachuca), Mexico. All these states contain numerous mining districts—cities, towns, camps—which it would take too much space here to enumerate. With the exception of the few modern installations most of the mines are worked by the primitive Mexican system of winding up the ore in raw-hide sacks, hauled by means of cables made from *maguey* fibre, upon a mule-actuated windlass—the *malacate*. In some cases the miners carry huge pieces of ore on their backs, from 100 lbs. to 200 lbs. in weight, along the galleries to the shaft. Interior transport and haulage are primitive.

The principal ore of silver is the sulphate, although native silver is also freely encountered in some districts. The ores were very generally decomposed to a depth of about 300 feet. Argentiferous galena is plentiful, and silver is freely found in conjunction with copper ores. The *caliches*, a chalk-like substance, easily worked, is another rich form of occurrence of the metal, and there are others less important. Various different methods of separating silver from its ores are used; the prevailing ones being those of smelting, lixiviation, and the *patio* process, which last has accounted for 90 per cent. of the production. Indeed, the recovery of silver by the *patio* process has always been one of the most important industries of Spanish-American countries, especially in Mexico, Peru, and Chile. In Mexico it has been employed continuously since the year 1557, when it was invented by Medina at the *hacienda* Purisima Grande. This was the first application of amalgamation to silver ores, and permitted the treatment of the vast quantities of low-grade ores, which did not pay to smelt. To-day great quantities of ore are still treated by this method. The process is too well known to require much description here. Its main points of advantage are the simplicity—in practice, for its chemistry is complicated in theory—of its methods and appliances. The principal agents employed may be said to be mercury and horseflesh, or rather mule-flesh; the mercury forming an amalgam with the precious metals under the incorporation brought about by the trampling hoofs of the mules. The trampling and incorporation of the *torta*, or charge of pounded ore, mercury, water, salt, copper sulphate, and other constituents, mixed into a paste, was originally performed by barefooted natives, but the practice of using mules for the purpose came from Peru, in 1783, as before mentioned. The *patio*, as its name implies, consists of a paved yard upon which the crushed mineral is treated. This is in some cases of very large capacity, one of the most important in the country, that of the Guadalupe works at Pachuca, which treats nearly a thousand tons of ore a week, being as large as the *plaza* of a city. Upon this the *torta* is spread, and bands of a dozen mules, or mules and horses, harnessed together, are driven up and down from morning till afternoon, through the slushy mass. The animals are then bathed to remove the chemicals, but notwithstanding this the work is deleterious, and they last but a few years—the old ones but a few months—as they become poisoned by the copper sulphate. At some of the *haciendas* of Pachuca six hundred horses are employed in this work, and the total throughout the country is considerable. Constant efforts have been made for the use of mechanical appliances, to take the place of the equine mixer, but these have not been found to give the same efficiency. The process is typical of the country and the race—time, space, and material are plentiful, and labour is cheap, and horses—well, they were made for man's use! The innate tendency of the Spanish-Americans to do without mechanical appliances also is indulged.

The growth of the silver-producing industry of recent years is shown by the returns, giving approximately a value of seven million Mexican dollars for 1890 and fifty million for 1902, for export alone. The total value of the silver production for 1907 was eight million sterling, which was more than that of the United States, and so Mexico led the world in that year.

Gold.—The gold which was formerly produced in Mexico has come principally from the silver ores, with which it is generally associated, and has been obtained from the amalgamation of these. More recently gold-bearing quartz lodes are being worked, and are producing important quantities of gold. Among the foremost of these are the mines of the district of El Oro, in the State of Mexico, somewhat less than a hundred miles to the north-west of the capital. They produced in 1905 about ten million dollars in gold, or about 800,000 dollars per month. Whilst Mexico has not generally been looked upon as a gold-producing country, it is undoubtedly the case that it will, under the present rate of development, rank among the foremost of these. At present Mexico holds sixth place with a production for 1907 of 3¾ millions sterling. Gold-bearing lodes are being discovered and worked in most of the States, and thousands of such deposits are being prospected, or awaiting such, whilst numerous crushing plants are treating ores in those districts most accessible to the railways. The enterprise known as El Oro Mining and Railway Company may be looked upon as a well-managed and prosperous concern, controlled by British capital. It was first acquired by a British company in 1815, and it is stated that it yielded five or six million pounds sterling of gold. Later it was abandoned, taken up in 1870 by native capitalists, and at the end of last century purchased by an American company, to be again acquired by British interests in 1899. The enterprise controls a large area of ground of more than 500 acres, a short railway to the Mexican National Line, and some valuable forests which afford fuel. With its battery of 200 stamps and large cyaniding mills, it has a capacity for ore treatment of 20,000 tons per month. The yield per ton of ore is given for 1900 at slightly under £3 per ton, at a cost of about 25s., and for 1907 35s. per ton, at a cost of slightly under 20s. The tonnage treated for these years were 53,500 tons and 263,000 tons respectively, and all the intervening years show the steady increase. The output for 1907 was more than a million tons of ore, due to the added capacity of the new stamp mill, whilst the monthly profits for that year and for 1908 fluctuated between £14,000 and £18,000.

Other successful enterprises of El Oro region are the Somera Gold Mining Company, affiliated with the foregoing, and the Mexico Mines of El Oro. The latter company's mill has a capacity of 250 tons of ore daily, and the recent monthly profits have been, it is stated, upwards of £15,000. These are also controlled by British capitalists, as is the "Esperanza" Mine of El Oro, it is stated, which has produced since 1895 a value of 4½ millions sterling, with a profit of nearly 2½ millions. The "Dos Estrellas" Mine is yet another example of this successful district. It is said to have made profits since 1902 of 2½ millions sterling, and to have ore for future work in large quantities. It is interesting to note that this excellent performance has been made on ground which had been condemned by mining experts![34]

34 These figures are from the Mexican Year Book, 1908.

Other prosperous mining concerns in different parts of the country, generally owned by native capital, include the "Real del Monte" Mines of Pachuca, elsewhere described: the "Maravellas and Anexas Mining Company," principally silver producing; the "Santa Gertrude Mines," a silver property; "La Blanca and Anexas," gold and silver—all of which are in the Pachuca district. The Parral mining district, in Chihuahua, is one which has recently received attention, although it is not new, having yielded silver from the middle of the sixteenth century. Some six millions sterling represent the investments in the district during the last fifteen years in these mines. The famous Peñoles Mine is among the most prosperous in the country. This is a lead-gold-silver-producing enterprise in Durango, at Mapimi, worked first in Colonial times. Now it owns large smelters, a line of railway, and an extensive property. In 1907 this enterprise produced 58,000 kilograms of silver, 504 kilograms of gold, and has an annual output of some 20,000 tons of lead.

In Sonora various gold-mining properties are at work. Among them is the Consolidated Goldfields of Mexico, Ltd., British capital: the Creston-Colorado Mines, worked by American capital, including the old British-worked Minas Prietas mines: there are other gold mining companies old and new under British enterprise, and the Bufa and the Trinidad Companies, producing gold, silver, and copper. In fact, the State of Sonora is a rich field for the working of the precious metals, and offers great possibilities.

In Chihuahua are some important gold and silver-producing enterprises, among them the Greene Gold-Silver Company, owned by Americans, and the Palmarejo Mines, a British enterprise. Indeed, with its numerous important mining centres, this State is held to be the foremost in Mexico, and a large output of the precious metals is being made.

Lower California contains a great deal of resource in gold-quartz lodes, and some important *placer* deposits. This territory is one of the richest mineral regions of North America.

The principal gold-producing States are Chihuahua, Sonora, Zacatecas, Guerrero, Oaxaca, Mexico, Lower California, Hidalgo, Chiapas, Coahuila. No less than eighteen of the States of Mexico contain gold-bearing districts.

Hydraulic, or *placer*, mining for gold has not been much considered as a source of supply, as there are no great alluvial deposits, so far known, such as exist in other parts of North and South America. Nevertheless, something has been done in this way, principally in the States of Chihuahua and Guerrero. The geological formation, however, does not point the probability of the existence of great alluvial deposits, and the *placers* take the form of river bars principally.

The rise of Mexico's gold-production has been rapid. The country now holds sixth place. In 1893 its value was less than 4 per cent. of that of the silver output, whilst in 1894 it jumped to 14 per cent., and in 1902, 20 per cent. The export of gold bullion in 1890 was only half a million Mexican dollars, whilst in 1903 it had risen to 11½ millions. The value of the total gold production for 1907 was 3¾ millions sterling.

Among other producing mines is the Providencia, of Guanajuato, yielding gold, silver, and iron. Yet another is the "San Rafael and Anexas," a regular dividend-payer, whose net profits for 1907 are given as three-quarters of a million dollars. The famous region of Tlalpujahua is once more receiving attention.

Copper.—The rise of Mexico as a copper-producing country has been remarkable. Less than fifteen years ago the Republic was unheard of as a source of the red metal, now it ranks second in the world's output, coming next to the United States with a production for the year 1907 of 56,600 tons. The following States are those which are most important as copper-bearing: Chihuahua, Sonora, Coahuila, Zacatecas, Jalisco, Michoacan, Puebla, Querétaro, Tamaulipas, Lower California, and Colima.

In Sonora the following mines are at work: The Bufa Mining and Smelting Company; the Trinidad Mining Company, upon which large sums of money have been spent; the Montezuma Mine, an important enterprise, formed with an outlay of millions of dollars upon its appliances and workings, and having a daily capacity of 250 tons of ore, belonging to American capitalists. The Cananea Consolidated Copper Company, a remarkable enterprise instituted by American capitalists. Cananea is considered to be one of the most important copper regions in the world, and a considerable preliminary outlay made has been justified in the results; the works exporting several thousand tons of copper monthly. It forms one of the most complete installations of its nature. The Yaqui River Smelting and Railway Company is a custom smelter, and affords a market for much local copper ore. There are other copper-producing enterprises under development, and the State of Sonora is thus a most productive source of the red metal.

In Chihuahua active development upon copper mines is being carried on, and the production stimulated by the establishing of smelting works. There is also an important copper foundry at Monterrey, in the State of Nuevo Leon.

In Lower California are the large copper mines and smelting works of Boleo, owned by a French company. This is an important enterprise, supporting a population of 8,000 souls, and its eight smelters are of a capacity of 150 tons daily, giving an output of copper of 11,500 tons per annum. With its own railways, harbour, and town, the enterprise is a self-centred community of much prosperity.

The State of Guerrero affords some copper ore deposits probably of great extent, and among these are several mines which are being developed.

In the State of Zacatecas is the important British enterprise of the Mazapil Copper Company, with an extensive property, smelting furnaces, and railway line, with also a long overhead cable system of ore-carriage.

Iron.—Deposits of iron ores are found in several of the states. In Durango is the much described *Cerro de Mercado*, a hill of iron ore calculated as containing 460,000,000 tons of iron ore, assaying 70 to 75 percent. pure iron. This remarkable hill was discovered in 1552.

The city of Monterrey, in the State of Nuevo Leon, contains a large ironfoundry and steel-producing plant, and two iron and brassfoundries, establishments which are of much importance to the country. Guerrero has valuable deposits of iron ore near Chilpancingo.

Quicksilver.—In the State of Guerrero are the quicksilver mines of Ahuitzuco, which have produced quantities of mercury. Durango has deposits of cinnabar at Nazas and El Oro.

Coal.—In the State of Sonora are extensive fields of anthracite, with seams in some cases 14 feet in thickness, and these are being developed by an American company. Near these are others, equally important, and the whole area is very considerable. Coahuila contains perhaps the most important coal-beds in the Republic, and a considerable output of coal and coke is being made. Other states contain coal-fields.

Petroleum.—In the State of Tamaulipas are the petroleum deposits of "El Ebano," worked by an American company. In July, 1908, an enormous "fresher" was struck at San Geronimo, near Tampico, and this became ignited and burned fiercely for two months, with a pillar of flame 1,000 feet high, which was visible for 100 miles. So rapid was the flow of oil when this was extinguished that earthen dams were hastily constructed to save the oil. Several other states have oil deposits.

Salt.—In Tamaulipas, on the Gulf of Mexico, the salt mines of Matamoros and Soto la Marina produce quantities of salt. On the Pacific side of the country, Carmen Island, off the Gulf coast of Baja, California, exists one of the largest salt-beds in the world.

Lead is distributed through numerous states. It occurs largely as high-grade argentiferous galena. The output for 1907 was 73,000 tons.

Antimony.—The value of the production of this for 1907 was about £140,000.

Tin has not been worked commercially, although great deposits of the ores of this metal are shown to exist, especially in the State of Durango, where there are several districts, Guanajuato and Aguascalientes. It was one of the metals used by the Aztecs.

The value of the total mineral production of the Republic, in round numbers, as shown by the fiscal returns, including the product of reduction works and the exports of metals, ores, and bullion, is taken at £15,000,000—an excellent showing.

The number of mining properties held under title for 1907 are:—gold and silver, 14,950; gold and silver with other metals, 9,050; other metals and mineral substances, 2,350, or a total of 26,350, equal to an area of 873,000 acres. The method of acquiring mining property in Mexico is relatively simple. As to ownership, the only cause of forfeiture is default in payment of the taxes upon the title-deeds.

In Mexico the foreign capitalist and miner will find endless scope for his money and energies. Yet it is a feature of the industry, and of the excellent conditions obtaining in the financial world of the Republic, that good mines are easily financed within the country itself. Details of the conditions of the mining regions are further set forth in the chapter devoted to the natural resources of the various states.